P9-BZS-699

UNDERSTANDING & DISMANTLING RACISM

UNDERSTANDING & DISMANTLING

RACISM

THE TWENTY-FIRST CENTURY CHALLENGE
TO WHITE AMERICA

JOSEPH BARNDT

FORTRESS PRESS

MINNEAPOLIS

DISMANTLING RACISM
The Twenty-First Century Challenge to White America

Copyright © 2007 Fortress Press, an imprint of Augsburg Fortress. All rights reserved. Except for brief quotations in critical articles or reviews, no part of this book may be reproduced in any manner without prior written permission from the publisher. Visit http://www.augsburgfortress.org/copyrights/ or write to Permissions, Augsburg Fortress, Box 1209, Minneapolis, MN 55440.

Cover image and design: Design Works
Book design: Zan Ceeley/Trio Bookworks

Library of Congress Cataloging-in-Publication Data

Barndt, Joseph R.
  Understanding and dismantling racism : the twenty-first century challenge to white America / by Joseph Barndt.
     p. cm.
  Includes bibliographical references and index.
  ISBN-13: 978-0-8006-6222-6 (alk. paper)
  ISBN-10: 0-8006-6222-9 (alk. paper)
  1. Racism—United States. 2. Pluralism (Social sciences)—United States. 3. Minorities—United States—Social conditions. 4. Minorities—Civil rights—United States. 5. Whites—United States—Attitudes. 6. United States—Race relations. 7. Racism—United States—Religious aspects. I. Title.
  E184.A1B249 2007
  305.800973—dc22
        2007016303

The paper used in this publication meets the minimum requirements of American National Standard for Information Sciences — Permanence of Paper for Printed Library Materials, ANSI Z329.48-1984.

Manufactured in the U.S.A.

Dedicated to the memory of five colleagues
Beloved friends in the struggle to undo and dismantle racism

Jim Dunn
Imani/Nadine Addington
Pat Simpson-Turner
Kenneth Jones
Gerry Conroy

Their lives have enriched all of us in the anti-racism community.

CONTENTS

Preface   xi

Introduction   **1**

The Happiness Machine—A Fable   1

The Dross of Racism   3

The Happiness Machine and Current Reality   4

A Book for White People   6

And Also a Book for People of Color   7

The Work of Crossroads Ministry and People's Institute   8

Language and Terminology   8

Other "Isms"—The Happiness Machine's Multiple Consequences   10

Writing an Ending to the Fable of the Happiness Machine   11

1. The Continuing Evil of Racism   **13**

The Complex and Bewildering Tangle of Racism   13

Our Colonial and Racist Beginnings   15

From Colony to Nationhood: The Deepening of Racism   17

Resistance to Racism: The Better Side of a Bitter History   25

The Civil Rights Movement: The Resistance Rewrites History   29

The Continuing Evil of Racism in the Twenty-First Century   33

Detecting and Measuring Twenty-First Century Racism   42

The Twenty-First Century: A New Beginning   48

2. Defining Racism **55**

The Need for a Common Definition of Racism 55

Introducing a Definition of Racism 58

Exploring Prejudice 60

Exploring Race 62

The Misuse of Power by Systems and Institutions 73

Summary 82

3. White Power and Privilege **85**

From "Black Like Me" to "White Like Me" 87

White Power: Not the Same as White Privilege 90

A Closer Look at White Power 91

A Closer Look at White Privilege 95

Responses to White Power and Privilege 107

Conclusion: You Can't Take It Off 110

4. Individual Racism: The Making of a Racist **111**

Power³: Racism at Its Worst 111

"Go Home and Free Your Own People" 112

What and Who Is a Racist? 115

"Racialization": The Mass Production of Racists and Victims 120

Racial Identity Formation:

The Shaping of Superior and Inferior Races 123

The Making of a White Racist 126

The Four Walls of Racism's Prison 129

Summary and Conclusion: None of Us Are Free 141

5. Institutionalized Racism **143**

The Misuse of Power by Systems and Institutions 143

Taking an X-Ray of the Happiness Machine 144

The Nature and Purpose of Institutions 145

Defining Institutionalized Racism 151

How It Got That Way:

A History of Institutionalized Racism 154

How It Stayed That Way:

New Forms of Institutionalized Racism 157

How to "See," Identify, and Analyze Institutionalized Racism 165

Conclusion: The Possibility of Authentic Institutional

Transformation 182

6. Cultural Racism   **185**

What Is Culture?   187
The Creating of Race-Based Cultures   190
Defining Cultural Racism   195
The Race-Based Cultures of Communities of Color   204
White Cultural Identity in the Twenty-First Century   207

7. Dismantling Racism   **219**

A Time to Tear Down . . . and a Time to Build   219
Building Antiracist Communities of Resistance   221
Planning a Jailbreak: Organizing to Dismantle Racism   231
Introducing a Tool to Measure Institutional Change   233
The First Half of the Continuum: Where Are We Now?   236
Principles of Organizing to Move Forward   243
The Second Half of the Continuum:
    The Three Stages of Institutional Transformation   255
Conclusion: Toward a Racism-Free Twenty-First Century   262

Notes   269
Additional Resources   277
Index   285

PREFACE

Understanding and Dismantling Racism is the fourth book on racism that I have written over the past forty years. In each of these books my primary goal has been to describe how white racism functions in the United States and how it has been changing—for better and for worse. In that sense, each book has been a kind of historical update. In a far more important sense, each book reflects the process of my own growth in how to understand and dismantle racism.

The first book, *Why Black Power?*, was written in 1968 in the context of the fiery hot cauldron of the movements for racial justice that were reshaping the social and political fabric of U.S. society. That book's answer to the question, Why black power?, was, and still is, "Because of white racism." It was written as a message to white people that black power—as well as red power, brown power, and yellow power—were an inevitable and essential response to white racism and to the irresponsible use of white power.

I wrote the second book, *Liberating Our White Ghetto*, four years later in 1972, just as it was beginning to be obvious that despite all the legal changes in the 1960s, little alteration was taking place in the imbalance of power relationships between white society and communities of color. In my personal understanding of racism, it was becoming increasingly clear that the central problem was not simply white unwillingness to change, but the imprisoning and self-perpetuating nature of systemic racism that captures, separates and destroys all of us—not just some of us. We needed then—and still need now—to comprehend the imprisonment of the white society in its institutional and cultural structures, and the necessity of the white society, and not only people of color, to be set free from racism.

The next twenty years were relatively quiet in terms of public protest against the continuing racism and racial disparity in our society. Perhaps, more than anything else, it was a time of recovery from the violent repression that brought the movements of the 1960s to a standstill. Especially during the 1980s, a pretense of peaceful progress and successful change was portrayed in virtually every institutional and community setting in our society, primarily through programs of "multicultural diversity and inclusiveness." When I wrote *Dismantling Racism: The Continuing Challenge to White America*, published in 1991, there were ever-widening cracks and fissures in these programs that began to signify the inevitable failure of multicultural diversity as a solution to racism. The book sought to be a part of a new wake-up call and to challenge white people to participate in the ongoing task of dismantling racism.

Now it is almost twenty years later, and the first decade of the twenty-first century is nearing completion. The failure of programs of multicultural diversity and inclusiveness is increasingly obvious, while public protest and new forms of organizing against racism are developing in ways that are irrepressibly strong and powerful. For some, the renewed turmoil is a depressing sign of defeat. For others—and I count myself among them—it is a wonderful opportunity, a new sign of hope and promise. This new book, *Understanding and Dismantling Racism*, tries to present new learnings about systemic racism from the past fifteen years and to describe exciting new organizing opportunities to transform structures of systemic racism. In this book, I attempt to portray how changes in recent years have brought about both progress and regression in the struggle to end racism, and I will share my own growth in understanding how racism can ultimately be dismantled.

Expressions of Gratitude

I am deeply grateful to all my friends and colleagues from Crossroads Ministry and People's Institute for Survival and Beyond. I know that because of their collegial and collective work, I have come much closer to understanding racism and how to dismantle it. I am especially grateful for the contributions of a reading committee appointed by the board of Crossroads Ministry, as well as permission from Crossroads and People's Institute to use their materials in this book. Where noted, some of the Crossroads charts and definitions have been somewhat altered to fit the context of this book.

It is impossible to name everyone to whom I am deeply indebted, but special thanks are due:

- to Ron Chisom and Barbara Major, for many years of mentoring and friendship—teaching, loving and supporting me when I needed it, and critiquing and correcting me when I needed critiquing and correcting;
- to Mel Hoover, with whom I shared a long and productive partnership as co-leader of Crossroads;
- to Chuck and Sue Ruehle, longtime friends and partners in antiracism work;
- to Victor Rodriguez, friend, colleague, and codesigner of programs of antiracism training and organizing;
- to Anne Stewart, the best of training partners who also provided strong leadership in developing the analysis of cultural racism;
- to Robette Dias, who has added richly to my understanding of the relationship between colonialism and racism;
- to Emily Drew, supportive friend and colleague who has been immeasurably helpful in advising me on content and style of this book;
- and above all, to Susan Birkelo, my spouse and closest companion, who has loved me and tolerated me at my best and my worst. Her love and support have made my life rich and this book possible.

INTRODUCTION

... The Right to Life, Liberty, and the Pursuit of Happiness.
—U.S. Declaration of Independence

The Happiness Machine—A Fable

Once upon a time there was a kingdom of people who pursued happiness. Nothing was more important to them than being happy. The happier they became, the happier they wanted to be.

The source of the people's happiness was a magic Happiness Machine. Whenever the people felt unhappy they would pour their troubled feelings into the Happiness Machine. The magic machine would melt their feelings down and purify them. The residue of their troubles became dross, and the dross was drained away and dumped into a distant part of the kingdom. The people would take their purified feelings and go away singing and feeling happy again. They were called the "Happy People."

As the years and centuries went by, the Happy People became happier and happier because of the wonderful effects of the Happiness Machine.

There was only one problem. Another group of people lived in a distant part of the kingdom where all the dross was dumped. The dross made them very unhappy. They were called the "Unhappy People." The more dross that was dumped on them, the unhappier they became. However, the Unhappy People were not permitted to use the Happiness Machine, because the one thing the magic machine could not do was purify its own dross.

The Unhappy People complained to the Happy People about the problems they had with the dross. But the Happy People ignored their complaints. When they were confronted with the troubling results of their happiness, the Happy People simply took their troubled feelings to the Happiness Machine, and it made them happy again. It was easy to believe that it was not the dross of their own troubles that made other people unhappy. Rather, they convinced themselves that the Unhappy People were just incurably unhappy and that they had nobody but themselves to blame for their unhappiness.

It was not long before the Unhappy People began to protest more insistently about their situation. They organized marches and demonstrations. They demanded that the dross be removed from their part of the kingdom. And they demanded a fair share of happiness for their people. But the Happy People turned a deaf ear to their protests, which only served to make the Unhappy People unhappier, and they protested all the more.

Finally, the Happy People could no longer ignore the protests. They used force to put down the protesters, and arrested and jailed the leaders. They passed laws and organized military force to control the Unhappy People. Many of the Unhappy People were killed. This only made them unhappier. They began to plot and plan how they could destroy the Happiness Machine.

The conflict and tension caused a severe drain on the Happy People's happiness. To make it worse, some of the Happy People were becoming increasingly troubled about the way the Unhappy People were being treated. All these new troubles made the Happiness Machine work even harder, and as a result even more dross was produced. They had to build an even bigger and better Happiness Machine to take care of the happiness needs of the Happy People. Consequently, the dross was piled higher and higher and spread farther and farther into other parts of the kingdom, which made more and more Unhappy People. It was not long before the Unhappy People were in a constant state of rebellion.

Then a new and even greater danger arose. The Happiness Machine had become so large and productive that there was no place left in the kingdom to put the dross. The piles of dross crept closer and closer to the homes of the Happy People and to the place where the Happiness Machine was operating. There was an ominous threat that the dross would back up into its own machine, and the machine would self-destruct. Now the Happy People were troubled not only by the rebellion of the Unhappy People, but also by their own Happiness Machine.

The new danger caused even greater internal troubles among the Happy People. Some people began to sorrowfully predict that the Happiness Machine would soon self-destruct. Others suggested that the only alternative was to build an even bigger Happiness Machine in order to deal with the crisis they were facing. Others began to see that the Happiness Machine was not the solution to their problems, but the cause. They wanted to reduce the size of the Happiness Machine, or even dismantle it altogether. Some even began to wish that they could join together with the Unhappy People and build a new society together without the help of Happiness Machines. . . .

The end of this story has not yet been written. This book is an invitation to readers to see themselves as part of the story and to help write its ending.

The Dross of Racism

As the reader has no doubt already recognized, this fable is about us and about real-life Happiness Machines. The real-life Happiness Machines are the structures and institutions of U.S. society. They belong to us, and they work for us. They produce food and clothing, cars and housing, resorts and recreation, law and order. Their purpose is to make us happy.

But, just as in the fable, our real-life Happiness Machines also produce unhappiness. They produce "dross." They produce poverty and segregated ghettos, unemployment and underemployment, and inadequate housing, health, and education. The very same systems that create and sustain our standards of living also create and perpetuate wretched conditions for millions upon millions of people, not only in the United States, but throughout the world as well. This fable is, in fact, no fable at all, but a story about the real world in which you and I live.

The subject of this book is racism. The "Happy People" in the fable represent the white society in the United States, and the "Unhappy People" represent people of color who suffer from white racism. Racism remains one of the most serious issues we need to face in the twenty-first century. Many, perhaps most, of us were hoping that problems of racial injustice in the United States had been sufficiently dealt with in the 1960s and in the years immediately after the civil rights movement drew to a close. We believed—or wanted to believe—that the social conditions of people of color, such as housing, education, employment, and health, would now be improving. We believed—or wanted to believe—that the increasing numbers of people of color in elected offices, media programming, and other public positions were a sign that things were truly changing. But it has become clear that these changes were more illusory than real. Racism still plagues not only the individual attitudes and behavior of white people but also, far more seriously, the public systems and institutions of white society.

I wrote this fable of the Happiness Machine more than thirty years ago, and used it in the introduction to two previous books: *Liberating Our White Ghetto* and *Dismantling Racism: The Continuing Challenge to White America*. Now, although there have been many surface changes for the better, I believe the underlying problems have remained the same or grown worse, and the basic message of the fable has not changed. One hundred years ago, W. E. B. Du Bois wrote in the introduction to *The Souls of Black Folk*, "the problem of the twentieth century is the problem of the color-line."[1] Du Bois's prophetic insight can be extended as well to the twenty-first century—the question of the color line is still central to and inseparable from all other social and political issues in our nation.

My purpose in writing this book is to examine how racism continues to function in the United States in the early part of the twenty-first century. I will explore the ways in which progress has been made toward racism's eradication over the past fifty years, and I will describe the ways in which racism continues unabated, even assuming new forms and disguises that make it more dangerous than ever. Most importantly, I will focus on the continuing task of dismantling racism, and the question of how we can work to bring systemic racism to an end and replace it with a racially just, multicultural society.

The Happiness Machine and Current Reality

As I write this book near the end of the first decade of the twenty-first century, there are three current news stories that provide vivid examples of the need to examine carefully current reality in the context of the story of the Happiness Machine. I believe that contemporary expressions of racism and the struggle to overcome racism can be found at the roots of each of these news stories.

News Story # 1: "Katrina" and the City of New Orleans

On August 30 and September 24, 2005, two hurricanes named Katrina and Rita, the most destructive to ever strike the continental United States, slammed into the coasts of Louisiana and Mississippi, killing thousands of persons, causing homelessness for millions, and destroying billions of dollars in property. Eighty percent of the city of New Orleans was inundated and destroyed, requiring the city to be virtually abandoned for months and to face years of rebuilding.

Normally, this terrible tragedy would be classified as a "natural disaster," its primary distinguishing characteristic being only its enormity. However, the classification of the tragedy as a "natural disaster" has been vehemently and angrily rejected by many people who view the devastation as quite unnatural and point to forces much more chaotic than the forces of nature. The basis for this reclassification as an "unnatural disaster" is the charge of racism in the preparedness, response, and recovery of New Orleans. During the weeks, months, and years of recovery, there have been—and continue to be—charges and countercharges, accusations and denials, investigations and counter-investigations, and acrimonious debate centered on the issue of racism.

News Story #2: The Immigration Crisis

It has been simmering for decades, but in 2006, the overheated political debate with regard to an estimated twelve million undocumented people in the United States began to boil over, significantly influencing preparations for the presidential elections in 2008. Legislative proposals to arrest and deport "illegal aliens" and to build hundreds of miles of walls along our national borders were countered with millions of people demonstrating in cities and towns across the nation, protesting unfair treatment of "undocumented workers."

As with the story of Katrina, at the roots of this story we hear angry charges of racism. The majority of the undocumented people are Latinos/Hispanics, particularly Mexicans, who cross our nation's southern border to work in fields and factories in unfilled low-income jobs that few others are willing to do. In retaliation for their presence, laws have been created to deprive undocumented people of health care, police protection, housing, education, and even driver's licenses. The results of these actions, along with attacks based on language, accents, culture, heritage, and skin color, are felt indiscriminately by all Latinos/Hispanics—documented or not.

News Story #3: Terrorism in Our Land

It is a story now so much a part of us, we refer to it in shorthand: "WTC on 9/11." On September 11, 2001, the twin towers of the World Trade Center in New York City were demolished by two hijacked commercial jet airliners deliberately flown into the buildings. Simultaneously, another hijacked plane was deliberately flown into the Pentagon in Washington, D.C., and a fourth hijacked plane, apparently intended to be smashed into the White House, was retaken by a rebellion of heroic passengers and crashed in a rural area in Pennsylvania. The resulting devastation caused by these horrendous events is immeasurable: 2,000 people killed, billions of dollars in property destruction, and the traumatic shock of a nation that has seldom experienced violent attacks from an outside enemy. The continuing effects of this story are not only global confrontations, but also the escalation of domestic racism toward Arabs and Middle Eastern peoples in the United States.

In ways that are similar to the news stories of Hurricane Katrina and the immigration crisis, 9/11 magnifies a view of the world with the reality of racism at the center. Many people from Arab and Middle Eastern countries, as well as people from underdeveloped and poverty-stricken countries around the world, increasingly consider the United States and the Western world an enemy of justice and freedom and a primary cause of decades and centuries of poverty and oppression. They also see a great deal of accuracy in comparing the horrific and unjustifiable attacks on 9/11 with the equally horrific and unjustifiable invasion of Iraq and other military and economic attacks in other parts of the world by the United States and their allies.

These three stories have common threads—the color-filled threads of racial tensions and conflict between white people and people of color, domestically and globally. And they clearly demonstrate what can be also demonstrated in a thousand similar stories: first, that racism has not disappeared; and second, that the continuing struggle to end racism is as relevant as today's newspaper. The story of the Happiness Machine is the story of our own lives.

A Book for White People

This book on racism is written especially for white people and about white people, and it is written by a white person. It is a book about our problem of white racism. More often than not, books about racial problems are about people of color—about African Americans, Native Americans, Asian Americans, Latinos/Hispanics, and Arab Americans. Those books are usually concerned especially with the problems that racism causes for people of color.

The purpose of this book is different. The central focus of this book is *not* about how racism affects people of color. Rather, the primary subject is how racism is caused by and how it affects white people and the predominantly white institutions and culture of our white society. I believe that we who are white need to come to new understandings about ourselves and about our racism, and we need to take responsibility for bringing racism to an end. The two primary goals of this book are, first, to help white people understand how racism functions and how it is perpetuated in our homes, schools, churches, and other institutions; and second, to help equip white people to combat and dismantle racism and to help build an antiracist/multicultural society.

While this book is addressed to white people, it is not an attack on white people; it is not based on accusations or blame, and does not seek to produce guilt. As I hope will become clear, my primary thesis about racism is that we are all "prisoners of racism," people of color and white people alike. Almost every leader in the struggle against racism, from Frederick Douglass to Martin Luther King Jr. and from Mahatma Gandhi to Nelson Mandela, has emphasized that racism is as debilitating to white people as it is to people of color, and that the goal of freedom is for all people. By the time the reader reaches the end of this book, I hope there will be new clarity on how we can all reach this goal.

And Also a Book for People of Color

Although this book is written primarily to white people and about white reality, people of color are also invited to read this book—if for no other reason than to assess whether the understanding of racism presented here corresponds to your own experience and understanding. The underlying analysis of racism presented here does not originate with me or any other white person, but has been taught to me by people of color, who are the true experts on racism. I hope that I have been able to maintain faithfulness to this understanding of racism that comes from the perspective of people of color, while applying it to the reality of white people.

During the past fifty years, my principal teachers about racism have been African Americans, and my predominant experience with struggles for racial justice has been in the context of African American communities. I have been profoundly affected by the centuries-long history of African American people surviving slavery and postslavery racism in the United States; and even more, I have been influenced by the central leadership that African Americans have given—and are still giving—to the struggle to end racism in our nation.

More recently, it has also become very important for me to learn how racism in the United States affects other communities of color. Native Americans, Latinos/Hispanics, Asian Americans, and Arab Americans have also been devastated for centuries by racism and have struggled valiantly for racism's defeat. As I have gained experience in and learned from all communities of color, I have come to a greater understanding of the complexity of multiracial oppression in our society, as well as the interrelatedness and interdependence of their separate struggles.

In my personal strivings to become an effective antiracist teacher and organizer, there has been nothing more important than listening to, learning from, and following the leadership of people of color, and to be accountable to people of color in my understanding of racism. I am especially very clear that it is neither the right nor the role of a white person to speak for people of color. Thus, wherever in this book I describe the reality of people of color, I try through direct quotes or through footnotes to attribute these descriptions appropriately to authentic sources of people of color. Where I have failed to do this, or where I have inaccurately heard, understood, or described the reality of people of color or the reality of racism from the perspective of people of color, I accept full responsibility.

The Work of Crossroads Ministry and People's Institute

The analysis of racism in this book is the product of collective work by many, many people. It especially reflects years of efforts by two antiracism training organizations: Crossroads Ministry, located in Chicago, and People's Institute for Survival and Beyond, located in New Orleans. Both of these organizations have developed significant new ways of teaching and organizing to understand and dismantle racism. The table of contents and chapter sequence of this book directly reflect the outline and progression of a Crossroads Ministry antiracism training workshop, and are also quite similar in outline to a People's Institute training workshop.

The People's Institute for Survival and Beyond was cofounded in 1980 by Jim Dunn and Ron Chisom, and Chisom is now its director. Although the People's Institute addresses the experience and issues of all communities of color, its leadership is primarily African American, and its analysis is rooted principally in the African American experience.

Crossroads Ministry, which I cofounded in 1986 and directed for eighteen years, is now codirected by Robette Dias and Chuck Ruehle. While the work of Crossroads, like that of People's Institute, began with an analysis principally rooted in the African American experience, it has a multiracial focus and seeks to address the ways in which issues of racism affect all people of color.

During the past three decades, thousands upon thousands of people have benefited from the work of these two organizations, and have been equipped with analyzing and organizing skills to work for community and institutional transformation and the building of an antiracist society. It is my deepest hope that readers of this book will explore further involvement and action in dismantling racism by connecting with the work of these two organizations. Information on both can be found in the resource section at the end of this book.

Language and Terminology

Since this book is written by a single author, but at the same time seeks to reflect the collective experience of many people, I have found it a little difficult to keep my pronouns straight. The reader will note at times the alternating use of "I" and "we" in reference to the voice that is trying to communicate this analysis. It is impossible for me to write in the first person without needing to also reflect the wisdom and authority of many people from the past and present who have informed me and who have spoken to me with a collective voice. Nevertheless, practical circumstances have dictated that this book be written by a sole author, and although this sole author accepts responsibility for errors and weaknesses in the content, I want readers to read and feel the wisdom and authority that comes from a collective analysis of racism.

Likewise, since I am particularly addressing white people about white racism, sometimes the "we" of the text refers to white readers, and sometimes "we" refers to all people reading the book. I have attempted to make the pronouns clear in the context of a given page or paragraph,

Other terms used in this book require some clarification. There are constant changes in U.S. society as to the commonly accepted names used to denote various racial groups. In the chapters that follow, there is extensive discussion of how the current uses of these terms evolved, how they are in the process of constantly changing, and why it is important to define and use these terms in a respectful and accurate way.

Prior to deeper exploration in the book itself, however, it is important to note here in the introduction that the term "people of color" will be used (rather than terms like "minorities" and "nonwhites," which are neither accurate nor respectful) to represent the five major racial groups other than white people: African Americans, Native Americans, Asian Americans, Latinos/Hispanics, and Arab Americans. The use of a unifying term like "people of color" represents a deeply felt need expressed within all of these groups to build unity and strength among themselves, and to no longer allow racism to divide them from each other and make them compete with each other for the leftovers of a racist society.

The term "white people" is used to designate all people who are not people of color, and in particular to describe the descendents of Europeans who are citizens of the United States. As will be explored more deeply, it was by legally defining "white people" and by the racial empowerment of all who fit this definition that the roots of structural racism in the United States were formed and sustained.

Each of the six major racial groups have other alternative names that I could have chosen to use. In consultation with colleagues of color, I have tried to use the presently most commonly accepted name within each group. The term "Latinos/Hispanics" is representative of an almost equal split in opinion at the time of this writing between the name "Latinos" or "Hispanic Americans."

At any moment, there may be differences or shifting of opinions as to the best terms to be used. As I will describe further within the book, the changing of names is often a very positive sign of struggle with identity and especially a struggle within each group to name themselves and not allow others to name them. By the time this book is being read, new names may be evolving, while old names used here may have been discarded. Even the term "people of color" is likely to be replaced by a more helpful or useful successor. In the naming or describing of people of color in this book, I have done my best to be faithful to the counsel of colleagues of color. If I have erred or offended anyone by terminology or description, however, I accept personal responsibility and ask for patience and forgiveness. I especially apologize if any of the terms I have used begin to take on an offensive meaning.

Other "Isms"—
The Happiness Machine's Multiple Consequences

While dealing with the subject of racism, we need to be aware that racism is not the only social problem of our society. The dross of our Happiness Machines produce other "isms" such as sexism, heterosexism, classism, nationalism, militarism, anti-Semitism, and environmental pollution—all of which cause tremendous suffering and endanger humanity's existence. The same fable could be used to describe the social reality of poverty-stricken people, women and children, gays and lesbians, oppressed religions, and political domination throughout the world. All of these social problems are interwoven into a single fabric of oppression, and they are not easily disentangled from each other. However, it is not possible to simply analyze and resist "oppression in general." Just as this book addresses racism, each of these other "isms" must be separately analyzed and addressed.

At the same time, even when we are working to address any one of these other "isms," it is important to understand how each of them are affected by racism. Wherever one goes, whatever the issue, whatever stone is overturned in the field of social turmoil, we encounter the persistent and ever-present problem of racism. An understanding of racism is needed, therefore, not only by those who are directly involved in issues of racial justice, but also by those who work with all the other issues of justice and social change. At various points in the book, I have made special effort to further explore the interrelationship of racism with other issues of oppression.

Even more importantly, the fable of the Happiness Machine is an international story. It does not only apply to life within the United States. The Happiness Machines and their dross have been globalized; they are everywhere. And struggles for freedom and equality are also taking place everywhere. Not just in the United States but all around the world—in every country on every continent—efforts are being made to end the destructiveness of the Happiness Machine. The struggle for racial and economic justice can not be successful anywhere if it is not successful everywhere. Although the focus of this book is on racism in the United States, it must be read in the context of struggles with all issues of political and economic injustice everywhere in the world.

Finally, an explanation is needed about anti-Semitism and how it is related to a book on racism. Anti-Semitism has produced centuries-long terrifying oppression of Jews throughout the world, including in the United States. Anti-Semitism must even today be constantly and vigorously resisted. However, I believe it is important to make a distinction between racism and anti-Semitism. In the United States context, Jewish identity is usually understood in religious, cultural, and national terms, rather than racial terms. In fact, there are Jews of every race, both in the United States and throughout the world. Nevertheless, as I will indicate further in chapter six, Jews have from time to time also been racialized in ways that subjected them to explicit racist oppression in the United States as well as elsewhere in the world. The major experience of the racialization of Jews was in Nazi Germany, where the identification of Jews as an inferior "race" reached devastating proportions and resulted in horrendous persecution and genocide. Clearly, anti-Semitism needs to be understood as a form of oppression that is closely related to and often overlapping with racism, and must be opposed in every way possible. Because of the way the concept of race developed historically and is used in the United States, however, I will not in this book be describing Jews in racial terms nor dealing directly with the subject of anti-Semitism.

Writing an Ending to the Fable
of the Happiness Machine

At various places throughout the book, I will return to the fable of the Happiness Machine and ask what kind of conclusion can be written to the story. I am also asking that you, the reader, help write the ending of the fable. A number of different endings are possible.

- *A win/lose ending:* In traditional fairy tales the perpetuators of evil are destroyed and everyone else lives happily ever after. Such a fairy-tale ending would therefore mean the destruction of the white society and the triumphant victory of people of color.

- *A lose/lose ending:* There could be an ending in which everyone loses as the Happiness Machine self-destructs, taking the whole world with it. This ending presumes the greed of the Happy People leading them to cling to their machines, their worldviews, and their pretense about reality—until it is too late. Such a terrifying conclusion to the story precludes any hope of transformation and change.

- *A win/win ending:* Many people, perhaps the great majority of us—people of color and white people alike—have in mind another ending to the story, an ending that provides freedom and justice for all people. Is such an ending possible—a win/win ending in which everyone gains and no one loses?

It is the belief in the possibility of the third ending to the story that informs the fundamental assumptions of this book. Millions of people in the United States are involved in antiracism organizing in order to create a win/win ending to our story. Through their teaching, protesting, advocating, mobilizing, and organizing for personal, political, and social change, they express their conviction—as I wish to express my conviction in this book—that the Happiness Machine can either be dismantled or transformed and redirected to serve everyone on an equal and just basis. They believe—as I believe—that those who are now in power will yet be able to read the signs of the times, and yield their power rather than bring about their own destruction. This book is written especially for those who have dedicated themselves to working for racial justice, and who seek to be better equipped to be a part of writing a win/win ending to the story.

THE CONTINUING EVIL OF RACISM

> While everybody was asleep, an enemy came and sowed weeds among the wheat, and then went away.
> —Matthew 13:25

The Complex and Bewildering Tangle of Racism

Racism is an evil weed sown long ago in the garden of humanity. Over centuries, the evil weed has grown wildly, ensnaring healthy plants and covering the landscaped pathways, creating a great maze, a labyrinth with twists and turns that have led humanity astray. The complex and bewildering tangle of racism that still entwines and entraps us all today is rooted in the past, long before any reader of these words was born.

The purpose of this book is to describe how racism functions in the United States in the twenty-first century, and how it is possible to dismantle racism and build an antiracist, multicultural society. If we wish to understand racism today, however, we must begin with history. Before we can begin to define and dissect how racism functions in our nation in this present day, it is essential to realize how deeply the roots of racism are embedded and intertwined in the life and history of our world, and especially of our nation.

In the words of Pastor Johnny Ray Youngblood, speaking of the need to go back into this painful history: "The only way out is back through. In order to get well, you have to go back through what made you sick in the first place.[1]

Have you ever heard this disclaimer by a white person: "Slavery and segregation happened a long time ago; why should I be held responsible for what people did before I was born?" There is a sense in which this is true; no one can be blamed today for the evils perpetuated by their foreparents. However, there are other questions that need to be asked:

- To what degree are the actions of the past still influencing our lives today?
- Have the evils of the past been eradicated, or are they still affecting all of us today?
- How does the racism of the past continue to handicap people of color or reward white people?
- We may not be responsible for the past, but how are we responsible for what is happening now?

We cannot know the answers to these questions unless we know our history. It is simply impossible to understand the role that race and racism play in our lives today unless we know how we got here.

We are a people whose memories have been shortened by amnesia and anesthesia and whose knowledge of history has been distorted. New generations of people have reached adulthood since 1960. Many have little awareness of the civil rights movement or of the legal system of institutional racism that existed before that time. They have never known separate toilets and water fountains, segregated buses, restaurants, and accommodations, and all the other insulting and exploitative indignities. This history dare not be forgotten, particularly since it still exerts such a powerful influence over all of us.

In this initial chapter I want to lead readers through a bare outline of this history—a skeletal framework. Then, as this book progresses, I will put flesh on these bones as a way of building an understanding of the path that leads from the past to the present. Throughout this book readers will be asked to probe this history, learn more, and seek to interpret it. We will explore how racism has gone through many changes and adaptations as it moved from its brutal beginnings to a far more sophisticated, subtle, and dangerous means of oppression. We will discover, however, that underneath the growing sophistication, the basic foundations of racism have remained unchanged. The very same evil weed that was sown centuries ago in the garden of humanity is still threatening us today.

A Path of Struggle for Freedom and Justice

While not ignoring the pain of the past, there is also a good side to this history; the evil of racism is only half the story. The other half is the tireless and heroic resistance by those who refused to tolerate evil. Through the courageous organizing efforts of millions of people who lived before our time, a path of justice has been opened through the maze of racism—the very same path many of us are now struggling to maintain and widen. To understand more fully our place in history as we stand now in the early years of the twenty-first century, and in order to better understand efforts to combat racism and build an anti-racist, multicultural society, we need to acknowledge, celebrate, and build on the heroic work of those who have been on this path before us. Let us move forward with courage to look at our shameful history of racism, and with joy to look at our history of resistance to racism and our movement toward justice.

Our Colonial and Racist Beginnings

It began in 1492. If we accurately trace the path of racism in our country, it will take us all the way back to our colonial beginnings. As we view this historical path, it is important to see how racism and colonialism have always been interwoven. The land that was originally occupied by indigenous peoples and that ultimately became the United States was colonized by a number of European countries: England (the original thirteen colonies and Hawaii), France (Louisiana Purchase), Spain (Florida, the Southwest, Puerto Rico), and Russia (Alaska and Pacific Northwest).

But we were not the only colonies on the earth. We were just a few among many European colonies throughout the world. The "discovery" of the Americas by Christopher Columbus and the colonization that followed were part of an enormous global European colonial enterprise. Not only the United States, but virtually every nation in the present world—whether in North America, South America, Africa, Asia, or Australia—has a history of being "discovered" and a story of colonial occupation and control by one or more European nations. Europeans once claimed ownership, by "divine right," of the vast majority of the world—its lands, its people, and its resources.

Told from the point of view of Europeans, this history of "discovery" and occupation is still held up today as a glorious and heroic accomplishment. Told from the point of view of the rest of the world, however, these stories describe the experience of violently destructive invasion and oppression. Most of these historically colonized territories are still trying to recover from this painful history. Moreover, colonialism and neocolonialism have not ended, but are still carried out today, not only by many European nations, but also by the United States[2] and other powerful nations.

Racism and colonialism are closely intertwined. The colonization and racialization of the non-European world were interlinked and virtually simultaneous. As I will attempt to explore further throughout this book, neither one could have taken place without the other, and neither one can be eliminated without the elimination of the other. Although awareness of the inseparable linkage between colonialism and racism is not new, I believe it is even more important today than ever to understand how colonialism and racism in the United States are interrelated, as can especially be seen in the continuing oppression of Latinos/Hispanics and Native Americans.[3]

Racism's Two Original Sins: Genocide and Slavery

During the colonial years of our nation, racism was perpetrated in the form of two unspeakably horrible and devastatingly evil activities—the genocide of indigenous peoples and the enslavement of African peoples. Moreover, these atrocities did not end when our colonial status ended; they continued long after we became a nation. The consequences of genocide and slavery still form deep and unhealed wounds in the heart and soul of our country. As a nation, we remain in deep denial about their having taken place and even more so about their ongoing effects. Genocide and slavery are the deep and foreboding roots of today's continuing racism. It takes courage and commitment to explore these two great crimes in our nation's history.

Genocide. From the perspective of most white people, the "discovery" of America was a marvelous accomplishment. Columbus is seen as a good person, a courageous sailor, and a hero who opened up the doors of opportunity for the people who came from Europe to this land that we now call "ours." The defeat and destruction of indigenous people is described as a victory of which we can be proud; it is still portrayed and celebrated in "cowboys and Indians" movies. We still describe Indians as savage and evil, deserving to be subdued and destroyed by our moral and upright soldiers and frontiers people.

From the perspective of most indigenous people of the Americas, however, along with other people of color, Columbus is not seen as a hero, but as the cruel and violent originator of Europe's colonial invasion and conquest of their land. Native Americans describe their resistance to colonial invasion as heroic acts of proud people.

The United States has never formally admitted to the crime of genocide. Nevertheless, conservative estimates are that during a period of approximately 375 years, between the time of the "discovery" of America in 1492 and the conclusion of the "winning of the West" in the mid-1800s, more than 90 percent of the indigenous population was either killed or died of related causes. According to historian Howard Zinn, "the Indian population of 10 million that lived north of Mexico when Columbus came would ultimately be reduced to less than a million."[4]

In the words of Bartolomé de Las Casas, a priest who traveled with Columbus and who protested Columbus's cruelty:

> . . . we dare confidently aver, that for those Forty years, wherein the Spaniards exercised their abominable cruelties, and detestable tyrannies in those parts, that there have innocently perish'd above Twelve millions of souls, women and children being numbered in this sad and fatall list; moreover I do verily believe that I should speak within compass, should I say that above Fifty millions were consumed in this Massacre. . . . For the Spaniards so contemned them (I now speak what I have seen without the least untruth) that they used them not like beasts, for that would have been tolerable, but looked upon them as if they had been but the dung and filth of the earth . . .[5]

Slavery. The enslavement of Africans by Europeans began in 1441. As many as fifty million enslaved Africans were forcibly removed from African soil, about one-third of which—ten to fifteen million—were brought to the Americas. No one knows the number for certain, but as many as half of those enslaved and carried away were killed or died on the journey. There is no way of understanding this deadly enterprise as anything other than global genocide, a holocaust initiated by Europe and continued by the United States.

In 1619, enslaved Africans were first brought to the American colonies, and a legalized system of chattel slavery was established. The system of slavery provided a primary source of labor and was a major economic pillar in the building of our country. Laws governing the slaves and their masters gave the slave owners full rights to treat the slaves as property like any other animal they owned, and the slaves had little or no rights at all. During America's 246 years of legalized slavery from 1619 to 1865, there were somewhere between eight million and twelve million slaves owned in our nation, with at least double that number having died on the journey between Africa and North America.[6] However much the horrors of slavery are researched and documented, they can never be effectively imagined or described. The system of slavery produced incalculably destructive results—to African people and to the soul of our nation.

From Colony to Nationhood: The Deepening of Racism

In the American Revolution in 1776, our status as a colony of England was brought to an end, and the United States became a nation. The passage from colony to nationhood served only to intensify and deepen our racist foundations, however, with the genocide of Native Americans and the system of slavery continuing unabated. The United States was designed as a race-based nation, and racism became embedded in our national identity in three primary ways: first, by becoming a white supremacist nation; second, by subjecting and enforcing the servitude of people of color; and third, by becoming ourselves a colonial power.

1. A White Supremacist Nation. The United States is a race-based nation. It always has been and it still is now. Every person born in the United States or who is naturalized as a new citizen of the United States is given a racial identity and assigned to one of six primary racial groupings: white, Native American, African American, Latino/Hispanic, Asian American and Arab American. Each of these racial groups has been carefully and legally defined.

More importantly, not only are we a race-based nation, but from the very beginning we intentionally defined ourselves as a white supremacist nation. The purpose of creating and maintaining racial categories was to make certain that the United States would exist exclusively for white people. From the moment of independence from Britain, the United States was intentionally designed with a racial hierarchy dominated by the white race. Racism became part of our national fabric, first of all, through the ideology and practice of white supremacy. The benefits of nationhood, the land, and all its resources were clearly identified as existing solely for white people. The Constitution of the United States was written exclusively for white people in the context of an explicit ideology of white supremacy. Moreover, all of the systems and institutional structures that were put in place under the shadow of the constitution's wings were openly and explicitly designed exclusively for white people.

These intentions of our nation's forefathers to be and to remain a white country were made even more explicit one year after the constitution's ratification. New citizens of the United States were required to be white. As Ian F. Haney-Lopez described in his book, *White By Law*:

> In its first words on the subject of citizenship, Congress in 1790 restricted naturalization to "white persons." Though the requirements for naturalization changed frequently thereafter, this racial prerequisite to citizenship endured for over a century and a half, remaining in force until 1952. From the earliest years of this country until just a generation ago, being a "white person" was a condition for acquiring citizenship.[7]

After the Naturalization Act of 1790 was passed, the Supreme Court was given the responsibility of defining who and what is a white person. Although the Court occasionally modified its definition of a white person, allowing some immigrants of color to be redesignated as white immigrants, the primary precepts of the Naturalization Act of 1790 and the reserving of citizenship for white immigrants remained in effect for more than 160 years, until the time of the civil rights movement.

It could not have been stated more clearly. The United States was designed as a nation exclusively for white people. People of color were permitted to be present for the sole purpose of serving the needs of a white nation. It is a surprise for many people to realize that the primary indicators of the foundations of racism in our nation are not just the ways that were devised to oppress people of color, but even more importantly the intricately designed blueprint and legal structures that proclaimed and guaranteed that the entire nation with all of its resources would exist exclusively for white people. That which still plagues us today, far more than the legacy of subjugating people of color, is the continued functioning of systems of white power and privilege that are still bearing the structures created exclusively for white people under the ideology of white supremacy. The preserving of white power in the legal framework and institutional structures of the United States ensured that the wealth of our nation would be amassed and passed on to succeeding white generations, creating a gap between white people and people of color that has barely—if at all—begun to be closed.

2. The Shaping and Subjugation of People of Color. After establishing white supremacy, the second step in building a race-based nation was to ensure that all people of color would be subservient to the white society and to create societal structures to place them in the service of white people. In the most explicit way possible, people of color in the United States were grouped into five separate, legally defined racial identities, and each racial group was given a role and function in the society. This was carried out openly and with full legal support during the first 160 years of our life as a nation—until the time of the civil rights movement in the 1950s and 1960s. Since that time, even though the explicitness of this function and purpose has been removed, the function nevertheless remains, though hidden and more difficult to perceive.

Originally, there was only one racial category for people of color: "nonwhite." However, the "nonwhite" category eventually evolved into five primary legal racial categories: Native American, African American, Latino/Hispanic, Asian American, and Arab American. These five categories have more recently become even more complex, refined, and subdivided, even to include legally recognized categories of "multiracial" and "other." However, the idea of "nonwhite" people in a white supremacist, race-based nation has never changed.

In later chapters, the absurdity of these racial categories will become even clearer, as will the evil purpose of the white society in creating these "races."

For the moment, in keeping with the need in this first chapter to review only a brief outline of the way in which racism has been structured in our history, the following descriptions will chart the path for later examination of the ways in which the lives of people of color were carefully and cruelly channeled to serve the purposes of the white society.

- *Native Americans: From Genocide to Reservations.* To put it as bluntly as possible, the United States wanted the Native Americans' land but it did not want the Native Americans. Thus, as the United States persisted in its frontier military enterprise of "winning the West," most of the indigenous people were killed through a "scorched earth" genocidal policy. For those who survived, a system of reservations was developed, which "gave" to Native American people relatively small parcels of land on which they were granted permission to continue as quasi-nations, and which would function under the watchful and controlling eye of the U.S. government. Parallel to the establishing of reservations was the creation of a system of Native American boarding schools, the purpose of which was to remove Indian youth from the reservations and put them through a socializing experience that would "get the Indian out of the Indian" and equip them to function off the reservation as second-class white people. Thus, the central goal of the United States was accomplished. We got the land, and we got the Native Americans out of the way.

- *African Americans: From Slavery to Segregation.* Not land, but labor is what the white supremacist system of the United States sought from African Americans. The inhumane system of slavery continued for seventy-five more years after ratification of the U.S. Constitution. Then, as a result of the Civil War and the Thirteenth Amendment, legalized slavery ended. The Fourteenth and Fifteenth Amendments theoretically guaranteed African Americans equal rights. It was a short-lived step of progress. Following a brief twelve-year period of Reconstruction, new methods to segregate and control African Americans were devised and legalized. Slavery was abandoned, but it was replaced by an alternate system of subjugation of the slaves' descendents. The goals of the new system were to prevent participation by African Americans in the political system, and to make certain their availability for the low-cost labor pool. This new system of subjugation of African Americans was firmly put in place when the Supreme Court decision of *Plessey v. Fergusson* in 1896 permitted the creation of a system of "apartheid—U.S. Style," which would stay in place for the next sixty years. Although the Ku Klux Klan and White Citizens Councils provide vivid reminders of the blatant cruelty of our shameful past, the system of segregation and apartheid was actively or passively supported in virtually every aspect of the white society, in the South and in the North.

• *Three More Races: Latinos/Hispanics, Asian Americans, and Arab Americans.*
The racialization of people in the United States began with the creation
of three races: a superior white race and the designation of two inferior
races of Indians and African descendents. However, the number of racial
identities was soon expanded to six with the addition of three new races:

1. "Latinos/Hispanics" as a racial designation was created out of a wide
   variety of Central and South American and Caribbean national and
   cultural groups whose only commonality is either the Spanish or Portuguese language and a shared early history of colonial oppression by
   Spain and Portugal. In addition to the goal of acquiring new land for
   the United States, the carefully defined role of Latinos/Hispanics is to
   also serve as a labor pool for the larger white society.

   The creation of this new racial category of Latinos or Hispanics
   began with the annexation of Mexican land in the U.S. Southwest in
   1848, and was followed by the territorial acquisition of Puerto Rico
   and Cuba following the Spanish-American War in 1898. Soon thereafter, this racial identity began to be applied to anyone who came to
   the United States from anywhere in Central or South America where
   Spanish (or Portuguese for the special case of Brazil) was the native
   tongue. Although new subdesignations and delineations for this racial
   grouping have come into being (for instance, Spanish surname, Hispanic white, Hispanic nonwhite, and so forth), a clearly racialized
   Latino/Hispanic racial identity has been established that applies to any
   non-European whose native tongue is Spanish, whatever may be their
   national, ethnic, or cultural heritage.

2. "Asian Americans" became a racial designation for laborers arriving in
   the United States from the Asian continent or Pacific Islands. It began
   with the importation of Chinese workers in the mid-1800s to build
   the railroads and to provide service in the expanding western frontiers
   of the United States. Then, other groups, including Filipino and Japanese people, arrived for similar purposes of laboring for white America.
   Like all other noncitizens of color who immigrated here as workers,
   citizenship was not open to them, and their status as temporary workers or undocumented "aliens" left them facing enormous legal rejection and social oppression.

   After the December 7, 1941, Japanese attack on Pearl Harbor,
   President Franklin D. Roosevelt issued Executive Order 9066. This act
   excluded persons of Japanese ancestry from residing in certain locations,
   particularly on the West Coast. As a result, there was a mass evacuation

and incarceration of more than 120,000 Japanese Americans, most of whom were U.S. citizens or legal permanent resident aliens. Their property was confiscated and they were detained for up to four years, without due process of law, and forced to live in bleak, remote camps behind barbed wire and under the surveillance of armed guards.

In relatively recent years, particularly as a consequence of U.S. military involvement in Asian countries, virtually every nation of Asia has been represented in the pool of immigrants into the United States. Each new group joins the hundreds of national and ethnic groups who are classified under this common racial identity of "Asian American."

3. "Arab Americans" are the newest addition to the list of racialized peoples in the United States. The Supreme Court and the Census Bureau have always been quite schizophrenic about the racial identity of Arabs and Middle Eastern people. At times, they have been legally designated as white people; at other times, they have been classified as nonwhite people. In recent years, and particularly since the events of 9/11, as is witnessed to in the following quote from Salah D. Hassan, from Cornell University, Arab and Middle Eastern people in the United States are more often than not considered a separate race within the United States, a race that is especially associated with the characteristic of "terrorist": "Unlike other racial constructs, which are now defined according to the census along a spectrum from white to black, the contemporary racialization of Arabs is linked primarily to US foreign policy in the Middle East, which is then translated into the domestic context."[8] It is difficult to predict how the process of racializing or deracializing Arab Americans and Middle Easterners will continue, since their racialized fate depends upon the outcomes of United States military adventures into the Middle East, as well as the responses of Middle Eastern countries to our economic and political presence in their countries.

3. The United States as a White Colonial Power. The third main aspect of our nation's history of racism is the role the United States began to play as a white colonial power. The interrelationship between racism and colonialism that was so clearly evident in European colonialism has been replicated dramatically in our national history. Even as the United States overthrew the colonial domination of England, and later also ended the colonial presence of Spain, France, and Russia, the nation took on the role colonizer—an expression of its white racial supremacy. As has already been indicated in the description of the purposes served by creating racial categories, the two major objectives of this exercise of colonial aggression were the acquisition of land and nonwhite alien labor:

- *Acquisition of Land.* As the United States' frontiers expanded westward, not only did the nation continue to occupy and colonize the land occupied by Native Americans, but also began to move into land that belonged to Mexico. All of the land in the Southwest United States, including California, Arizona, New Mexico, Texas, and six other states, once belonged to Mexico. Following the U.S. invasion of Mexico and the capturing of Mexico City, Mexico was forced to cede 55 percent of its land to the United States. The provisions of the Treaty of Guadalupe Hidalgo of 1848 included protection of language, property, and civil rights of Mexican nationals living within the new border—guarantees that were either quickly ignored or legally dissolved as new states were formed. It did not take long before most of the land belonged to white people, the language switched from Spanish to bilingual and then to English, and the Mexican landowners became farm workers and laborers for the new landlords.

  Then in 1898, fifty years after annexing half of Mexico, the United States began the colonizing of Puerto Rico, Cuba, and the Philippines, among others. Under the doctrine of "Manifest Destiny," the international role of the United States took on its invasive shape, fulfilling Thomas Jefferson's vision of the United States as an "Empire of Liberty." In succeeding decades, and continuing through today, scores of invasions by the United States military, and economic dominance by government and corporations have made the United States a dominant global colonial power.

- *A Source of Alien Labor.* The nation's greatly expanding economy required increasing numbers of workers for factories and farms. African American laborers and first-generation migrants from Europe were simply not enough. In order to supply additional labor, the floodgates were opened to import large numbers of Asian, Latino/Hispanic and Afro-Caribbean workers. The dilemma was how to make use of their services without being burdened with their permanent presence as citizens. The answer to the problem was a complex system of migratory labor that allowed "nonwhite foreigners" to become temporary residents, or even in some cases permanent residents, but to keep as many of them as possible from becoming citizens. Hidden beneath deceptive historical distortions is a simple fact: European immigrant laborers could become citizens and climb the ladder of success. All other immigrant laborers were declared to be "nonwhite" and remained disposable aliens, without the rights or the potential status of citizens.

An example: Chinese immigrants were imported in great numbers and exploited, especially in the West, as a source of cheap labor. The need for Chinese labor was reduced following the completion of the transcontinental railroad in 1869, however, and they were also perceived to be an increasing threat to the economy in California during the gold rush. Thus the Chinese Exclusion Act of 1882 was the first U.S. immigration law to target a specific ethnic group, denying citizenship for Chinese people who were already living as permanent residents in the United States.

A second example: following the annexation of huge portions of Mexico, Mexican and Mexican American farm workers joined African Americans as the labor pool for North American agriculture, and later for factories. In 1942, an official United States project, called the "Bracero" program, provided a legal basis for Mexicans to enter the United States for farm-labor purposes. It has often been called a program of "legalized slavery," and despite their enormous contribution to the national economy, the Braceros suffered harassment and oppression from extremist groups and racist authorities. Although the official Bracero program no longer exists, the use of undocumented Mexican immigrants remains an unofficial and unrecognized primary labor source for U.S. agriculture, but these workers nevertheless continue to be mistreated and victimized by both employers and law enforcement agencies.

A third example: the U.S. territory of Puerto Rico and other colonialized peoples of the Caribbean, such as people from Cuba, Dominican Republic, and Jamaica, also provided—and continue to provide—a significant amount of cheap migrant labor for the United States. Puerto Ricans in particular were given the schizophrenic identity (first as a colonial territory and later as a commonwealth) of semicitizenry and immigrant alien laborers. As Puerto Rican scholar and activist Victor M. Rodriguez has written:

Thousands of Puerto Ricans found themselves thrown into the migratory outflows created by economic and colonial policies. . . . Puerto Rican immigrants in the United States, particularly before U.S. citizenship was imposed on Puerto Ricans, found themselves in a vulnerable status. They were "stateless" in the sense that they were citizens of a colony with no international standing, and did not have the protection of a consulate or an embassy in the United States.[9]

Summary

A complex system of racial classification and racism was put into place in the United States from the time of "discovery" in 1492 through the time of the civil rights movement in the 1950s and 1960s. It was based on an ideology of white supremacy, it shaped a race-based government and society that was designed to exclusively serve the needs of white people, and it placed all people of color at white peoples' disposal. It is virtually impossible to describe the violent destruction that this system of white supremacy has caused and is still causing today.

The continuing imposition of racialized identities on people of color forms a constantly shifting racial hierarchy that dictates not only relationships of people of color to white people but also to each other. Particularly in chapters 2 and 6 I will more closely examine this racialized structure of the United States and how it perpetuates itself. As we progress in this and succeeding chapters to explore more deeply the presence of racism in our nation's past and present, we need to keep in mind the primary assertion of this book: that in the past fifty years, the dismantling of this complex racialized structuring of U.S. society has only barely begun. Despite the many legal and structural adjustments and cultural changes, the momentum of this past history still controls the lives of nearly everyone in our society.

Resistance to Racism:
The Better Side of a Bitter History

Racism is only half of the story. The other half is the tireless and heroic resistance on the part of racism's victims. No matter how bitter the history of violent oppression of racism, there is a better side, a side that is wonderfully inspiring. At every stage of history there has been a powerful and redeeming opposition to racism that has changed history and taken us a step closer to becoming the nation of justice that we claim we want to be.

This awe-inspiring and unrelenting journey toward racial justice has been a part of the history of our country from its very beginnings. For every act of racism there have been equal and opposite actions of resistance. Through the courageous efforts of millions of sisters and brothers who lived before our time, a broad path of freedom was cut through the jungle of racism. The path to freedom is more than five hundred years long; it is the very same path that so many of us are now struggling to maintain and widen. It is important to know that we are not the first on this path, and we are not alone. There is a great host of heroes and heroines who came before us, just as there is a great multitude of companions and co-strugglers who are with us now.

To understand more fully our place in history as we, in the early decades of the twenty-first century, seek to join our efforts to combat racism and build a multicultural society, we need to acknowledge and celebrate those who have been on this path before us. Those of us now gathered to help write an ending to the story of the Happiness Machines should be aware of those who came before us as well as those who join with us today in various parts of the world. All people were created to be free, and it is in the human spirit to resist when that freedom is being threatened. Again and again it has been demonstrated that, at the very moment of their subjugation and oppression, people commit themselves to survive, to resist, and to work for liberation.

As a white person reflecting on this wonderful history of resistance, I must be clear that this history was never taught to me by white historians. Moreover, as I will describe more fully in later chapters, I was carefully taught not to believe this history when it was told by people of color. It was only when I began to overcome this bias and to listen to history from the perspective of people of color that the blinders began to be removed from my eyes. I have been learning a corrected history that has become the basis for redefining the history of white people and people of color in the United States and throughout the world.

Led by People of Color—Joined by Many White People

First, and most important, this struggle against racism has always been led by people of color. African Americans, Native Americans, Latinos/Hispanics, Asian Americans, and Arab Americans have always been at the forefront, courageously standing and fighting the powerful forces of racism that seek to destroy them. When history's pages are accurately written, they will be filled with the names and deeds of these women and men who resisted the theft of Native lands and genocide, who rebelled against slavery, who opposed and fought against the exploitation of all people of color, and who rose up again and again to protest the desolation and death caused by white America. The names of these heroes and heroines need to be written in our hearts and more boldly than ever on the pages of history See page 266).

It is also important to remember and celebrate that throughout this history, an important role has also been played by a significant number of white people who were convicted by conscience and could not tolerate the racist acts of their fellow whites. In the Underground Railroad, for example, white station operators worked closely with black conductors in guiding runaway slaves to freedom. Likewise, white abolitionists and black leaders of slave rebellions inspired each other to greater acts of courage. In the distant past as well as in recent efforts for racial justice, white people have contributed significantly—even to the point of giving their lives—to the struggles of African Americans, Native Americans, Latinos/Hispanics, Asian Americans, and Arab Americans and Middle Eastern people.

The number of white people involved in these activities has never been large; nor can the celebration of their participation in resisting racism erase either the action or the acquiescence of the vast white majority. However, those who did join the resistance are a crucially important symbol and model for those who would follow their example today. These white people followed the leadership of people of color and stood courageously against the evil of racism. The names of these white heroes and heroines also need to be written on the pages of history and written on our hearts in a way that will never be forgotten.

Let us take a closer look at this better side of the bitter history of racism: the story of the resistance to racism.

Resisting Colonialism and Genocide

Our history books rarely inform us that when genocidal acts against Native Americans were initiated in 1492, a powerful resistance to racism also began. During our entire history, long before the revolutionary war and long after the shaping of the United States as a nation, indigenous peoples of the North American continent fought tenaciously and heroically against their European colonial oppressors. The Indian wars that white historians usually describe as European defense against Native American aggression are in fact the opposite. Since history is written by the victors, however, this amazing story of Native American resistance to colonial invasion and genocidal frontier expansion has either been unrecorded or unbelievably distorted by historians and particularly by the movie industry.

Nevertheless, this resistance *is* recorded, remembered, and celebrated by the survivors—the hundreds of tribes of Native Americans—who, though they were decimated, were not destroyed. Increasingly, across our country, this history is being lifted up and celebrated in Native American museums and in tribal celebrations, telling the stories of resistance and survival against the greatest odds.

Resisting Slavery and Apartheid

Likewise, the history of rebellion and survival by enslaved Africans has not been forgotten by their descendents, even though minimalized and distorted by the memories of white historians. When history's pages are accurately written, they are filled with the names and deeds of women and men who rebelled against slavery. These memories are preserved in stories and songs—including the powerful music of African American spirituals. Throughout the time of slavery, courageous and determined women and men followed a path of resistance "that with tears has been watered, treading a path through the blood of the slaughtered," to quote James Weldon Johnson's "Lift Every Voice and Sing," long considered the African American national anthem.

The rebellion and resistance of slaves began at the very moment when slavery was introduced in Jamestown, Virginia, in 1619; it gathered momentum during the 160 years of slavery during colonial times, and its full force was felt during the seventy-five years that slavery continued after the United States became a nation. They fought to survive bitter slavery and to demand the end of racial oppression. And at the end of the Civil War, the victory of emancipation was celebrated with cries and singing: "Free at last; thank God almighty, we're free at last." But it was a hollow victory, as the forces of white supremacy regathered and new forms of enslavement were devised. Racism continued, but so did the powerful resistance.

Following emancipation, during the brief twelve-year period of Reconstruction, black political and economic development took place in a way that was unmatched until the post–civil rights movement. Then the Jim Crow laws and Supreme Court decisions in favor of segregation were passed, shaping the new apartheid law of the land. In response, the resistance became even stronger. During the ninety-year period between emancipation and the beginning of the civil rights movement, powerful organizing took place at every level of U.S. society, including:

- legal organizing that would eventually be successful in challenging laws of segregation,
- self-defense organizations against the Ku Klux Klan and White Citizens Councils, and
- the powerful cultural developments of the Harlem Renaissance.

Nearly a century of constant and unquenchable organizing eventually brought to an astonished nation the birth of the civil rights movement.

More than Black and White: Red, Brown, and Yellow Resistance

This amazing history of resistance to racism has included all peoples of color. Far too often, the struggle for racial equality has been perceived, especially by white people, as a black/white issue. Before, during, and following the civil rights movement, media portrayal and popular thinking have far too often failed to recognize the racist oppression of other peoples of color as well as their stories of resistance. Latinos/Hispanics, Asian Americans, and Arab Americans have also struggled against racism in ways that have been heroic and momentous. They have risen up again and again to protest the desolation and death caused by white America. Tragically, the effect of racism has often made these different groups of people of color compete with each other for the meager resources that have fallen from white people's tables, and we have often failed to see and celebrate how their struggles against racism have complemented each other and created a strong and powerful defense against the common enemy of racism.

The Civil Rights Movement:
The Resistance Rewrites History

Occasionally in our lives, there comes a miraculous moment, after struggling for a goal against all odds, when we are least expecting it, that the barriers fall and victory is won. It is a moment when years of pressure against an immovable obstacle all of a sudden become enough, and the obstacle gives way. Most of us know such moments in our personal lives, and we also have pictures in our minds of phenomenal moments in history when long-awaited change suddenly happens: for example, the end of slavery in the United States, the fall of the Berlin Wall in Germany, the freeing of Nelson Mandela and the end of apartheid in South Africa. The civil rights movement in the United States in the 1950s and 1960s was also such a moment in history.

Throughout history, people of color suffering from injustice and oppression have had a deep belief in the final outcome of liberation. "Freedom now!" has been the rallying cry, the quiet encouraging voice, and the preacher's theme. The following excerpt from a sermon by Martin Luther King Jr. during the Montgomery bus boycott sums up this profound hope for freedom and justice:

> . . . the universe is on the side of justice. It says to those who struggle for justice, "You do not struggle alone, but God struggles with you." This belief that God is on the side of truth and justice comes down to us from the long tradition of our Christian faith. There is something at the very center of out faith which reminds us that Good Friday may occupy the throne for the day, but ultimately it must give way to the triumphant beat of the drums of Easter. Evil may so shape events that Caesar will occupy a palace and Christ a cross, but one day that same Christ will rise up and split history into A.D. and B.C., so that even the life of Caesar must be dated by His name. There is something in this universe that justifies Carlyle in saying, "No lie can live forever." There is something in this universe which justifies William Cullen Bryant in saying, "Truth, crushed to earth, will rise again." There is something in this universe that justifies James Russell Lowell in saying: "Truth forever on the scaffold / Wrong forever on the throne / Yet that scaffold sways the future / And behind the dim unknown stands God / within the shadows keeping watch above his own." And so here in Montgomery, after more than eleven long months, we can walk and never get weary, because we know there is a great camp meeting in the promised land of freedom and justice.[10]

The American Wall of Apartheid Falls

An amazing and extraordinary moment in cutting a path through the labyrinth of racism in the United States occurred in the lifetime of many readers of this book. It is still amazing to realize that only a few decades ago, a completely legalized apartheid system was still intact, controlling the lives of all people of color in the United States. Separate and unequal education was still the law of the land. Voting was blocked by an array of legal barriers. Residential housing and the use of all public accommodations were strictly segregated. Even though slavery had been abolished a full century before the civil rights movement, every African American was, for all practical purposes, still in chains; and Native Americans, Latinos/Hispanics, Asian Americans, and Arab Americans were subjected to similarly oppressive controls.

There were seemingly endless periods when one could believe that evil had triumphed, that those who controlled the chains and shackles would never yield. But, after centuries of genocide, trails of tears, broken treaties, slavery, segregation, and overpowering and overwhelming repression—in what now seems like a series of sudden and miraculous events culminating in a few strokes of the pen—the oppressive and carefully crafted legal system that mandated and supported segregation and discrimination was demolished.

Of course, as we shall remember and make clear a few pages from now, the successes of the civil rights movement and the other movements for justice were only partial, and much of what was given was then all too quickly taken away. Nevertheless, this was a time of incredible achievements by the forces of resistance to racism. Future generations must not be allowed to forget the scenes of hundreds of thousands of people rising up to protest, march, and demonstrate, to face police, dogs, fire hoses, and gunfire, to accept the punishment of prison, torture, and death—to bring down the walls of U.S. apartheid, making possible another great step of freedom and justice for humanity.

The Many Movements

Once again I want to emphasize that this story of resistance and struggle is not just a black/white story. There were other movements of resistance that paralleled and co-defined the civil rights movement, joining together to bring about so many achievements. These other movements of people of color included, among others, the American Indian Movement, the United Farm Worker Movement, the Brown Berets, La Raza, the Puerto Rican Independence Movement, and the Yellow Power movement among Asian Americans. The participation of each of these groups in the struggles of the 1950s and 1960s marked a new level of awareness of the interdependence of peoples of color in the struggle against racism; and it carved a new level of cooperation and mutuality that would greatly influence their relationships in the decades that followed. "Never in American history," writes historian Howard Zinn, "had more movements for change been concentrated in so short a span of years."[11]

This was also the time of the antiwar movement in opposition to the war in Vietnam, which also contributed enormously to both the upheaval and the accomplishments of this period. There were many ways in which it seemed that movements for racial justice, which were predominantly led by people of color, and the antiwar movement, which was mostly white, were in opposition to each other. The greatest moment in bridging this gap came when, on April 4, 1967, Martin Luther King Jr. took a public stand in an address at Riverside Church in New York City, declaring that it was impossible to disassociate the war against racism in the United States and the racist war in Vietnam.[12] There are many people who would also suggest a link between Dr. King publicly and visibly identifying himself with the antiwar movement and his assassination exactly one year later.

Violent U.S. Government Opposition to the Movements

Even while celebrating the powerful accomplishments in the 1950s and 1960s, it is impossible to ignore the tremendous forces of racist reaction during this period that sought to prevent the civil rights movement from being successful. Cruel acts of violence were perpetuated against those who worked for justice, not only by the Ku Klux Klan, White Citizens' Councils, and other reactionary white groups, but also by local, state, and federal police and other governmental agencies. Readers whose memories go back that far will recall such events as the murder of Emmett Till; the bombing of a Birmingham Sunday school, the attacks on the Freedom Riders; the hateful and violent attacks on demonstrations in Selma, Chicago, and many other cities; and the assassinations of Dr. Martin Luther King Jr., Malcolm X, Medgar Evers, Viola Liuzu, James Reeb, Jonathan Daniels, the three Philadelphia Mississippi registration workers (James Chaney, Andrew Goodman, and Michael Schwerner), and hundreds of others.

At the center of governmental racist reaction was the secret program in the basement of the FBI called "COINTELPRO" (Counter Intelligence Program). Even while the executive and legislative branches of government were writing and approving civil rights laws that would finally implement the Thirteenth, Fourteenth, and Fifteenth Amendments that were passed one hundred years before, another branch of the government was plotting to destroy the civil rights movement. J. Edgar Hoover, director of the FBI, created COINTELPRO and its stated goal "to expose, disrupt, misdirect, discredit, or otherwise neutralize" the activities and leaders of these dissident movements they considered dangerous. COINTELPRO committed acts of political terror and assassinations, and secretly infiltrated racial justice and antiwar organizations with *agent provocateurs* who sought to turn these organizations toward violence and thus justify police violence against them. They especially targeted the Southern Christian Leadership Conference (SCLC), Black Panthers, and other black civil rights groups, Nation of Islam, La Raza, Puerto Rican independence groups, the American Indian Movement, and a number of mostly white antiwar movements, including Students for a Democratic Society and the Student Nonviolent Coordinating Committee.[13]

Ultimately, in a report by an investigating governmental committee, COINTELPRO was exposed in the following words:

> Many of the techniques used would be intolerable in a democratic society even if all of the targets had been involved in violent activity, but COINTELPRO went far beyond that . . . the Bureau conducted a sophisticated vigilante operation aimed squarely at preventing the exercise of First Amendment rights of speech and association, on the theory that preventing the growth of dangerous groups and the propagation of dangerous ideas would protect the national security and deter violence.[14]

It is important to remember that the civil rights movement and these other movements did not die natural deaths. They did not run out of gas. They did not give up the fight. Their demise was neither accidental nor coincidental. Rather, they were systematically and intentionally dismantled, through acts of police violence and oppression, which were mostly coordinated by the U.S. government. As a result, by the end of the civil rights movement—around 1973—there were very few leaders of the movements who were not dead, in jail, or in exile.

Once More the Path Is Hidden

Surprisingly, even in the midst of this violent suppression, there was a sense in which there seemed to be some forward movement. Despite opposition, despite violence and death, by the early 1970s a fairly wide swath had been carved through the poisonous jungle of racism. Even more important, as the protest marches receded into the background, the legislative and judicial apparatus seemed ready to pick up the pace on the important new civil rights legislation they had created in response to the insistent demands of the resistance movements.

Many readers will still remember how good it felt when the civil rights movement drew to a close, and in the immediate years following, civil rights legislation and the war on poverty began to be implemented. Millions of people in our country affirmed that they wanted the future to look different from the past. Inside our government, during a brief, almost Camelot-like moment, the executive, legislative, and judicial branches of government demonstrated what could be accomplished if the will was there.

But the sense of progress was short lived. The nation began to balk and to grow tired of civil rights, of the Vietnam War, of the antiwar protesters, of being challenged and confronted. The elected leaders of the United States said, in effect, "We've had enough." Tragically, they didn't know they had barely begun.

Imperceptibly at first, and then with alarming speed, the newly carved path of justice once again began to be choked with the weeds of racism. The voters elected leaders who would, through active decisions and passive and malignant neglect, reverse the forward motion. Near the end of the 1970s, all the branches of government that just a few years earlier had appeared ready to do the right thing now seemed to coalesce and conspire on how they might do the wrong thing. The Supreme Court, well on its way to becoming the "Reagan Court," announced a series of decisions that undermined the effects of earlier hard-won victories. Bit by bit, decision by decision, they stripped away the power behind legislation affecting school integration, affirmative action, and other steps taken to eliminate discrimination. In 1989, looking back upon the wreckage of more than a decade of judicial deconstruction, Dr. Benjamin Hooks, executive director of the National Association for the Advancement of Colored People (NAACP), described the Supreme Court as "hell-bent on destroying the few gains that women and minorities have made."[15]

The Continuing Evil of Racism in the Twenty-First Century

We now come to the final part of this brief tracing of the history of racism and resistance in the United States—and we have also come to the central purpose of this book: to examine how racism is still functioning today. What has happened since the end of the civil rights movement is not past history. Rather, it brings us to the very moment in which you, the reader, are reading these words. It is the moment when the baton is passed to us by those who have run the race before us.

The primary purpose of this book is to examine how, despite all the heroic efforts to eliminate it in our past, racism continues to function in the United States today; and to ask how you and I can be a part of developing new and ongoing organizing strategies to dismantle racism. In order to do this, we need to examine and analyze carefully what has happened in the decades since the civil rights movement. What has changed? What progress has been made? How has racism continued? What has yet to be accomplished to bring this evil to an end? Why is changing hearts and minds not enough? Above all, we need to explore our own roles and how each of us is called to be a part of a continuing movement in this country and in this world to resist and to dismantle racism.

Nearly half a century has passed since the civil rights movement and other movements for racial justice came to an end. During the past fifty years, efforts to implement the accomplishments of the freedom movements have been often exciting and have even been partially successful. But there have also been terrible setbacks and failures. One thing is clear: the specter of racism is still present among us.

In matters of race relations and racism, the United States is a forgetful country—a nation in denial. An unfortunate and inaccurate impression has been created in the minds of many people that racial problems were solved in the 1960s. The common belief is that the barriers of racism have been removed and nothing more needs to be done, other than to wait for those who were left behind to catch up. Moreover, there is a kind of selective historical amnesia about the events of the 1960s themselves.

We need to restore our collective memories. We must not forget that an incredibly powerful struggle for justice took place in the 1960s, and that it transformed the face of the United States. The great accomplishments of that era need to be celebrated and not forgotten. At the same time, we need to be clear that racism was not eliminated in the 1960s; the evil is still present with us. The transformation was a long way from completed. We need to ask: What has changed and what has gotten better? And what has not changed or gotten worse? Our answers to these questions will help us determine what has yet to be done, and what our role is in taking next steps to further the dismantling of racism.

Better or Worse?

Today there is a great debate about the accomplishments of the movements of the 1950s and 1960s and about the progress or lack thereof in the years that followed. This debate is crucial for our task. Have we progressed? Have we regressed? On the one hand, a case can clearly be made that progress has been made and there is much that is better. But an equally strong case can demonstrate that there is much that is worse.

What do you, the reader, think? Consider for a moment what has taken place in recent years, and especially during these first years of the twenty-first century. What do you think is better? What do you think is worse?

Much Is Unquestionably Better

From one perspective, there is much that is unquestionably better. There are very few areas of life that have not at least to some extent improved for people of color during the past decades. It is hard to believe such repression was taking place just a few years before. In fact, many of our youth are now having trouble remembering or even believing that such oppressive laws existed in our country.

It is important to remember, and to affirm and celebrate these achievements:

- The laws of segregation are gone. With new civil rights laws enacted, access is guaranteed to all areas of public accommodation—restaurants, hotels, theaters, churches, etc.
- Equal Employment Opportunity (EEO) is a requirement for all public institutions, along with equal provision for advancement and promotions.
- Affirmative action in many public and private institutions provides advanced opportunities for people of color.
- Elected and appointed officials of color in local, state, and federal government institutions have significantly increased.
- Economic improvement has resulted in increasing numbers of people of color with middle and upper incomes.
- There are increased opportunities for education and increased levels of educational achievement among people of color.
- Personal attitudes and actions have changed, with growing individual and mutual acceptance based on a sense of equality. The ideology of white supremacy is decreasingly determinative of interpersonal relationships.
- There have been a number of public apologies for racism and even, in the case of Japanese-American people, reparations for incarceration.
- There is increased emphasis on multicultural diversity and inclusiveness, which reflects a desire to become a more diverse and inclusive society.

Of course, this is only a partial list. It could be much longer. As this list indicates, there are many dramatic changes for the better, and there can be no going back. There is an old saying that you can't put toothpaste back in the tube. As a result of the accomplishments of the civil rights movement, a level of transformation has taken place in our society that is, for all practical purposes, irreversible. The overt, intentional, and legalized system of apartheid has been virtually eliminated. The publicly proclaimed and accepted, explicit and unabashed doctrine of white supremacy that was the ideological foundation of our nation for the nearly five hundred years since Europeans came to these shores has been officially rejected.

It is true our nation has yet to admit culpability for these things having taken place, and the debate about reparations has only begun to open up the question of the need to take responsibility for the damage that was done. And it is certainly true, as we shall examine as deeply as possible in the course of this book, that new forms of racism have emerged that will take the United States to even deeper levels of transformation in order to eradicate them. However, without the achievements of the 1960s we would not even be able to begin to address these issues.

But Much Is Also Unquestionably Worse

Tragically, for every area in which there has been positive change, it is also necessary to recognize there is also much that is unquestionably worse. The pursuit of racial justice is not only incomplete, but in many ways we have taken giant steps backward.

- The reality of segregation continues. Despite desegregation, integration, and diversity, our society is more segregated—residentially and educationally—than it ever was.
- Our nation's wealth and power, which has for hundreds of years been passed on to white people by the momentum of history, has only barely begun to shift toward equalization with people of color.
- The changes that affected other people of color had virtually no effect on the lives and conditions of Native American people living on reservations or living off reservations in many of our nation's inner cities.
- Explicit racism has been replaced by forms of racism that are more hidden, more subtle, and more sophisticated.
- Despite some new opportunities, the quality of education, including achievement levels, for most people of color remains far below that of whites.
- On almost every measurable level, equal opportunity has not produced equal results—not even close.
- New legislation, public backlash, and court decisions are weakening or eliminating affirmative action.
- Increased numbers of people of color in governmental positions has not nearly been matched proportionally by increased power, at least partly due to regionalization and privatization of governmental functions.
- Poverty among people of color is still disproportionate, and the economic gap (including the "poverty gap" and "wealth gap") between white people and people of color has not significantly lessened.
- Inequality in the criminal justice system is pervasive, and the incarceration rate of people of color, especially African Americans and Latinos/Hispanics, is excessively high.

- There is a growing "permanent underclass" in our society, where hopelessness engenders a culture of violence and drugs.
- There is a great amount of denial that racism still exists. A "colorblind" ideology has replaced white supremacy as a way of avoiding the issue of racism.
- Multicultural diversity and inclusiveness is often superficial and ineffective, providing a thin veneer of change that covers unchanging conditions and power relationships.
- Immigration issues, particularly with regard to Latinos/Hispanics, indicate an extremely high level of unwelcomeness and political discrimination.
- Since 9/11, discrimination against and incarceration of Arab American and Middle Eastern people has dramatically increased as a reaction to terror threats against the United States.
- Global economic apartheid has increased, making increasingly acceptable the divisions between the developed and underdeveloped world, resulting in governmental power decreasing, while multinational corporate power is increasing.

Just as with the list of things that are better, this is also only the beginning of a very long list. If it were complete, it would go on for pages. What would you, the reader, add or change on these lists of the ways that race relations and race-based societal conditions have improved and how they have gotten worse since the 1960s? How do you assess what has happened to the forces of racism and resistance during these first years of the twenty-first century?

It is clear that racism has not gone away. The list of how conditions have gotten worse is as long as—or longer than—the list of positive changes. Despite the many accomplishments, despite the efforts extended and the lives expended, despite the changing of the legal structures, the power of this evil is still with us.

How Racism Is Different: The "Iron Fist" and the "Velvet Glove"

Even more important than the question of how it is "better or worse" is the question, How is racism different? How is racism expressed and felt today in ways that are different from the past? Racism is like a cancer that has the capacity to assume new forms and mutate into new expressions. We need a clear analysis of how racism is functioning today, and we need to analyze these new forms, and learn how to resist and reverse them.

A 1960s analysis of racism is not adequate to work for elimination of racism in the twenty-first century. The central issue is no longer public displays of bigotry and intentional, legalized discrimination. And the solution is far more complex than responding with marches and demonstrations.

Racism can be simple or complex; it can be expressed as an iron fist or a velvet glove. In the past, its main expression was the overt and blatant iron fist, but its newer forms are more subtle and less visible. When the iron fist is no longer possible, it shifts toward the more subtle and sophisticated form, with a velvet glove disguising the reality underneath. It is the velvet glove covering the iron fist that we seek to examine more closely in this book. As I will try to make clear, it is the velvet glove of racism that deceptively tries to give the impression that things are better and that the struggle against racism is nearly complete.

The "Iron Fist": Diminishing but Not Disappeared. Open and explicit racism has far from disappeared, even though it has been dramatically reduced. Racism in the vicious form of an iron fist is still quite visibly and dangerously active today. Hate groups are still organizing. Violent hate crimes are reported every day. Cross burnings, church burnings, race-based vandalism, beatings, and murders are part of our everyday headlines and experiences.

The Southern Poverty Law Center has been documenting hate crimes against people of color since 1981.[16] In addition, the federal government, mandated by the Hate Crime Statistics Act of 1990, provides documentation of violence and other hate crimes against people of color, as well as similar crimes by people of color against white people.[17] The statistics reveal that overt and violent forms of racism have not come to an end. The most publicized incidences of hate crimes are lodged in the memories of all those who work and pray for their end: Vincent Chin's brutal slaying in Detroit, the dragging death of James Byrd in Texas, the arson-engulfed churches throughout the South, to name a few. We still have visible and well-known hate groups that publicly espouse white supremacy and violence against people of color, such as the Ku Klux Klan, the World Church of the Creator (now named the Creativity Movement), The Militia, Aryan Nations, and other supremacist movements—including the Minutemen, purportedly guarding against terrorists on the border between the United States and Mexico.

Although these groups are usually described as "fringe" groups, it is important to recognize that in many ways they act out the beliefs and values of a much larger number of people who quietly agree with and encourage their activities. These white supremacist groups are the tip of an iceberg, and are indicators of far more serious problems that still lie beneath the surface.

But it is not only the fringe groups that exhibit explicit hatred and violence. As we have seen again and again in the past few decades, the law enforcement agencies of our cities throughout the United States—the police, the courts, and the prison system—are responsible for untold race-based harassment and brutality. Vivid pictures keep replaying of police violence against Rodney King in Los Angeles, Amadou Diallo in the Bronx, Donovan Jackson-Chaves in

Englewood, Timothy Thomas and Nathaniel "Skip" Jones in Cincinnati, Sean Bell in New York City, once again just to name a few.

But the problem is not just the nationally publicized cruelty caught by video cameras. Less visible in the national view, but painfully present in local communities, is the continuing cruel and inhumane treatment by the courts and prison systems. One example among many: in rural southwest Georgia, the work of the Prison and Jail Project, directed by John Cole-Vodicka, focuses on exposing and seeking to end explicit racism that persists in the legal system as though the civil rights movement and passage of civil rights acts had never taken place.[18]

The iron fist of overt and blatant racism is still present with us, and we are still not doing enough to eliminate it. Nevertheless, a case can be made that in the United States, with painful steps and slow, overt acts of hate-based violence are growing fewer. If this were the worst expression of racism, then we could feel gratified that we are working on the last vestiges of a disease that is on the path to extinction.

Racism Mutates: The "Velvet Glove" Covers the "Iron Fist." Instead of disappearing, however, racism has mutated into new forms that are in fact far more devastating. The velvet glove symbolizes and represents racism's almost magical power to hide and delude. Racism has assumed new sophisticated forms that are not as readily apparent and whose primary weapons of enforcement are bureaucracy, psychology, and public relations. The "velvet glove" of racism creates the illusion that it does not exist and therefore is far more difficult to detect and eliminate. Yet its power to oppress is no less than that of open and blatant racism. Iron fist or velvet glove—the results do not change, as figure 1.1 demonstrates:

Cause	Results
Iron Fist: Under the blatant form of racism's iron fist, laws explicitly dictated where people of color could live, the limits of their education, and the kind of work they must do.	People of color were ghettoized, undereducated, and underemployed.
Velvet Glove: Under the more sophisticated and "gentler" velvet glove, members of a subjugated race no longer have explicit boundaries dictating where they may live, no legal limitations on their education, nor restrictions on the kind of jobs they may have.	People of color are still ghettoized, undereducated, and underemployed.

Fig. 1.1.

Iron fist or velvet glove—the means are different, but the end is the same. Yet there are many people who believe that because the iron fist can no longer be seen, the power of racism has been removed. There are many people who actually say things like, "There is a level playing field now, and the rest is up to them," and "I don't know what they are complaining about; racism is no longer a major factor in their lives."

Here, then, is the dilemma that needs to be dealt with: racism continues its destructive actions as before, but in ways that are more hidden, more disguised, more sophisticated. From the outside, because we have lost sight of the iron fist and can only see a velvet glove, many people in the white community are all too easily convinced that racism has lost its power over people of color and is going away. Yet, for a person of color who is the target of racism, the velvet glove still feels like an iron fist and does not produce different results than the iron fist. A person of color who is still unable to get a job despite decades of "equal employment," or whose child's education is still inadequate after half a century of desegregation, will not be taken in by the new velvet glove covering racism, because it still feels like the old iron fist. As one commentator described the effects of racism's sophisticated new forms: "It may not be cross-burning, but it still grinds exceedingly small."[19]

Racism Is "Bigfoot"

To change the metaphor, these new forms of racism can also be described as a "kicking foot." The People's Institute for Survival and Beyond, the antiracism organization in New Orleans that I described in the introduction to this book, has developed a "Foot Identification" exercise that demonstrates the power of racism. The purpose of the exercise is to do a "power analysis"; that is, to portray how people of color experience the power of racism in their daily lives.

The Foot Identification exercise is a vivid portrayal of contemporary racism at work. In the exercise, academic or social-work language is replaced with street language. A person being interviewed in a local neighborhood might not say, "I am feeling powerless as a result of my being oppressed by racism," but rather, "I am getting my ass kicked every day of my life." The goal of the exercise is to reveal the power of racism by identifying the "feet" that are kicking people every day of their lives. The "feet" are identified as the systems and institutions that function differently within communities of color than they do in our white, middle-class communities—the banks and financial institutions, the school system, retail stores, the employment system, the criminal justice system—the police, courts, and prisons—the health-care system, the social-service system, the church, the media, and so forth. Each of these systems is felt as a kicking foot, partly because of the poor services they provide, but even more so because each of these systems and institutions is controlled from outside communities of color and is in no way accountable to these communities. Racism is seen and felt as "Bigfoot," the mysterious monster that can only be detected by its footprint, by the effect of its kicking foot in the lives of people of color every day of their lives.[20]

Whether or not the community of color in this Foot Identification exercise is an African American ghetto, a Latino/Hispanic barrio, a Native American reservation, an Asian American "Chinatown" or "Little Saigon," or an Arab American "Little Beirut," the results of the Foot Identification exercise are always the same. The "Bigfoot" of racism is quite real. The decision-making power that determines the daily life of communities of color comes from the outside, and it decidedly disadvantages the people who are trapped in their poor communities.

C. Eric Lincoln describes vividly the powerlessness of those who experience the "Bigfoot" in their daily lives in the African American ghetto:

Each morning all over America the great American tragedy was reenacted each time a black man looked at himself in a mirror as he shaved, and each time a black woman put on the face she would wear in her efforts to find bread for her family in the kitchens of the elegant houses far from the decaying flats and tenements of the racial compound to which she was assigned. What each saw in the looking glass was a cipher citizen, an American who would have no serious input in any of the decisions which would determine the quality of his or her significant experiences for that day, or any day; whose life chances had already been programmed with sinister predictability by persons unknown, or, even if known, unavailable and unconcerned. . . .

Freedom implies power—*the power to be responsible*. Such power was unthinkable because black responsibility lay well beyond what liberal White America envisioned when it endorsed the black mission to overcome. The power that shaped life in the black ghetto was not, and is not, of course, black power. It does not originate in the ghetto. It is power from the outside. It is alien power, with many faces. It is the nonresident merchants who come into the ghetto with the sun in the morning and who leave with the sun in the evening, taking with them the day's toll for their visitation. It is also the vexatious blue presence, that alien, anonymous, contemptuous phalanx known as "the law" but more often than not considered an army of occupation pursuing its own private system of spoils. It is the ubiquitous presence of alien school teachers, case workers, process servers, rent collectors, repossessors, bailiffs, political hustlers, and assorted functionaries and racketeers whose economic stakes in the black ghetto require their temporary and grudging presence imposed upon a community they detest and which detests them in return.[21]

Detecting and Measuring Twenty-First Century Racism

Thus, from the perspective of communities of color, the continuing presence of racism in the twenty-first century is easy to detect. For those who do not directly experience it, however, its presence is not so easily perceived. Whether it is described as "Bigfoot" or as a velvet glove covering an iron fist, racism has become more hidden and disguised, so that it is easy for white people to become convinced that it has gone away, or at least that it is rapidly diminishing and disappearing. In fact, the very effectiveness of the twenty-first century forms of racism is measured by its *not* being seen at work. So, the question is how to expose racism's new disguises?

The critically important question for this book is how is it possible to see the new forms of the old racism that are operating in ways that still devastate people's lives? How does a person "see" the velvet glove and detect the old iron fist that is being covered and disguised by a velvet glove? How can a society measure the presence and the effects of racism? In the chapters that follow, the goal is to reveal the ways in which new forms of racism comprise the powerful continuation of racism in the twenty-first century. Only as the eyes of each of us are opened and as we begin to understand how racism functions in our society today will we be able to devise new ways to oppose racism and to dismantle it.

To put the question another way, How can we really know whether racial conditions are getting "better" or "worse"? How can we know that racism is present, and how will we know when it is truly disappearing? Or, more simply put, how do we measure change from racial injustice to racial justice? Are there common criteria and standards of measurement that will produce agreement on the status of racial equality and inequality in our society? It is important to have effective and consistent means of quantifying the presence, absence, and intensity of racism, as well as its increase or decrease over a period of time. Since some people claim racism is disappearing, and others claim that it is as strong as ever, it is important that we use common methods of measuring.

We've Actually Never Measured Racism Before

To begin answering these questions, it is important to recognize that they are relatively new questions for our society. Prior to the 1960s, our nation neither measured nor even cared about measuring racism. Since the objective of the legal structures of white supremacy was to ensure that there would be differences, the only reason for measuring disparities between the white society and people of color would be to gauge and celebrate the success of these racist intentions.

Now, however, the law has set a new goal of equality. It is "officially" and "legally" no longer desirable that people of color be treated differently from white people (even if there are still uncounted numbers of people who "unofficially" wish these changes were not taking place). And so now, because it has officially become important for our society to be seen as changing with respect to race relations and racial conditions, one of the new public activities in recent years is that we are also deeply invested in measuring whether change is actually taking place. There are major enterprises in our government, in universities, and in private industry with the primary objective of measuring the differences and similarities of condition of life between the white society and the various groups of people of color.

The practical aim of this measuring is to create benchmarks by which forward or backward movement is detected. As we shall see, there is still a great deal of controversy over what needs to be measured, and the most accurate way of measuring it. Nevertheless, the good news—that which is essential to transformation taking place in our society—is that we are now measuring. And this measuring reflects a new instinct in our society: to desire equality officially and to care about whether it is being achieved.

Measuring change includes especially finding out if the "gaps" are opening or closing: for example, the residential gap, the educational gap, the employment gap, and the economic gap. Wherever there has been inequality and disparity between the races, there is measuring taking place to see whether and by how much the disparity is increasing or decreasing. In fact, our society is measuring just about everything that is measurable, with the theoretical goal and the projected hope that one day these measurements will bring back reports of achieved equality. Extremely sophisticated methods of measurement have been developed in order to determine what has gotten better and what has stayed the same or gotten worse.

Measuring the "Gaps"—Three Popular (but Insufficient) Methods

During the past forty or fifty years, three main methods of measuring have been generally accepted as ways of determining progress with regard to issues of racial equality in the United States. These three measuring categories are "legality," "opportunity," and "intentionality." As we shall see below, serious questions need to be raised as to whether these are the most valid measuring methods. For the moment, however, let us first see what is learned by using them.

1. "Legality": Equal Rights Under the Law. For more than 450 years the system of white supremacy and racial domination in the United States was defined and upheld by the law. Then major changes in our legal system took place during the civil rights movement. As a result, it is theoretically no longer possible to use explicit legal measures to defend or enforce white supremacy in the United States. Thus, since the first step on the path to eliminating racism was changing the law, the first thing that needs to be measured is whether the laws enforcing racism have been effectively reversed, and whether the new laws to end racism are being effectively enforced.

For example, segregation took place in the United States by making it the law of the land. Then the Supreme Court decided that segregation laws were not legal, based on other laws that take precedence, including the Thirteenth, Fourteenth, and Fifteenth Amendments to the Constitution, which guaranteed the end of slavery, equal protection under the law, and the right to vote. As a result of this decision by the Supreme Court, civil rights laws were passed, seeking to guarantee equality under the law.

In hundreds of ways, laws have been changed in order to create new legal foundations for racial justice in the United States. As a result, white supremacy, a fundamental principle of our nation from 1492 to 1954, is theoretically no longer supportable by the law. And any violations of this principle are challengeable under the law.

Thus the first method to measure change is to evaluate changes in the laws. For several reasons, however, just changing laws is not enough. To begin with, the mere existence of a law does not guarantee that it will be implemented and enforced. Furthermore, as we have experienced repeatedly in recent decades, laws can be weakened and even eliminated by the interpretation of the courts. And a far more serious problem is that racism can circumvent the law, operating in increasingly subtle, sophisticated, and extralegal ways, always one step ahead of the law.

2. "Equal Opportunity": A Level Playing Field. The second method for measuring change is the presence or absence of equal opportunity. Assuring equal opportunity has been a guiding principle and a means of measuring progress toward racial justice since the 1960s. A popular image is that we need to create a level playing field for all people. A great deal of new legislation was created that seeks to guarantee equal opportunity. Nearly every public institution in our society now has a public declaration on the wall at the entrance, stating that this institution provides equal opportunity without regard to race, gender, religion, and (more recently) sexual orientation.

As a result, a number of doors were opened for people of color that had been closed. These open doors created new opportunities in education, jobs, housing, politics, and many other areas of life. Hundreds of thousands of people of color have walked through these doors. New opportunities have produced a significant increase in the size of the "minority middle class," representing new and potentially powerful leadership for the future: educators, communicators, business people, social scientists, political leaders—and the list goes on. The importance of this new generation of highly skilled people is just beginning to be felt.

As part of creating new opportunity, a controversial concept is that of "affirmative action." Its validity is regularly debated in the media and contested in the courts. There seems to be little question that affirmative action provides greater opportunity for people of color, along with women and other groups that have been disproportionately left behind in our society. However, the debate is whether it creates a form of discrimination that has been determined to be outside the law. As we shall see in chapter 3, the way a person feels about affirmative action revolves to a great degree around the question of the need for corrective action for centuries of historical affirmative action for white people.

3. "Intentionality": Measuring Racism Committed "On Purpose." The third category of measuring is the "intentionality" of racist behavior. This concept is, to a great degree, subjective, since intentionality often has to do with personal attitudes and actions. However, "intentionality" is also a legal term that is increasingly used in courts of law to determine whether or not those accused of illegal actions actually intended by their actions to do harm on the basis of race. Only if the perpetrator of a violent action says the "N-word," or otherwise gives evidence of racist intent just before plunging the knife into the victim, may it be considered a racial hate crime. There is, of course, serious debate as to whether intentionality as a legal concept is a valid means of measuring the presence or absence of racism. Indeed, criminal behavior can have racist results even if it is perpetrated by people who have no racist intent. Nevertheless, this means of measuring the power of racism has become well accepted within the criminal justice system, even if it may have only limited usefulness.

There is no denying that these three methods of measuring racial conditions—legality, opportunity, and intentionality—are important, but they fall seriously short of being adequate to measure twenty-first century racism as it is expressed with a velvet glove. In fact, by using only these three standards of measurement it is possible to make an argument that quite a bit of success has been achieved in working toward the elimination of racism in our society. The laws have successfully been changed; opportunity has been greatly increased; and intentional hate crimes have been diminished. But, despite the indications of success by these three measuring tools, there is still a long list of things that are much worse rather than better in racial conditions in our nation.

Why are these three measuring tools not enough to measure the continuing power of racism? The simple reason is because they measure the starting line of the race, and not the end of the race. None of these measuring tools measure final outcomes. None of these methods of measurement is able to tell us if equality between white people and people of color in the United States has actually been achieved. These three measuring tools tell a story of wanting to do better, but they do not tell us if we have accomplished our goals. Tragically, when we only use these three measuring tools, they actually become a part of the velvet glove, and a part of the new disguise for racism's continuation.

The Missing Fourth Criteria: Measuring Results

It is the contention of this book that a fourth and far more important measuring tool must be used in conjunction with these other three: the measuring of results. Simply stated, this means that the absence of equal results means the continued presence of racism. If, despite decades of effort, there is still a wide gap between people of color and white people in the statistical measurement of housing, education, employment, wages, leadership distribution, decision-making power, or any other area of public life, there is an unavoidable conclusion that racism is still at work. Conversely, when—and only when—there is parity between people of color and white people in these statistical measurements, the claim can be made that racism is being overcome and eliminated.

Of course, as anyone familiar with statistical measurement will quickly note, it is not quite as simple as all that. There may be other complicating factors to explain disparities. To measure conditions within a society and to explain deviations from the norm is a very complex process. For every statistical deviation there are many possible explanations, such as historical background, cultural variations, and differences in values. Nevertheless, it is also possible to make statistical adjustments that take such factors into account. When this is done, it is possible to measure the results of racism with accuracy.

The Results Have Not Changed

If we measure results, it becomes quickly obvious that racism has not been overcome. There is more than adequate documentation to identify the continued presence of both the iron fist and the velvet glove of racism. From the list of things that are better and things that are worse on the previous pages, it is clear that racial conditions are in some ways improved, but that in a myriad of ways they have not improved. Likewise, any number of studies and surveys conducted since the end of the 1980s and continuing into the first decade of the twenty-first century reveal that in some areas there has been a lessening of the gap between people of color and white people, but that in other areas the gap has widened. On average, despite changes in the law, despite new opportunities, and despite good intentions, the differences in basic living and working conditions between people of color and white people have remained more or less the same.

To be sure, there has been a gradually increasing middle- and upper-income group within people-of-color communities. But it has not been large enough to diminish the lower income and poverty status of the majority significantly. And it has not diminished the *de facto* segregation between white communities and communities of color. When statistics about a growing "middle class" among African Americans, Latinos/Hispanics, and Asian Americans are misused to cover the continuing economic and social poverty of the majority of people of color, then even the improvements become a part of the velvet glove of continuing racism.

Although there is room enough in this book to provide only samples of documentary evidence of the continuing results of racism, more complete sources of documentation are listed in the footnotes and bibliography.[22]

- *The Economic Gap.* There is an enormous economic and poverty gap, forming a "permanent underclass" in the United States, the world's richest society. In 2004 African Americans, Latinos/Hispanics, and Native Americans each had poverty rates nearly three times as high as those for whites. Poverty rates among African Americans were 24.7 percent, among Latinos/Hispanics 21.9 percent, among Native American and Alaska Natives 24.3 percent, but among whites only 8.6 percent. The odds of economic and social success are stacked against children who are born into communities weakened by poverty, broken families, substance abuse, violence, unemployment, and substandard schools.

- *The Education Gap.* Higher education is key to increasing income and wealth over a lifetime. Educational attainment rates have improved for all racial and ethnic groups since 1960, but there is still a long way to go to close the gap. More than 27 percent of whites had achieved a bachelor's degree or more in 2003, but only 17.3 percent of African Americans and 11.1 percent of Hispanics/Latinos did. In 2000, 11.5 percent of American Indians and Alaska Natives had completed higher education.

- *The Housing Gap.* Although home ownership by people of color increased between 1989 and 2003, a wide disparity still remained: 72.1 percent of whites own their homes, but only 48.1 percent of African Americans and 46.7 percent of Hispanics/Latinos.

- *The Social Service Gap.* From 1985 to 2005, while government funding for the military increased by 37 percent, there were decreases by an average of 40 percent for low-income housing, low-income employment services, child care, health care for migrants, and maternal and child health, taking away major pieces of a social safety net for those who need it most. Societal response systems, emergency and otherwise, are far more effective for white people than for people of color, as was demonstrated once again quite clearly in the face of Hurricane Katrina in New Orleans and other parts of Louisiana and Mississippi. This gap is seen and felt in the every day life of people of color in every part of the United States.

- *The Criminal Justice Gap.* Our punitive criminal justice system is weighted against poor people of color, with a disproportionate number ending up in jail. Bureau of Justice Statistics data show that of the 1.4 million people serving more than a one-year term in state and federal prisons by the end of 2003, 44 percent were African American, 35 percent white, and 19 percent Hispanic/Latino, a ratio that had changed little since 1995. Of the record-high 4.8 million adults on probation or parole nationwide, 30 percent were African American and 12 percent Hispanic/Latino. Unequal treatment of people of color has been well established at each stage of the criminal justice continuum, from profiling to sentencing. The greater protection and service given to white society by police, and the use of the media and the criminal justice system to demonize and criminalize people of color, results in a completely disproportionate presence of people of color in our prisons, and particularly on death row.

The list is almost unending. An inventory of the continuing disparities and divisions between white people and people of color would also include such issues as immigration, language, health care, governmental representation, media, arts and entertainment, and every other area of societal life, including even basic human issues of communication, fear, and mistrust.

The continuing results produced by the evil of racism cannot be denied, despite our efforts based on legality, opportunity, and intentionality. In the final appraisal, only results will indicate the overcoming of racism. As I will further argue in the analysis of racism presented in the coming chapters, there are clear reasons why these results have not yet changed significantly enough. And there are very clear steps that can and must be taken in order to close these gaps. The task is to continue to rebuild the path toward justice until fundamental transformation and true equality come to our society's racism-wracked landscape.

The Twenty-First Century: A New Beginning

The Call to a New Beginning

This portrait of U.S. society depicts us as a people more conflicted than ever over the subject of race and racism. Our nation's inconsistent behavior is obvious, but not easy to comprehend or explain. On the one hand, we pridefully describe our forward movement. With great satisfaction we make lists of improvements, not only on levels of personal relationships, but also in areas of changed laws and equal opportunity. On the other hand, we express deep-seated hostility to those who expose continuing racism and repeatedly resist acknowledging the need for further changes. This contradictory behavior reveals a schizophrenia that lies just below the surface of our collective psyche. It is a schizophrenia that leads us again and again into unresolved cyclical patterns of behavior.

In this first chapter I have sought to describe this continuously replaying cycle in the history of our nation. From 1492 to the present, this cycle moves repeatedly from racism, to resistance to racism, to new efforts to become a racially just people, and then the cycle of the evil of racism begins again. Our present situation cannot be understood outside of this cyclical history and all that it brings to our current situation. Our nation is today what our history has made us; each component of this repetitive cycle is still playing out among us. The unfinished task of resolving these contradictions is before us.

What does it mean for the United States to be faced with this unfinished task and the dynamic of the cycle once again turning inexorably toward us? It can be seen as a depressing repetition of history, holding little promise or possibility. Or it may be perceived as the sign of new opportunities for struggle and change. It depends on where we stand. For those who have hoped and prayed for an end to complacency and longed for a new commitment to racial justice in our country and in our world, these are not so much indications of defeat as they are opportunities for a new beginning.

The circles of history do not have to be vicious cycles in which we are condemned to face the same problems and make the same mistakes over and over again. The continuing challenge to all of us, but especially to white America, is to come to grips with this unfinished task and with the forces that seek to prevent us from taking the next steps forward. Our challenge in this book is to analyze and understand, and to equip ourselves with what is needed for a new way forward.

A new beginning for our nation starts with a renewed struggle for racial justice. Looking back at the last half-century of reversals and regression, looking at the present moment of continuing racial divisions and racism, and looking ahead to the call for a new moment in history, it is time for us to turn once again to the reopening and creating of a yet wider path, a broad highway of justice through the maze of racism in America.

New Contexts for a New Beginning

As we start down this path once again, it is important to recognize that things have changed since the last time we passed this way. The first years of the twenty-first century are very different from the 1960s. We are building on the accomplishments of past struggles. There are at least five ways in which the situation has changed, providing new contexts and new definitions for our struggle.

1. *The law has changed.* Prior to and during the civil rights movements, the only weapon against racism was moral pressure. Now, the laws that explicitly defined white superiority have for the most part been removed, and an entirely new set of laws seeking to control discriminatory behavior have been created. Even though these laws are often being undermined and are not being effectively implemented, racial injustice is theoretically illegal. Laws and policies promoting equality and seeking to end racial discrimination exist not only in our federal, state, and city governments, but also in most corporations, business and industry, and in unions, universities, and churches.

Several things have been gained. In the first place, a legal standard against which the existence of racism can be measured is beginning to emerge. In the second place, continuing racism exposes an internal contradiction in our legal structure. Society's own laws are being disobeyed, not just the mandates of religion or the dismissible moral imperative of a liberal fringe. Ultimately, if a society based on law is to survive, it will enforce its laws and protect those victimized by the violation of those laws. Therefore, we who work to eliminate racism in the United States have a new and powerful weapon with which to accomplish our goals: racial injustice is against the law.

But changing the law is not enough. Despite the law, racism still thrives and prospers. Notwithstanding many positive changes, racism continues to infect and affect nearly every area of our national life. In many ways, racism has become more deeply imbedded, more carefully disguised, and more difficult to eradicate. The separation between white people and people of color has widened; tension and hostility have deepened, producing in communities of color a greater sense of despair and abandonment than ever. For those who know that legal issues are only part of the equation, this book asks the question, How can we build on the accomplishments of the past and redefine the task of dismantling racism in a way that moves toward more effective change?

2. *A central focus is now on economics.* Once the battle against segregation and discrimination in public accommodations was won, a far more serious problem needed to be addressed: racism in economics. A popular expression says it all: "It doesn't help to have the right to eat in a restaurant if you can't afford the prices on the menu." Economics has always been at the core of racism. The elimination of segregation and discrimination in public accommodations and at the voting booth were necessary first steps. But they were merely

preludes to the more central struggle against segregation and discrimination in the marketplace, and even further, the testing of whether racial justice is even possible under the present economic system.

But economic change is not enough. Money does not measure everything. Centuries of white supremacy created more than economic dominance. There are other dimensions of life that measure the peopleness of a people, such as values, culture, religion, and identity. All of these have been subjected to the destructive power of the Happiness Machine. In the following chapters the reader will be invited to explore not only the centrality of economics in defining new directions to confront and eliminate racism, but these other dimensions as well.

3. *Partial success is disguising the unfinished task of dismantling racism.* White people in the United States are divided by two primary divergent streams of thought and belief. The mainstream contains those who believe that the task is completed and little more needs to be done. Within this same stream, there are also differing viewpoints, with some people feeling a sense of accomplishment and others resentful that it was done in the first place. Both groups in this stream, however, have little awareness of the unfinished task. In recent years, this mainstream group has been taught to define its relationship with people of color in terms of an insidious color-blind ideology that describes reality without race and tries to make the problem of racism go away by pretending that race has gone away.

The second stream contains all of those who are quite aware that the task is still incomplete. However, there is a great deal of difference and disagreement within this stream about what needs to be done and how it should be carried out. At one end of the spectrum are those who advocate "more of the same"—continuing with the same strategies of the past decades since the civil rights movement. At the other end of the spectrum are those who view the continued pursuit of the present path of change as ultimately destructive and are seeking new understandings and new strategies for change. The purpose of this book is to address this second stream of thoughts and beliefs—to be in dialogue with all those who are quite clear that the task is incomplete, but are not clear what yet remains to be done. The goal is to explore the possibilities of growing closer to a common understanding of racism and what can be done to overcome it.

4. *Changing demographics are producing new battle lines, new strategies, and new leadership.* At some point in the twenty-first century, the white population will no longer be the majority. Dramatic new possibilities are inherent in recognizing that those who have tried so unsuccessfully to maintain their

identity by the myth of the melting pot can soon be outvoted. Behind the reluctant willingness to permit integration, and behind the erratic movement toward multicultural diversity, has been the assumption that white people would always maintain ultimate control. If white society can get past the fear of loss of control, it may be possible to comprehend the extraordinary potential of these momentous changes.

Especially important to this evolving reality is the emergent leadership roles of people of color. Unfortunately, it is easier to comprehend this intellectually than to follow in practice. The priorities of white people in achieving racial justice are often quite different from those that are defined by people of color. Throughout this book, white readers will be encouraged to develop a stronger commitment to follow the strength and leadership of people of color.

5. *Racism is a global issue.* Racism in the United States is linked to and inseparable from racism and other forms of oppression and suffering throughout the world. Many of us became especially aware of this during the final struggle against apartheid and efforts to build multiracial democracy in South Africa during the 1980s and 1990s. Most nations of the third world still suffer from the long-term effects of colonialism, neocolonialism, and contemporary global imperialism. Economically, politically, and morally, global apartheid can no longer be ignored or excused. No longer can a small minority of predominantly white nations be permitted to maintain themselves with incredible privilege at the expense of the majority. Although the primary focus of this book is to portray how racism functions within our own country, the assumption behind this portrayal is that resolution of racial issues within individual countries, including our own, can no longer be dealt with in isolation from global issues of racial and economic injustice, and our own nation's role in perpetuating them. As Cornel West has written,

> Let us not be deceived: the great dramatic battle of the twenty-first century is the dismantling of empire and the deepening of democracy. This is as much or more a colossal fight over visions and ideas as a catastrophic struggle over profits and missiles. Globalization is inescapable—the question is whether it will be a democratic globalization or a U.S.-led corporate globalization (with thin democratic rhetoric). . . .
>
> . . . we must remember that the basis of democratic leadership is ordinary citizens' desire to take their country back from the hands of corrupted plutocratic and imperial elites. This desire is predicated on an awakening among the populace from the seductive lies and comforting illusions that sedate them and a moral channeling of new

political energy that constitutes a formidable threat to the status quo. That is what happened in the 1860s, 1890s, 1930s and 1960s in American history. . . . We must work and hope for such an awakening once again.[23]

In this chapter, I have attempted to show that our nation's twenty-first century reality is a product of a long history of racism and resistance. We now face a new context and are called to a new beginning in the struggle to understand and dismantle racism. In chapter 2, the next step is to explore a common understanding and definition of racism.

2

DEFINING RACISM

"I'm not a racist, but . . . ," claims a person talking about his racial beliefs.

"The police have determined that the crime was not an incident of racism," reads a quote from a newspaper article.

"The problem isn't racism; it's an economic problem," argues a person in a debate about racial issues.

"I don't see color," claims a university student, defining herself as a "nonracist."

"Reverse racism" is charged in a lawsuit by a white man as the reason he did not get a job.

As the above examples demonstrate, the word *racism* is understood differently by many people, and is used in many confusing and contradictory ways. It is a powerful word that carries with it a great deal of emotion-laden implications. It is a word that brings about defensiveness and denial in white people, especially when they are accused of being racist. At the same time, racism is a word that people of color have used for centuries to describe the conditions under which they are forced to live in the United States.

The Need for a Common Definition of Racism

The goal of this chapter is to develop a definition of racism. The way a problem is solved depends on how it is defined. It is impossible to resolve a problem or treat a sickness without a proper diagnosis. And yet we have a long history in the United States of trying to solve the problem of racism without agreeing on what racism is. If we don't have a shared definition and analysis of racism, we will never be able to agree upon shared solutions. In order to reach the end of this book with a common analysis and a commonly agreed-upon way to dismantle racism, there must be a clear definition that will be used consistently throughout the book.

Thus, the first step to comprehending racism and how it functions in the United States is to come to a common understanding of what we mean by the word *racism*. We need to begin by recognizing that there are, in fact, many different understandings of racism, and there is no commonly agreed-upon definition. In fig. 2.1 below is a list of words and phrases that are often used in the United States to define or describe racism.

Do you agree this is a representative list of some of the many ways racism is defined or described? What would you add? It should be obvious by looking at this list that there are multiple ways of defining racism.

```
Racism is . . .
Personal prejudice
Systemic power
Bigotry
Institutional
   discrimination
Hate
Oppression
Bias
Segregation
Personal dislike
Economic inequality
Political control
Stereotyping
White supremacy
Personal belief in
   superiority
```

Fig. 2.1.

Is Racism an Individual Problem?

Now let's rearrange the words on this list into two categories *See* fig. 2.2). Some of the words in the above list describe individual attitudes and actions of individuals, and some of them describe the actions of groups and institutions. More often than not, when racism is discussed in our society—on TV, radio, in newspapers, or in popular conversation—it is described in terms of an individual issue, a matter of personal attitudes and actions. Especially in the white community, the word *racist* is often used to describe individuals who are racially prejudiced, biased, or bigoted in their attitudes or actions. For most of us who are white, racism is perceived as the same thing as racial prejudice, individuals having bad feelings or opinions about another person simply because of her or his racial identity.

. . . Or Is Racism a Collective Problem of Systems and Institutions?

Other people—and from my experience it is more often people of color than white people—define racism in terms of the power that systems and institutions have on their lives: schools, banks, police, government, businesses, churches, and so forth. If we listen carefully to the way people of color describe their experience of racism, it will not usually be described in terms of individual attitudes and actions, but rather using terminology similar to the list of collective actions in the box below (fig. 2.1): issues of power, control, and oppression. They will describe the difficulties of finding a job, having a decent home, getting a good education, or being treated fairly by the criminal justice system. Of course, they may also speak of white individuals as racist. But most people of color are clear that the power to hurt and control them does not come so much from individuals as from the power of the systems and institutions of our society.

And so, we have two different approaches to defining the problem of racism. One is based on individual attitudes and actions; the other is based on the actions of systems and institutions. One approach is heard mostly from white people and the other is heard mostly from people of color. Not surprisingly, very often when white people and people of color attempt to communicate with each other about racism, we end up talking past each other, because we have two totally different understandings of the word.

Racism can be seen as a problem of *Individual Attitudes/Actions* by a person of one race toward a person of another race	Or, racism can be seen as a problem of *Collective or Group Actions* of one racial group toward another racial group
• Personal prejudice • Bigotry • Hate • Bias • Personal belief in superiority • Stereotyping • Personal dislike	• Systemic power • Institutional discrimination • Oppression • Segregation • Economic inequality • Political control • White supremacy

Fig. 2.2.

Different Definitions Produce Different Solutions

As stated above, the way a problem is solved depends on how it is defined. These two different kinds of definitions of racism suggest two very different solutions to the problem. If racism is defined in terms of individual attitudes and actions, then the way to end racism will be to change individuals, to reduce or eliminate racial prejudice. In fact, that is how we who are white commonly talk about solutions to racism. We work at reducing or eliminating our prejudices, changing our attitudes and actions. We work on getting along with each other, improving race relations, and seeking racial reconciliation.

We seek to build personal relationships with people of color that demonstrate that we are not prejudiced and that we like people of color. As white people, we want to feel good about ourselves, and we want people of color to feel good about us, too. One of the expressions we use very often in the white community is "Some of my best friends are . . ."

Of course, no one can deny that it is important for all of us—white people and people of color alike—to work on personal prejudices. It is a good instinct for an individual person to want to be free of prejudice. The problem is that just focusing on individual attitudes and actions cannot end racism, because individual attitudes and actions are only a small part of racism. Simply working on our personal issues and relationships does not make racism go away. In order to get to the root of the problem of racism, it is necessary to probe deeper than the issue of individual race prejudice. We need to include the other items on the list—the ways racism expresses itself systemically and collectively.

By paying attention to the voices of people of color and defining racism as not only a problem of individual attitudes and actions but also a problem of the collective actions of systems and institutions, the solution to racism takes on new dimensions. It calls not only for change on individual levels, but also on institutional levels. If the problem is only individual attitudes and actions, then individual change is enough. But if the problem is also systems and institutions, then individual conversion is not enough, and the solution must include institutional and systemic transformation.

Introducing a Definition of Racism

I want now to propose a working definition of racism. It is intended to be a definition that readers of this book can explore and test, and if it passes the test, then it can be a common definition that can be used on a common path toward dismantling racism.

Before introducing the definition, I want to set up some very stringent criteria that I believe such a definition must meet:

- The definition must speak to both the individual and institutional aspects of racism. The definition must adequately describe the terrible destructiveness of racism as a systemic and collective evil, yet include the racist acts of one individual or the sufferings of a single victim.
- The definition must not oversimplify or avoid the most painful and difficult aspects of racism; it must reflect accurately the historical and present-day realities described in the previous chapter.

- The definition must take into account racism's persistence and resistance to change, while at the same time recognizing ways in which it is successfully being overcome.
- The definition must clearly expose racism's causes and unflinchingly name those responsible for it, and at the same time be inviting to all those who wish to work for its elimination.
- Finally, the definition must leave room for debate and disagreement on the part of the reader, and at the same time be consistently applied throughout this book.

This is a tall order. Let us see how close we can come to fulfilling it. The definition I would like to introduce is this:

RACISM

=

Race Prejudice

+

the Misuse of Power by Systems and Institutions

Many readers will have seen some variation of this definition before. This is not a private or unique definition that I have created, or that is used solely in this book, but is a definition that is used in one form or another by a great number of antiracism organizations throughout the country. Any organization worth its salt that teaches about racism will seek to communicate that racism is more than prejudice and is the expression of systemic power over people of color.

At the same time, the particular expression of this definition and the following breakdown and explanation are derived from the specific work of the People's Institute for Survival and Beyond and of Crossroads Ministry. As I stated above in the introduction, my own personal growth in understanding racism comes from extended work with both of these antiracism training organizations.[1]

Race Prejudice Is Not the Same as Racism

What this definition says is that racism is more than race prejudice, and it emphasizes the need to distinguish the differences between them. Each of us—white people and people of color alike—are racially prejudiced to one degree or another. No matter what our race or color or background, we all have distorted and unsubstantiated opinions and stereotyped beliefs about other racial and ethnic groups. And we don't give up these prejudices easily; many of us vigorously resist alternate points of view that conflict with our distorted racial biases.

But the point of this definition is that no matter how serious and damaging they might be, prejudice and bigotry are not the same as racism. The reason for this is that not everyone's race prejudices are backed up by the power of society's systems and institutions. Even though the name-calling of individual racial prejudice can be destructive and hurtful, it is immeasurably worse when backed up by collective force.

Race prejudice is transformed into racism when the racial prejudices of one racial group are enforced by the systems and institutions of a society, resulting in greater rewards and privileges for the racial group with power, and fewer rewards and privileges for the racial groups without power.

Racism is more than simple prejudice or bigotry. Everyone is prejudiced, but not everyone is racist. Racism goes beyond prejudice. It is backed up by power. The distinctive mark of racism, according to this definition, is *power*: collective, systemic, societal power. Racism is at work when institutions such as the police, the schools, government, corporations, or churches are structured to function in ways that favor or benefit one racial group more than other racial groups. Racism is the collective power to enforce prejudice. More simply stated, racism is prejudice plus power.

Breaking Down the Definition: Looking at Prejudice, Race, and Power

This is the definition of racism we will be exploring together throughout this book. However, I am not asking that you the reader buy into this definition before you have had opportunity to try it on and see if it fits you. First, we need clarification about the words and concepts contained within this definition. For example, what is race, and what is systemic power? For the rest of this chapter, we will explore much more closely each of the words in this definition:

1. First, we are going to look at the word *prejudice*;
2. Then we will explore the word *race*;
3. Finally we will look more closely at the issue of *systemic and institutional power*.

Exploring Prejudice

Prejudice, as defined in Webster's Dictionary:
1. a judgment or opinion formed before the facts are known; preconceived idea, favorable or, more usually, unfavorable.

2. a judgment or opinion held in disregard of facts that contradict it; unreasonable bias, as a *prejudice* against Northerners.[2]

The least difficult of the concepts contained in this definition of racism, as well as the least controversial, is the idea of prejudice. What is prejudice? From the Latin roots of the word comes the meaning to *prejudge* a situation, a person, or an object. The prejudgment of prejudice is made without sufficient knowledge or a fact base and is more often than not inaccurate. The common understanding of prejudice is to be "biased," to have opinions without knowing the facts and to hold on to those opinions, even after contrary facts are known. For example, I might have biased beliefs about food, about one university over another, or about people from Chicago or California.

A person's prejudice can be hateful and hurtful; but it also can be relatively harmless, such as believing that one's grandchildren are the smartest, most beautiful children in the world. Prejudice can even produce beneficial effects, such as when we teach our children not to take candy from strangers. Prejudice can be as mild as "taste," such as an opinion on what looks good in clothing, or what is the best kind of a car to buy. In the original English use of the word in the nineteenth century, a "gentleman of fine prejudice" was a man of good taste.

There is a kind of prejudice that is not harmless, however, that refers to unfounded fear, mistrust, or hatred of a person or group, especially toward people of a race, religion, ethnicity, nationality, sexual orientation, or social status different from one's own. This kind of prejudice automatically carries with it the suggestion of intolerance, unfairness, and injustice. There is nothing harmless about this kind of prejudice, and there is especially nothing harmless or beneficial about race prejudice.

Racial prejudice is, of course, terribly painful. I do not like to be prejudged because I am white, any more than others like to be prejudged because they are African American, Native American, Latino/Hispanic, Asian American, or Arab American. Our racial prejudices are very harmful to ourselves and to other people.

All of us, white people and people of color, are racially prejudiced. We have all learned or been taught distorted and unsubstantiated opinions about people from other racial backgrounds. They are taught to us and passed on to our children. We've all got them. Prejudice is in the air that we breathe; it is our toxic environment. Even as we look deeper into our definition of racism, we need to affirm the importance of all of us acknowledging our racial prejudices, and working hard to reduce and eliminate them.

However, the word that makes the phrase *race prejudice* so volatile is not just the word *prejudice* but also the word *race*. If we are going to understand *racism*, we have to first of all understand *race*. Let's take a look at the word *race*.

Exploring Race

What is race? We use this word all the time to describe ourselves and each other. But do we know what we mean by it? Take a look in a mirror. Do you see a person of a particular race? Walk down the street in the middle of the city or town in which you live. Do you see people of different races? Read this morning's newspaper. How many articles have something to do with race? We live in a race-based society, and almost everything that happens has racial implications. Race is part of all of our lives.

Yet do we know what race is? Racism cannot be understood without understanding race. Some people would say that race is a myth without any foundations. Others say race is scientifically based and can be described through laboratory analysis. Still others define race culturally. We live every day of our lives consciously and unconsciously accepting race as real and important. Yet there is no common understanding of what race is.

Race: Legally Required, Yet Undefined

"Race" is a legal concept in the United States. Legally, everyone has to have a race. Perhaps this is the first important thing to recognize as we begin to explore race—in this country, race is not a matter of choice. Race is an assigned legal identity. A person can't simply decide not to have one, or switch to another race. And, it is virtually impossible to have one's racial identity accepted as biracial or multiracial.

Again and again, we are asked to check the box that pertains to our racial identity. And if you cross off all the boxes and write in "human," you will have a race assigned to you anyway. One way or another, each of us is "racialized," placed in one of six different racial categories: White, African American, Native American, Latino/Hispanic, Asian American, or Arab American. Later, in chapter 6, we will explore more deeply this process of "racialization," and the way we are all socialized to accept the construct of race as well as our own individual racial identity.

But first, we need to explore further this introductory question, What do we mean by this concept of race? The plain fact is that we do not have an official, legal, or commonly shared definition of race. Everyone has a race, and we use the word with great casualness all the time, but we do not mean the same thing by it. We think different things when we think about race, and we see different things when we observe different races. And most of us have very specific and deeply felt beliefs about race that are often in conflict with what others believe about race. We simply don't know what a "race" is.

So it is not enough to be working on a definition of racism; we must also develop a clear and acceptable definition of race.

What Race Is Not. Perhaps it is better for me first to be clear about what I do *not* mean by *race* when I use the word in this book. Here are is a list of what I believe race is not, a list that may be very surprising, since they are popular ideas and believed by many people:

- *Race is not scientific, it is not biological, and it is not based on genetics.* It is important to our understanding of racism that in the following discussion we come to a common agreement that race is not scientific, nor can our racial identity be scientifically determined. At one time, race was considered by everyone to be based on science. For a long time—for several centuries, in fact—it was believed that intelligence and physical capacity were determined by a person's race. But no longer today. There are very few scientists today who do not scoff at the idea of a scientific basis for race. Even the U.S. Supreme Court decided in 1922 that scientific definitions of race were unacceptable.[3] Nevertheless, there still remains today a popular belief that race is a scientific concept.
- *Race is not defined by color or other physical attributes.* Race is usually and popularly thought of as having something to do with skin color and differing body characteristics, such as hair and lips. Actually, it is true that most dictionaries do define race in these terms. As we shall see clearly in a few pages, however, our legal racial identity in the United States is not based on these factors. A person can have all the physical characteristics of a white person and still be legally categorized as a person of color. And a person can have physical characteristics of a person of color and still be legally determined to be white. Although we use color codes to talk about race (red, brown, yellow, black, and white), it is inaccurate to define race by color or any other physical characteristic.
- *Race is not the same thing as culture.* A single culture can include people of more than one race, and people of a single race can have more than one culture. Culture has more to do with worldview, values, and lifestyle and does not describe race. At the same time, there is something called "cultural racism." We will look more closely at the relationship between race and culture when we explore cultural racism in chapter 6.
- *Race is not the same as ethnicity.* Ethnicity is a description of linguistic, tribal, and/or national heritage, and does not describe race. A single ethnic group can be made up of more than one race; and people of a single race can be composed of more than one ethnic identity. For example, there are many white ethnic groups in the United States and in Europe, but they are all of the same race. Likewise, although African people are

historically considered to be of a single race, they are composed of multiple ethnic and tribal identities.

- *Race is not the same as religious identity.* A single religious group can be made up of more than one race, and people of a single race can have more than one religious identity. It is especially necessary to emphasize this distinction in the post–9/11 world, where great injustices are taking place against both Arab Americans and the Muslim religion, with little distinction made between the two. We need to also remember what happened in Nazi Germany, when Jewish people experienced horrible persecution and genocide as a result of their being identified as people of an inferior race.

The suggestion that race is none of the above may come as a surprise to many readers, since it is quite contrary to popular opinion. All of these ideas about race that I am suggesting are incorrect are still commonly believed in our society. In fact, even most of our dictionaries and encyclopedias still define race in terms of one or more of the above categories—color, body shapes, science, culture, ethnicity, or religion. For example, *Webster's New Twentieth-Century Dictionary* defines race by describing it as biological, scientific, and determined by nationality, ethnicity, and tribe:

> *Race*
> 1. (*a*) any of the major biological divisions of mankind (sic), distinguished by color and texture of hair, color of skin and eyes, stature, bodily proportions, etc. . . . three primary divisions, the Caucasian (loosely, *white race*), Negroid (loosely *black race*), and Mongolid (loosely, *yellow race*). . . .
> 2. a population that differs from others in the relative frequency of some gene or genes: a modern scientific use.
> 3. any geographical, national, or tribal ethnic grouping.[4]

A similar definition or race can be found in almost every dictionary and encyclopedia in our libraries—with at least one surprising and helpful exception. The current edition of the *Encyclopedia Britannica* contains a lengthy article on the subject of race, written by Audrey Smedley, which suggests a very different approach to understanding and defining "race." Following is a quote from Smedley's article:

> *Race*
> . . . the idea that the human species is divided into distinct groups on the basis of inherited physical and behavioral differences. Genetic studies in the late 20th century denied the existence of biogenetically

distinct races, and scholars now argue that "races" are cultural interventions reflecting specific attitudes and beliefs that were imposed on different populations in the wake of western European conquests beginning in the 15th century.[5]

As Smedley suggests, and as will be seen in the following pages, race is actually a very different concept than is commonly understood. And, if we understand race differently, it will also lead us to a very different understanding of racism.

What Race Is. So then, what is race? If I am arguing that the above list is what race is not, then what do I believe race is? What should we mean when we refer to a "race of people," or when we name six racial groupings in the United States: the "white race," the "African American race," the "Native American race," the "Latino/Hispanic race," the "Asian American race," and the "Arab American race"?

Let's follow the trail of history suggested in the above quotation from Smedley and the *Encyclopedia Britannica* to see if we can find out the answer to that question. In the following pages, we will trace the concept of race, beginning with its origins in Europe during the time of colonialization, then continuing to its importation as a central concept for the ordering of society in the American colonies, and finally to the process of race becoming embedded legally and culturally in our nation. Only as we see this derivation of the idea of race will we understand how it resulted in a race-based country and produced the race-based confusion and conflict in which we find ourselves today. After we have looked at this history, I will propose a definition of race that is derived from this history, and we will then test this definition to see if it applies accurately to our situation as we experience it today.

The European Invention of Race
It may be a great surprise for some readers to discover that the concept of race as we know it today is a relatively recent development. It was only five hundred years ago that the Western world began formally to divide and categorize groups of people into something called races, with one race being dominant and oppressive over the others.

Obviously, when race began to be used as a basis for oppression, it was not the first time humans oppressed each other. For thousands of years before we had races, there were many other ways humans practiced cruelty and injustice against each other—tribe against tribe, religion against religion, class against class, nation against nation. The tragic significance of the invention of race is not that it initiated human cruelty, but that it provided a new way for humans to be cruel and oppress each other. Moreover, when race was invented five hundred years ago, it became and has remained one of the primary means of human cruelty and one of the most vicious and destructive forces in the world. As we take this brief look at the development of race, we need to keep uppermost in our minds that the primary original purpose of racial classification was to determine superiority and inferiority and thus provide a way for the superior race to dominate the inferior races.

Although there are many ancient paths that led to its formal and official starting point, the idea of race as we know it today began to be first articulated in the sixteenth and seventeenth centuries when for the first time in the history of humankind, all human beings were classified into something called "race".[6] There were two simultaneous and interwoven activities that made this a moment in time that would bring into being a concept that would divide all the world's peoples into races:

1. Race developed as an academic and scientific idea
2. Race developed as a political ideology

1. The "Science" of Race: Caucasoids, Mongoloids, and Negroids. Let's tackle the academic and scientific ideas first. At the time of its invention, race was promulgated as a scientific concept, and race was considered to be scientifically based for a long time after that. Even today, as we have noted, many people still believe a person's racial identity is scientifically derived.

During the sixteenth and seventeenth centuries, the natural sciences such as biology, botany, and anthropology were coming into being in the universities of Europe. These scientific endeavors had never formally existed before this. One of the major activities by the developers of these new sciences was to create systems to identify and classify everything on earth—living or non-living. Almost everything we know today that has a Latin name—especially plants and animals—got their names from early scientists such as François Bernier, a French physician, Carolus Linnaeus, a Swedish naturalist, Johann Blumenbach, a German anthropologist, and others.[7]

While these early natural scientists were classifying plants and animals, it naturally followed that they also decided to classify people. They created the concept of "the races of men," with the world divided into various racial groupings. Beginning with Bernier in the sixteenth century and further developed by Linnaeus, Blumenbach, and others in the seventeenth century, they divided and classified humankind into three species or races: Caucasoid, Mongoloid, and Negroid. A fourth category, Australoid, was added by some, not only to refer to the indigenous people of Australia, but as a catch-all category for any species of humans that did not fit into the first three. By the end of the seventeenth century, the subcategories multiplied and many others were added. It was a little like the racial categories in the U.S. census today, which also began with four or five categories, but has now expanded to twenty or thirty categories, providing enough choices for everyone, while at the same time preserving the concept of race.

Caucasoid Supremacy. Most important to this scientific theory of the "races of men" was that it seemed quite clear to these academic thinkers that not all humans are equal; the four races were classified in descending order from superior to inferior: Caucasoid, then Mongoloid, then Australoid, and finally Negroid. They found the Caucasoid race to be exceedingly superior in every aspect—mentally, physically, and spiritually. Even further and disastrously, it was deemed obvious to these early scientists that the lowest race—namely, the Negroid—was not even human.

The clearest mark of Caucasoid preeminence was what appeared to these earlier scientists as superior intelligence. Evidence and explanation of this phenomenon was founded in beliefs about the size of the brain. While these academicians were measuring and comparing everything else—skin color, facial structure, body structure and posture, hair texture, and so forth—that which was most important to their measuring enterprise was the calculation and comparison of "cranial capacity." Their theory was simple, albeit totally erroneous: that the larger head size held the larger brain; and the larger brain denoted the smarter person. In order to prove their theory, they performed measurements on a small skull collection that had been garnered from all over the world. Perhaps it should not be surprising, given their subjective and very unscientific measuring methodology (the measurers themselves being of the same Caucasoid category they were attempting to prove superior) that the results of their measuring indicated—once again erroneously—that the racial grouping with the larger cranial capacity was Caucasoid. For the next nearly five hundred years, the academic world, dominated by universities in Europe and the United States, was able to maintain overwhelming consensus regarding the validity of the concept of race and the certainty of Caucasoid supremacy.

2. Race as a Political Ideology: The Colonial Enterprise. The creation of the construct of race was not simply an academic enterprise, however. The greatest encouragement toward the acceptance of race as a lens through which to view the world came not from the academic community, but from the governments of Europe during the sixteenth and seventeenth centuries as they were carrying out their highly profitable colonial enterprises. As has been noted earlier in chapter 1, virtually every nation outside of Europe—in North and South America, Asia, Africa, and Australia—has a history of being "discovered," occupied, and controlled by one or more European nations. Although all of these lands were already occupied by previous owners, they now had new owners. European colonizers presumed the right to appropriate the land, the people, and the resources of any and all places defined by them as available real estate.

Moreover, these colonizing nations were determined to think well of themselves and not to think of themselves as "evil empires." Therefore, the need for justifying their appropriating activity was high on their agenda. More than any other source, this justification came from the ideology of race and in particular from the concept of "Caucasoid supremacy." The superiority of the Caucasoid race and the inferiority—even the lack of humanity—of all others, who were more often than not typified as "savages," became the primary ideological principle to undergird and validate colonialism.

In latter days this ideological principle would be referred to as the "white man's burden." In these earlier days, however, it was simply the common assumption that Europeans had not only the right, but the responsibility to subdue and rule over the rest of the world's "lesser" peoples, while also claiming full proprietary rights over the land and the resources. It is of major importance to our understanding of racism to see that the process of colonialization of the world and the racialization of its peoples were coinciding and interdependent events. As concluded by Michael Omi and Howard Winant:

> The conquest, therefore, was the first—and given the dramatic nature of the case, perhaps the greatest—racial formation project . . . just as the "big bang" still resonates through the universe, so the overdetermined construction of world 'civilization' as a product of the rise of Europe and the subjugation of the rest of us, still defines the race concept.[8]

Religion and the church also played a significant role in the origins of race. That which was accomplished by the universities and governments of Europe could not have taken place without divine approval. The development of the concept of race and its practical application in the colonial enterprise required the endorsement of the church. From the sixteenth century through the mid-twentieth century most of the churches, like the rest of the white Western world, got it wrong about race. Especially in the sixteenth and seventeenth centuries, the Roman Catholic Church, along with the newly created Protestant churches of Europe and the Church of England, provided theological and ecclesiastical support for the construct of race, the concept of white supremacy, the right to colonial domination, and—as we shall see in the next few pages—the establishment of the race construct in the United States.

"Made in America": Race in the United States

If the formal beginnings of the construct of race took place in Europe, the next question is, How did this European idea become such an important part of life in the United States? How was this understanding of race imported into the United States, and how was it adopted and adapted, and then used to justify a national political and societal structure of white supremacy?

The United States was born as a child of the European colonial enterprise, one of those hundreds of global sites that Europeans "discovered" in the seventeenth and eighteenth centuries, and claimed ownership of the people, the land, and the resources. As with all the colonial enterprises of the time, the colonialists carried their primary assumptions and worldviews from the old land to the new, including the newly developing concept of race. When the earliest settlers came to North America and began to create colonies, they brought with them a racial hierarchy, with all its rationalizations and justifications. And at the top of the racial hierarchy was a deep belief in European/Caucasoid superiority. In one sense, therefore, it is important to emphasize that the race-based structure of the United States was not invented here, but is a product imported from Europe.

But in another, far greater sense, race is not a European import, but an American invention. Race may not have been born here, but it came as an immigrant child, was adopted while still in swaddling clothes, and raised from childhood as an American citizen. It was in the context of the American colonial experience that race and racism were developed into the uniquely American understanding we now have. Moreover, this "made in America" product was to be then later exported worldwide with earth-shaping and earth-shaking implications and consequences.

From the beginning, the American colonies were designed in every aspect as race-based societies, with all power and privilege belonging to European people, who would soon thereafter be legally denoted as "white." The ideology of race evolved one step at a time, just one step ahead of the need to defend the rights and privileges of white people and to deny the rights and privileges of all others. A century and a half later, when the colonies became the United States of America, this same concept of race was nationalized and constitutionalized.

Of course, race was not the only oppressive social classification in the colonies. There were other dominating and repressive categories in this new society, transplanted and enhanced from the old. A rigid class system and male authoritarianism were also automatically assumed and institutionalized. In addition, a religious hierarchy was clearly established that resulted in various expressions of Christianity being placed in the top positions, and non-Christians, particularly Jews, at the very bottom. But the first qualification for the elite and ruling class was white skin, and while there was a powerful white hierarchy of men with money at the top, the vast majority of other white people—both men and women—who did not find themselves on top identified with and maintained their loyalty to the white ruling elite.

Red, Brown, Yellow, Black, and White. The shaping of the concept of race in the American colonies, and later in the nation of the United States, produced our own unique racial language, ideology, and practices. Colors were used not only to designate European people as white people, but to name all the other races as they came into legal recognition. The European designations previously known as Caucasoid, Negroid, Mongoloid, and Australoid became red, brown, yellow, black, and white.

It is important to understand that the use of color-coding to describe racial identity was (and still is) politically motivated and not literally or scientifically based on the color of individuals or groups. We have already stated above that race cannot be defined by color. No individual matches any of the five colors in any literal sense, and no group is consistently of one shade or hue.

But the use of colors to describe race accomplished quite effectively the political purpose that was intended. That political purpose, encased in the legal structures and cultural worldview of our nation, was to enforce the clear understanding that the resources of this country were reserved exclusively for white people. The other races—the nonwhite people—existed for the sole purpose of serving the interests of white people. As has already been described in greater detail in chapter 1, there were at first during the colonial period only three races, three colors: white, red, and black. The American concept of race evolved primarily around these three:

- European immigrants, soon to be known as *white people*, with a clear ideology of white supremacy;
- Indigenous natives, to be called *red people* and clearly denoted as nonhuman, uncivilized savages;
- Imported African slaves, named *black people* and legally defined as less than human, merely property in the context of chattel slavery.

Later, during the nineteenth century, after the United States became a nation, two more colors—yellow and brown—were incorporated into the national racial vocabulary:

- *Brown*, referring at first to Mexicans and Puerto Ricans at the time of territorial annexation, and later to immigrants from other countries in Central and South America, and still later to Arab/Middle Eastern peoples;
- *Yellow*, describing at first Chinese laborers, and then to immigrants from all countries of Asia or from any Pacific island west of San Francisco.

This color-coded construct of race that began in colonial America was then written into the legal codes of the United States when we became a nation. They were enforced by the courts, and became deeply imbedded in the social fabric of our nation. Everything about life in the United States took on racial connotations and was separated by color. Then (as I already have referred to in chapter 1) in 1790, two years after the ratification of the U.S. Constitution, the first Naturalization Act was passed, which limited new citizenship to white people. The act stated that: ". . . any alien, being a free white person, may be admitted to become a citizen of the United States. . . ."[9]

From that year until 1952, when the naturalization act was repealed, the United States was legally defined as a white nation. The Supreme Court was given the responsibility of defining "whiteness." Until the early 1920s, the court understood race as a scientifically determined designation. In the early 1920s, when this no longer seemed viable, they changed to the basis of "common knowledge" to establish the category of whiteness. During all this time, from the standpoint of the Supreme Court, the five races of the United States were more often than not reduced to two races: white and nonwhite. These two legal expressions clearly meant that white stood for "something" and nonwhite stood for "nothing." To be white was to have an identity of worth to be nonwhite was to be worthless.

Before moving to some conclusions and to a proposed definition of race for the reader to consider, there is one final historical point to be made. It is extremely important to note that while many other changes took place during the civil rights era in the 1960s and 1970s, the legal concept of race did not change. Although civil rights laws and other laws ended discrimination by race, they did not attempt to challenge or change the concept of race; nor did they seek to end classification and categorization by race. And since that time, although there have been many other legal efforts to change how the different races are treated, the fundamental construct of race has been left untouched, and in many ways has even been strengthened.

Conclusions about Race

What can we conclude about all this? I believe that any understanding of race needs to recognize a critical and somewhat shocking fact: whatever else race is, it *has always had something to do with determining who gets how much of what in any society; and it still does.* Throughout the history we have just traced, and still today, the quality of our life is dramatically affected by which race we belong to. Like it or not, the concept of race is directly related to old and supposedly outmoded ideas of classifying groups of people as superior and inferior, and based on those ideas, allotting to each group their societal status, role, and power.

We must be thoroughly honest about this: the primary purpose of racial classification has always been to classify people into a hierarchy of superior and inferior, to identify one group as "better than" and another group as "less than" others. Although you and I may consciously reject those ideas as false, every time we say the word *race* we are giving credence to these ideas as though they were real and true. Whenever we categorize of people into races, we are using a classification based on that original concept of superior and inferior groups of people. Any realistic understanding of race must deal with this absurd historical assumption that a person's race determines his or her status and power, and that one race should get more status and power than other races because that race is better than the others. And any use of the word or concept of *race* today must deal with the fact that the word *race* still carries that meaning.

Today, race and racial identity are still legal concepts. We are still identified and counted by race. The present racial identities of white people, African American people, Native American people, Latino/Hispanic people, Asian American people, and Arab American people are still based on the legal and cultural meanings given to them in the past. Most importantly, still today—just as throughout the five hundred preceding years—we are still without a commonly accepted definition of the word or the concept of "race."[10]

A Definition of Race

It is now time to propose a definition of race for readers to consider. The definition is derived from the history of race I have just reviewed. I began by observing that although our society uses race to classify people, we have no commonly recognized definition of race. I continued by discussing what race is not, and then presented a brief history of the developing of the legal and social concept of race—first in Europe and then in the United States.

A definition of race cannot ignore this historical reality. From its inception, race has never been a neutral category that just happens to be misused in racist ways; rather, the concept of race itself was created for racist purposes. It is a concept and a construct that is in itself indelibly racist.

The following definition of race I want to propose is a somewhat edited version of a definition created by Dr. Maulana Karenga, professor in the black studies department at California State University in Long Beach, best known as the founder of Kwanzaa:

> Race is an arbitrary (specious, false) socio/biological construct created by Europeans during the time of world wide colonial expansion and adapted in the political and social structures of the United States, to assign human worth and social status, using themselves as the model of humanity, for the purpose of legitimizing White power and White skin privilege.[11]

What this definition says is that race as we know and use it today is neither scientific nor logical, neither neutral nor harmless, but rather is a concept and a societal construct that was designed and used for evil purposes. Race is an arbitrary and artificial political construct created to serve the purpose of control and exploitation. Most importantly, it is the clear assumption of this definition, as well as the supposition of this book, that when we say the word *race* today or use it in our daily lives, the word still carries that same meaning and power.

This is the definition of race I will continue to explore and use in the rest of this book. As with all other definitions and ideas presented here, the reader is encouraged not to simply accept or reject this definition out of hand, but to explore it and consider it in the next chapters before making up your mind as to its accuracy and acceptability.

Summary

- *Race, not just racism, is at the root of the problem.* If we are going to define racism as "race prejudice plus the power of systems and institutions," then we need to first of all agree on a definition of race. We need to understand race if we are going to understand racism.
- *Race is at the same time myth and reality.* Race is a fiction—arbitrary and artificial; it is unscientific, deceptive, misleading, and insane. At the same time, race is very real. Race is a sociopolitical construct that originated in Europe, but developed its present-day design in the United States. Race is an enforced myth that dictates the very identity and condition of each of our lives.
- *Racism created race.* Race as we know it today is not a legitimate concept that is misused by racism. Rather, race in itself is racist and was created by racism. The purpose of race is to define humanity in a way that gives the highest worth, social status, power, and privilege to white people. The foundation for our race-based society in the United States is not legitimately rooted in science or theology, but in a political construct designed to preserve white supremacy.
- *Ending racism must include ending the use of the concept of race as we know it.* We live in a race-based society that is set up so that all people in the society willingly or unwillingly become a part of its race construct. Our goal must not be only the eradication of racism, but the eradication of race itself as a construct on which society is shaped.

The Misuse of Power by Systems and Institutions

The third and final step in the introduction to our proposed definition of racism is to examine the concept of power. Racism is about power. Racism is race prejudice *plus the misuse of power by systems and institutions.* We have briefly looked at the first two concepts in this definition: prejudice and race. Now we need to look at the third part of the definition: the misuse of power by systems and institutions.

Racism is more than prejudice; the distinctive mark of racism is power—collective, systemic, societal power. Not simply the power of one individual over another, but shared power expressed through political and economic, educational, cultural, religious, and other societal systems and institutions. Racism victimizes entire racial or ethnic groups for the purpose of maintaining the benefits and privileges of the racial group in power. When an institution such as the police or the schools or the church is structured to function in a way that brings white people more favor or benefits than it does for people of color, that is racism's power at work.

Power: A Good Thing

Just as we have carefully defined prejudice and race, in order to begin this discussion of racism's power, we need to have a definition of power itself. From the perspective of this book and this analysis of racism, I want to be clear about three assumptions that will determine my approach to a definition of power:

1. *Power is not evil.* Power is often inaccurately described and defined as evil. Lord Acton, a British historian, is often quoted: "Power corrupts, and absolute power corrupts absolutely." However, we would be making a serious error if we cynically said that power is evil and that therefore no one is capable of using power beneficially or well. For the purposes of this discussion, that would mean that racism is inevitable and ineradicable.

2. *Power is not neutral.* Very often, power is also wrongly defined as neutral—neither good nor bad. This would suggest that power has no inherent moral content, but can be used arbitrarily either for good or for evil purposes. The definition presented here will assume that power is not neutral, but carries within it an inherent moral content and purpose.

3. *Power is good.* The point of view of this book is that power is neither evil nor is it neutral, but that power is good and is intended to be use for good purposes. From this perspective, having power and using it justly and well is a fulfillment of universal purpose. Even most of our religious thought describes power as belonging to God who is the all powerful one, and humans have power as a gift of God. This understanding of power, whether or not seen from a religious perspective, will shape the assumptions and discussions about power in this book and of our definition of racism. Power is the ability to act, to determine individual or collective direction or movement, and is intended to provide positive human experience for individuals and groups in society.

Misuse of a Good Thing

Of course, although power is in itself good, it can be and often is used for evil purposes. We often experience power as the efforts of others to control us, to assert their will and dominate us. It is important to see such experiences as the *misuse* of power, the *misuse* of a good thing. It is critically important to be clear that when we speak of power in our definition of racism we are clearly speaking of the *misuse* of power.

Defining Power and the Misuse of Power

Power is the individual or collective ability to be or to act in ways that fulfill our potential. Its purpose is to be used for good, but it can be misused to control, dominate, hurt, and oppress others.[12]

This question of whether power is good or evil is important not only to defining racism, but even more so to the task of dismantling racism. When we later in this book come to the discussion of how to end or eliminate racism, the goal will not be to advocate the ending of power for anyone, but the turning of the misuse of power into the proper use of power. The question is, How can power be restored to its proper use?

In the 1960s, the "black power movement" in the United States was a frightening thing for many white people. However, black power—along with red power, brown power, and yellow power—is, in light of this definition of power and our definition of racism, a very positive thing. The absence of power by any group in a society is an unacceptable result of oppression. Power, when rightly restored, will be equally shared by all groups in a society. Many programs in our society are aimed toward "empowerment." This also suggests that having power is a necessary thing, and that our discussion about the misuse of power must ultimately reach the question of the right use and the proper distribution of power.

Institutions and Institutional Power: Also Very Good

Not only is power good, but so is institutional power. As I will more deeply explore in chapter 5, the purpose of institutions is to produce, manage, and distribute the resources of a society. Institutions are crucial to the fabric of a society because they enable us to live together cooperatively and have our needs taken care of. In a democratic society, institutions are given legitimation by the government in order to ensure proper control and access by all people to resources.

At the same time, as our definition of racism emphasizes, institutional power can also be misused for evil purposes. At the center of racism is the misuse of institutional power. Nevertheless, since any discussion of institutional racism is going to be critical of institutions and how they misuse power, it is necessary first to insist that racism misuses something that is in itself necessary and good.

Institutionalized racism exists in a society when one racial group acquires the power to control an institution in such a way that they have more access to benefits and privileges, while the other groups have less access to benefits and privileges. In chapter 1 we saw that in the United States, unequal institutional power was intentionally designed in two very specific ways. First, from the very beginning, our nation was structured legally and intentionally to ensure that all its resources would exist exclusively for white people. All of our institutions were constructed to place ownership of land, economic power, and governmental power in the hands of white men and for the exclusive benefit of the white society.

Second, and also from the very beginning, our nation was structured legally and intentionally to ensure that all people of color would function as powerless instruments of service to the white society. Not only were people of color denied access to societal institutions, but they were legally defined as having the sole purpose of helping to make these institutions serve white people.

The power of race and racism became institutionalized and legalized. Every imaginable law was passed by the states and by the national government to define white institutional power and privilege and to define institutional subservience of people of color. The highest courts of the nation were given the responsibility of interpreting these laws, and the criminal justice system was given the responsibility of enforcing them.

As will be explored in much greater depth in chapter 5, the central argument in this book is that the changes in the laws of segregation and discrimination in the 1960s did not go to sufficient depth to change the original institutional structures or the institutional misuse of power. The reality is that our institutions are still structured to ensure control predominantly by white people, and that white people will still have greater access to the benefits of institutions than people of color. The most important task in this book is to propose how this reality can be changed.

Three Ways Racism Misuses Power

In order to pave the way for deeper exploration of systemic and institutional racism in succeeding chapters, I want to be more specific in describing the "misuse of power by systems and institutions." I want to identify three ways in which racism misuses power, three ways in which racism expresses itself through the systems and institutions of our society. I have given a different name to each of these three ways power is misused: "Power[1]" (power to the first power), "Power^2" (power to the second power), and "Power^3" (power to the third power).

- *Power^1* is racism's destructive power *over people of color.* This is racism's ability to hurt, control, and dominate people of color: African Americans, Native Americans, Latinos/Hispanics, Asian Americans, and Arab Americans.
- *Power^2* is racism's beneficial power *for white people.* This is racism's ability to provide and preserve power and privilege for the white society.
- *Power^3* is racism's ultimate power to control and destroy *everyone.* This is racism's ability to make everyone serve its purposes, and destroy everyone's humanity in the process.[13]

The use of mathematical symbols indicates that each of these expressions of power expands exponentially and is progressively more powerful than the one before it. Readers may recognize this as a method that is also used to measure the expanding power of tornados and earthquakes. As we further explore each of these expressions of racism's power, we will see each of them increasing in power exponentially until reaching Power^3, which will be seen as racism's most devastating and destructive form.

These three misuses of power provide a framework for looking more deeply at how racism continues to function in the United States today. Let us take a closer look at each of these.

Power^1 — Racism's Destructive Power over People of Color

This first expression of racism's power is quite familiar to most of us. Racism is a powerful dominating force *over* people of color. Whatever else we may know or not know about racism, most people know that racism controls, disadvantages, and hurts people of color. Racism has the power to control, hurt, oppress, and disempower African Americans, Native Americans, Latinos/Hispanics, Asian Americans, and Arab Americans. I am naming this expression of racism's misuse of power *Power^1*.

Power^1 is the devastating effect of racism's power that I highlighted in chapter 1 in describing the continuing evil of racism in the United States. Whether in the form of an iron fist or a velvet glove, Power^1 is the foot of oppression, the systemic control and domination that people of color have experienced in their long history of oppression. The list of burdens and hardships suffered individually and collectively—lower salaries, unemployment and underemployment, housing, unequal education, ineffective public services, and so forth—are familiar to anyone who reads the newspaper or watches TV news.

But Power[1] is only the first of three aspects of racism's power that we are going to examine. Although it is critically important for all of us to be aware of Power[1], there is a serious problem if this is the only aspect of racism that we know about. For most white people, this is the limit of our exposure to racism: we know that people of color are hurt by it. Even though this expression of racism needs to be recognized clearly in all its deadliness and destruction, it is not enough information about racism to solve the problem.

Fixing People of Color. As I stated at the beginning of this chapter, the way we define a problem will determine our solution to it. If the limit to what we know about racism is the way that it hurts people of color, then the solution will focus only on people of color and the need to change them. We will seek to *help* people of color, to *change* people of color, to *heal* people of color, to *minister* to people of color, or to *rescue* people of color. Whatever descriptive language we use for our activity, our solution will be driven by the assumption that "they" are the problem, and "they" are the ones who need to be changed.

Take a look at our nation's attempts to solve the problem of racism. They are mainly based on the diagnosis that people of color have been broken by racism and they need to be fixed. The primary thrust of almost all of our nation's social and political initiatives for solving racial problems is to attempt to change the victims of racism and the conditions within their communities. Virtually every program sponsored by government, universities, foundations, and churches, even though they are created by concerned people who firmly believe that racial problems must be solved and racial conflicts reconciled, are designed to focus time, effort, and money on efforts to help African Americans, Native Americans, Latinos/Hispanics, Asian Americans, and Arab Americans with *their* problems. Every program imaginable has been created to help and heal people of color—everything from soup kitchens to Head Start, all the programs of charity, all the programs of empowerment, and all the programs of equal opportunity, inclusiveness, and diversity.

Changing the wrong people. There is no question that most, if not all, of these programs accomplish some good. The question is whether they change the underpinnings of systemic racism. Our erroneous fundamental assumption has been that if we pour enough money into changing the victims of racism, they will catch up with us and will achieve a state of equality. But it isn't happening. Why? Because we are trying to change the wrong people.

Focusing on changing people of color requires little or no change of white people or the white society. Moreover, it requires no essential change in the power relationships between people of color and the white society. It is still "we" who have the power to help "them" change. Instead of being identified as part of the problem, the white society is identified as the solution. While we are working to help them change, we are avoiding the need to change ourselves. If we are going to understand and solve the problem of racism, we need to go further and deeper than dealing with the hurts of people of color.

$Power^2$—Racism Provides Power for White People

Racism is not only power *over* people of color. Racism also provides power *for* white people. If we define racism as the misuse of systemic and institutional power, then the bottom-line questions are: Who's got the power? and Who is misusing power? The answer is obvious. In the United States, only one racial group has the power to claim the major part of the land and resources for itself, as well as to impose its will upon and exploit other racial groups. $Power^2$ is racism at work *for* white people.

The most important issue in understanding racism is not what it does to *hurt* people of color, but what it does to *help* white people. Oppressing people of color is not the end goal of racism, but only a means to its primary end of enriching white people. Providing power and privilege for the white society is racism's central function and the main reason racism exists. $Power^2$ is the name I am giving to this second aspect of racism's misuse of power, and it is exponentially more powerful than $Power^1$. $Power^2$ is the principal reason racism exists.

For many white people, seeing racism from the perspective of $Power^2$ is quite new and often shocking. It is a major turning point in understanding racism to become aware that the primary purpose and end-goal of racism is not to hurt people of color, but to provide and maintain power and privilege for white people. $Power^2$ turns the focus away from the victims of racism to a new focus on the people and institutions who are not only the cause of hurt for people of color, but who also benefit from it. $Power^2$ moves us from the question of how can *we* help *them* change to the question of how we ourselves can be changed.

The Purpose of Oppression: To Gain Power and Privilege. The goal of *any* oppression is to gain power and privilege. Oppression takes place in order to establish dominance, to gain the benefits of dominance, and to make certain that those who are oppressed serve the purposes of those who dominate. For example, the purpose of class oppression is to establish an elite societal group with economic power and privilege, and to organize the rest of society so that the energies of the lower classes support and help to maintain those with class privilege. Likewise, the purpose of gender oppression, which in our society translates as male dominance, is to establish power and privilege for men and to define the role of women in ways that their energies enforce and support male power and privilege. The same is true of the oppression of one nation against another nation, which serves the purpose of establishing the dominating nation's power and riches, and using the energies of the dominated nation to strengthen and serve the power and privilege of the oppressive nation.

Just as this is true of all other forms of oppression, it is also true of racism. The purpose of racism is to gain and maintain, perpetuate and enforce power and privilege of one race over another. As we have seen in the history of the evolving of the concept of race in the previous chapter, white racial supremacy was established as a means of accruing control, authority, advantages, and benefits for members of the white race.

Those of us who are white find it very hard to recognize and acknowledge this, because we are accustomed to our own happiness and lifestyle depending on these institutions and structures in their present form. Remember the story of the Happiness Machine and the problem of its dross? No one has made us see that the forces responsible for the problems of people of color in our society are the same forces that sustain our own lives. No one has made us see that the condition of the minority of our citizens is a direct product of the majority's struggle for happiness. It is therefore not surprising that all our effort to solve the problems in our communities of color have caused so much frustration and met with so little success. We have tried to limit the effects of the dross of the Happiness Machine without cutting off its flow. We have tried to help others to change without realizing that it requires change in ourselves.

Solving the Right Problem. We have been trying to solve the wrong problem. In the United States, racism is primarily a white problem. This conclusion will be traumatic for many readers of this book. It is difficult for us as white people to grapple with the assertion that racism is a disorder of white people and not of people of color. If this assertion is true, however, it changes dramatically the way we look at and attempt to solve the problem of racism.

For years, we have been trying to change the wrong people. Even when we had the best of intentions we were aiming in the wrong direction. The racial problem of the United States is not a minority problem. It is a majority problem. The cause is in the white society. The effects of racism that are felt in communities of color—the problems of African Americans, Native Americans, Latinos/Hispanics, Asian Americans, and Arab Americans—are only the symptoms of our nation's sickness. Treating the symptoms without treating the cause will not heal the disease. All the programs in the world aimed at changing the victims of racism will ultimately be useless if the institutions and structures that create and control the conditions in the first place are not changed.

It is not, of course, that people of color do not need to change or do not want to change. Just the opposite is true. However, we all too often assume their problems are caused by the victims themselves rather than the institutions of the victimizers. And we assume that the cure for their illnesses begins with them and needs to be administered by us. And then, to add the final blow, the "cure" is attempted by the very institutions that created the problem in the first place.

It is as though an airplane were spraying poison gas over a city, causing the inhabitants to sicken and die. The owners of the airplane neither admit to the poisoning nor promise to stop. They do, however, sign a contract to develop an antidote for the gas. While the antidote is being developed, the gassing continues. When the antidote is ready, the pilots are directed to spray it, together with the poison gas, when they fly over the city.

If we were to double or triple our efforts to bring about change for the victims of racism through increased housing, better education, more employment, and other social improvements, we might achieve some statistical progress. However, we would set two forces in the white society into even greater contradiction with each other: the one that creates and perpetuates inhuman conditions, and the one that tries to correct the results.

The name of the problem that must be dealt with is *white racism*. It is the misuse of power by systems and institutions in order to perpetuate white power and privilege. And the only way to deal with it is by changing the systems and institutions of the United States that are structured to benefit the white society and to dominate, control, and exploit people of color. Simply changing attitudes are not enough. Helping the victims of racism is not enough. Only by changing and transforming white power and privilege will it be possible to make significant progress in dismantling white racism.

Power³—Racism's Ultimate Power to Control and Destroy Everyone

The next chapter is devoted to a deeper exploration of Power²—white power and privilege. Before moving further in that direction, however, I need to introduce the third and most powerful aspect of racism's misuses of power, which I have designated as *Power³*.

Racism takes all of us prisoner. Its ultimate design is to control and destroy everyone. Power³ is the third and most powerful expression of racism. This is the most devastating and destructive power of racism, because it subjects all of us to its will, people of color and white people alike.

You cannot cut the body of humanity in half and not have both halves bleed to death. The results of racism are far more devastating and destructive than its hurting of people of color (Power¹) and benefiting of white people (Power²). In this, the greatest and worst expression of racism's power, we can see its ability to make everyone serve its purposes, and to destroy everyone's humanity in the process. In Power[3] we can see that racism is far more than actions of evil and greedy people; it is an evil and destructive power in itself that has taken on its own self-controlling and self-perpetuating characteristics. At its deepest level, racism is a massive system of intertwining and choking roots that wrap and wind themselves around every person, institution, and manifestation of society. We need to explore how all of us—white people and people of color alike—are imprisoned by this power and cannot easily set ourselves free. We need to see how all of us face destruction as long as this evil power is at work to divide and take life from us.

Racism is able to make all of us—white people and people of color alike—cooperate with it and participate in its workings. Each and every one of us is socialized to become the person that racism wants us to become and to perform the function that racism wants us to perform. Racism actually claims the power to shape our identity, to tell all of us who we are, white people and people of color alike.

This socializing process is part of the identity formation that starts at the very beginning of each of our lives. Every white person is taught to behave according to a racist society's standards for white people, and every person of color is taught to behave according to a racist society's standards for people of color. In our further exploration of Power[3] in chapter 4, we will call these identity-shaping processes "the internalization of racist superiority" and "the internalization of racist oppression." And, in chapters 5 and 6, we will see that this same identity-shaping power of racism has deeply affected the nature of our institutions and our collective culture in society.

As we examine Power[3] more closely we will see the ways in which all of us—people of color and white people—are imprisoned by racism. But we will also be clear that our prisons are very different. Although racism is destroying us all, it is designed to make people of color feel uncomfortable and hurt, and to make white people feel comfortable and good. But ultimately, we are all deceived, dehumanized, and destroyed by racism. To paraphrase Malcolm X, we've all been misled, we've all been had, we've all been took, hoodwinked, and bamboozled. We are all defined and controlled in ways that threaten to destroy our very being. We will not fully understand racism until we recognize how all of us, including white people and white society, are destroyed by white racism.

Summary

In this chapter we have presented and begun to explore a definition of racism that we will deepen and widen in the following chapters of this book. Because we have covered so much complex material in this chapter, following is a summary of the major points that have been made.

What Is Racism?

Racism is race prejudice plus the misuse of power by systems and institutions. Racism is more than race prejudice; it is more than individual attitudes and actions. Racism is the collective actions of a dominant racial group. Racial prejudice becomes racism when one group's racial prejudices are enforced by the systems and institutions of a society, giving power and privilege to the racial group in power and limiting the power and privilege of the racial groups that are not in power.

Contrary to the assumptions of most white people, racism is not an individual, relational, or attitudinal issue. Rather, it is a systemic, institutional issue. People of color are not hurt by white individuals as much as they are hurt by white institutions.

Systemic racism cannot be measured nearly as accurately in terms of how it hurts people of color, but rather, how it helps, benefits, and empowers white society. The purpose and end-goal of racism is the creation and preservation of power and privilege for the white society. Therefore, hurting people of color is not the end-goal of racism, but a consequence. This is the "big secret" of racism: by focusing on the hurting and harming of people of color, we cover up the real reasons behind racism.

What Is Prejudice?

Prejudice is the prejudging of a situation, a person, or an object in ways that are more often than not inaccurate and made without sufficient knowledge or a fact-base. Prejudice can be as mild as taste and as vicious as bigotry. Individual prejudice, however, including race prejudice, carries little power and can do relatively little damage unless it is enforced collectively by one group over another.

What Is Race?

Race is a racist concept created to support racism. It is an arbitrary (specious, false) sociobiological construct created by Europeans during the time of worldwide colonial expansion and adapted in the political and social structures of the United States, to assign human worth and social status, using themselves as the model of humanity, for the purpose of legitimizing white power and white skin privilege. There are beautiful physiological differences among various peoples of the world, along with a great diversity of cultures and ethnicities. Race was not created to celebrate this diversity, however, but rather to categorize people into superior and inferior groups with differing degrees of power and privilege.

What Is the Misuse of Power by Systems and Institutions?

The purpose of systems and institutions is to produce, manage, and distribute the resources of a society. The two primary means of measuring power in an institution are who is in control of the institution and who has access to an institution. Racism exists in a society when one racial group acquires the power to control an institution in such a way that they have more access to benefits and privileges, while the other groups has less access to benefits and privileges. In the United States, unequal control and access to institutions on the basis of race was created to ensure that all U.S. resources would exist exclusively for white people, and to ensure that all people of color would function as instruments of service of the white society.

Three specific ways in which systemic and institutional power is misused by racism are:

- *Power*[1]—Racism's destructive power *over* people of color;
- *Power*[2]—Racism's beneficial power for white people;
- *Power*[3]—Racism's ultimate power to control and destroy everyone.

These three misuses of power provide a framework for looking more deeply at how racism continues to function in the succeeding chapters of this book. In chapter 1, we have already summarized the destruction caused by Power[1]. In the next chapter, we will explore Power[2] more closely, and in chapter 4, we will do an in-depth examination of Power[3].

WHITE POWER AND PRIVILEGE

To be White in America is not to have to think about it.
—Robert Terry, *For Whites Only*

To white readers: we are not only trying to solve the wrong problem; we are also studying the wrong people. We need to study us.

For many years our attempts to understand racism have been guided by a false and misleading assumption: that in order to study racism we need to study people of color. Think about that for a minute. It is certainly true that if we want to study the *results of racism*, people of color are the ones to put under a microscope. If we want to study *racism*, however, it is us—white people—who need to be investigated carefully.

We need to study us.

Specifically, we need to study white power and privilege. As we have seen in the previous chapter, white power and privilege are at the center of racism and are the reason and purpose for which racism exists. This is the problem we need to study and solve if we are going to be effective in our efforts to end racism. In the code language of this book, I have given the name "Power[1]" to describe the results of the oppressive power that controls people of color and compels them to use their lives and energies to serve and support white people. And I have given the name "Power^2" to describe the power that causes this oppression and at the same time provides disproportionate benefits for the white society. It is not enough to focus on Power^1—the problems experienced by people of color. The real problem is Power^2, the structures of our society that are designed to create and preserve power and privilege for the white society.

The goal of this chapter is to study Power^2, white power and privilege. Let's begin by shifting the imagery a bit. In chapter 1, I borrowed an image from the People's Institute for Survival and Beyond in their portrayal of institutions as having "feet" that kick communities of color, resulting in hurting, controlling, dominating, disempowering, and destroying people of color.

Now, building on that image, besides having "feet," an institution can also be portrayed as having other body parts such as hands and arms, head and heart. If Power^1 describes the feet of an institution kicking people of color, then Power^2 will describe the rest of the institution's body as serving the white society. In this chapter, we will study how the hands and arms, head and heart of institutions in our society serve white people, producing Power^2, white power and privilege.

For the most part, this chapter is addressed to white readers, especially on how white power and privilege affect our lives. If the reader is a person of color, it is important for me to acknowledge that as a person of color you are probably already aware of much of the information within this chapter. In your life's experience you have had to learn about white power and privilege in order to survive. It may be difficult for white people to realize it, but the fact is that you as a person of color probably know more about us as white people than we know about ourselves. I hope you as a person of color are willing to continue reading this chapter, to test the validity of this information from your own perspective, as well as to test your own knowledge about white people.

The specific objectives of this chapter are as follows:
- To gain a more complete understanding and analysis of the system of power and privilege in the United States that benefits white people;
- To comprehend the ways in which white power and privilege is concealed and disguised—including the ability of white people to deny its existence;
- To enhance the ability of readers to perceive, describe, and accept the reality of white power and privilege in our society;
- To create a personal awareness within white readers of our own personal power and privilege based on our whiteness.

From "Black Like Me" to "White Like Me"

It requires a major transition in our thought processes to turn from the subject of studying people of color to the subject of studying white people. Since our society has been studying people of color for such a long time, and we already have many models for studying people of color, it might be easier to use one of these models to help us turn to this new subject of studying white people.

One of the classic efforts to study people of color is described in a book published in 1960 entitled *Black Like Me*.[1] John Howard Griffin, a white journalist in New Orleans, used skin coloring and injections to turn his skin dark. With the appearance of an African American, he traveled around southern Louisiana, southern Mississippi, and eastern Texas, experiencing what it is like to be black. His goal was to write a book about black people that would help white people better understand the reality of racist oppression. Millions of white people have read this book and have been helped through Griffin's experiences to better understand the reality that black people have to go through in our society. When the thirty-fifth anniversary edition of *Black Like Me* was printed in the mid-1990s, it was still an international bestseller with sales of more than ten million copies. A movie version with the same title and starring James Whitmore was also produced in 1964.

As a way of preparing to study white people, what would it be like to turn *Black Like Me* around and to write a book entitled *White Like Me*? It would not be a book by people of color about white people, but rather it would be a book written by us about ourselves—specifically about our whiteness. We wouldn't even have to change our skin color to do the research. Although everyone's life experience is different in many regards, I am assuming that all of us who are white have a great deal in common with regard to our racial identity, and especially with regard to white power and privilege. My suggested goal for each white reader is to develop the ability by the end of this chapter to begin to describe your experience as a white person, perhaps even to write an autobiographical sketch entitled *White Like Me*.

Actually, in 2004 antiracism activist Tim Wise published a book by this very title: *White Like Me: Reflections on Race from a Privileged Son*. In his book, Wise describes his life as "a white man, born and reared in a society that has always bestowed upon me privileges and advantages that it has just as deliberately withheld from people of color."[2] Wise is very clear in his book—as I will try to be in the discussion of Power[3] in the next chapter—that racism not only gives white people advantages, but is also ultimately destructive of white people, and our own humanity is at stake when we take on the task of resisting and eradicating racism.

In addition to Wise's book, additional evidence that we are not alone in our exploring white power and privilege is in the growing numbers of colleges and universities that in recent years have developed "white studies programs," resulting in a number of academic studies and books being published on the subject. In addition, a number of antiracism organizations are addressing the issue of white privilege. It is very important that these efforts be acknowledged. Much of the information in this chapter is a product of the collective efforts of a growing number of people.[3]

Studying Us

Where do we begin? How much do we know about ourselves as white people? How much time do we spend thinking about what it means to be white? It is probably an accurate assumption that discussions of white power and privilege are not part of our normal dinnertime conversations. And yet—as I hope this chapter will effectively demonstrate—being white is probably the most significant feature of our identity that makes it possible for us to live the way we do, even more so than gender, class, and nationality.

Nevertheless, it is this feature of our identity—our whiteness—of which we are the least conscious. Robert Terry, one of the earliest researchers of white identity, put it this way in his book *For Whites Only*: "Being White means not having to think about it."[4] The very survival of a person of color requires thinking about what it means to be a person of color many times in a day. But we who are white don't have to think about being white. By not thinking about it, we also do not have to think about the issue of racism and the benefits it gives to us as white people. Racism is designed to work without our thinking about it. We have an unspoken agreement with the forces of racism that we will receive its benefits if we promise not to think about it. In fact, racism can't survive if we *do* think about it. The very act of thinking about and analyzing white power and privilege is an act of resisting racism that threatens it to the very core.

Most white people have a great deal of difficulty describing their feelings about being white. Since we never have to think about it, our first reaction is often the discovery that we have few thoughts and feelings about it. For many people, the second reaction is the feeling of invisibility of our white identity. As white people, we see neither our whiteness nor the results of being white. We are not aware (or we have learned to pretend not to be aware) of the fact that the color of our skin carries so much weight and power in this society. Thus, the starting place for our exploration of our white power and privilege is with the questions, Why is it so difficult for us to perceive them? and, How do we go about making them visible to ourselves?

Escape into Color Blindness

There is a connection between this sense of invisibility and the increasingly popular concept of "color blindness," one of the most dangerous and insidious ideas being perpetuated today. An entire generation of post–civil rights white children have been taught—and are still being taught—that they should train themselves not to see color. Not seeing the color of a person of color is said by this philosophy to be a way of practicing equality. In fact, the opposite is true. Although a person advocating color blindness may have good intentions, not seeing the color of a person of color is a way of making the person invisible. It also prevents us from seeing that the society is still structured in ways that are detrimental to persons of color. Not noticing a person's color may have the intention of correcting inequality, but it has the opposite affect of helping to cover it up.[5]

Advocating "color blindness" is also a way of avoiding seeing our whiteness. Just as "not seeing color" disguises the disadvantages racism causes for people of color, ignoring and not thinking about our whiteness is a way of covering up and denying the advantages provided for us because of our white skin. Peggy McIntosh from Wellesley College has done research and written several articles on white privilege. She compares white privilege to an "invisible weightless knapsack of special provisions, maps, passports, code books, visas, clothes, tools and blank checks." This knapsack is given at birth, and white people draw upon its assets throughout their lives. Dr. McIntosh began her exploration of privilege in a program of women's studies that addressed the issue of sexism and the phenomenon of male privilege. Emphasizing the way in which those with any form of unearned privilege are conditioned not to see their privileges, Dr. McIntosh writes:

> After I realized the extent to which men work from a base of unacknowledged privilege, I understood that much of their oppressiveness was unconscious. Then I remembered the frequent charges from women of color that white women whom they encounter are oppressive. I began to understand why we are just seen as oppressive, even when we don't see ourselves that way. I began to count the ways in which I enjoy unearned skin privilege and have been conditioned into oblivion about its existence.[6]

Some people explain the fact that it is so difficult to see our whiteness and our white privilege by using the image of a fish not knowing it is swimming in water. The environment has become so natural and the privileges have become so internalized in our subconscious that we do not notice them until they are taken away. The discovery of these privileges by those who previously were unable to see them can be a tremendous shock.

On the other hand, our white power and privilege are quite visible to people of color. Often, a person of color will state the belief that white people are deliberately lying when we say we don't see these privileges. However, there is something far more insidious here than outright lying. We are dealing with our lifelong conditioning not to see our whiteness and our white privilege.

The fact is, however—as I hope will be clear by the end of this chapter—our whiteness and our white power and privilege are not the least bit invisible. On the contrary, they have been blatantly and arrogantly flaunted down through the centuries. As we shall see, there has been nothing less than an exaggerated visibility to our power and privilege in the historical process that intentionally legalized the requirement of white skin in order to receive and exercise white power. We who are white need to come to the place where we can see that our whiteness and our white power and privilege are anything but invisible, to the place where they can be seen by us as one of the most visible aspects of our lives.

White Power: Not the Same as White Privilege

Before delving more deeply into this subject, I want to propose definitions of white power and white privilege. To begin with, we are talking about two different entities: white power is not the same thing as white privilege, and we must clearly distinguish between the two. White power is almost never individually possessed, but is held collectively and passed on collectively from generation to generation as an inherited birthright intended specifically for a race of people designated as white. White power functions through societal systems, institutions, and culture. As we shall see below, white power is the product of historical intentional design, and is still inherently present within our systems, institutions, and culture today.

White privilege, on the other hand, is the individual results or products of white power. It is individually received and experienced in the daily lives of individual white persons. White power produces white privilege. White power is collectively expressed, while white privilege is usually a personal and individual experience.

A white institution has the power to produce products and services that are designed primarily for the privileged use of the white community. To have white privilege is to be the consumer of these products and services. For example, an institution such as a bank, school, store, or government office that is controlled by and primarily addresses the needs of white people is an expression of white power. A white individual receiving products or services from such an institution that is designed particularly for his or her needs will be receiving white privilege.

Some white people find it difficult at first to see and feel a sense of white power. In fact, many of us are shielded from the necessity of participating in the direct management of the sources of our power. However, it is much easier to be in touch with, to see, and to feel our white privileges. Then, if we trace those privileges to their source, we will also be able to be in touch with, to see, and to feel white power.

Each white person perceives white power differently and experiences white privileges differently. To some of us they will be more obvious than others. These differences are influenced by a number of other factors besides our whiteness, such as our class and gender. For example, a rich white man will perceive white power and experience white privilege differently than a poor white woman. The rich white man will perceive white power as only one of a series of collectively empowering influences on his life, along with the power that comes with his class and gender. And he will experience his white privileges as a natural accompaniment to his class and gender privileges. The poor white woman, on the other hand, will have greater difficulty perceiving white power amidst all her other perceptions of powerlessness. And her white privileges will be in stark contrast to her lack of other privileges. She may even use her white privileges in an aggressive manner to demonstrate that she stands a little bit above someone else.

Since white power needs to be distinguished from white privilege, let's take a separate look at each of them, first a closer look at white power and then a closer look at white privilege.

A Closer Look at White Power

As we have already seen in the history of racism that was reviewed in chapter 1, rather than being invisible or hidden, white power emerged as a central characteristic of colonialism and was legally and intentionally decreed in the defining and shaping of our nation. For 90 percent of the history of our country—from 1492 until the time of the civil rights movement in the 1950s and 1960s—every aspect of life in our country was defined explicitly and intentionally as an expression of white power. The United States was built on the fundamental and blatant understanding that our nation and its resources were reserved exclusively for white people. The other races—the "nonwhite" people—existed for the sole purpose of serving and supporting the interests of white people.

Human Resources Reserved for the "Humans"

It is very difficult for many people to comprehend how the United States as an emerging democracy could fight a revolutionary war for freedom and at the same time be so oppressive. In order to understand this, we need to get inside the hearts and minds of the colonists, freedom fighters, and constitution writers of early America. As amazing as it may sound to us now, during our colonial years through 1776, and then for nearly a century after we became a nation, there was a commonly held legal and cultural assumption that no one else but white people were human. Each of the other racialized groups was defined in terms that made them less than human. Thus it was a natural thing for our forefathers and foremothers to create systems and institutions for white people exclusively. While a small minority of white people believed this was wrong, the majority simply believed that white people were the only human beings around!

Let's look at the beliefs a little more closely. There were two fundamental assumptions between the years of 1492 to 1865 that were the major building blocks for the constructing of a nation based on white power:

1. White people were the only humans. We were civilized. We had souls. We were Christian. We were in charge. And all the land and resources belonged to us. Although there was a constantly changing definition of which European groups belonged to the category of white people, you had to be classified as white to qualify for citizenship and to receive the privileges that came with it.

2. People of color were not considered to be human:
- Native Americans were defined as "not human." From a legal and cultural point of view Native Americans were considered to be savages, without souls, and without human rights. Therefore it was possible to kill a Native American without fear of persecution or prosecution. This assumption made possible the genocide that wiped out more than 90 percent of the Native American population.
- African Americans were defined as "not human." Throughout the entire period of slavery until 1865, African Americans were legally defined as chattel property with no human rights. The highest degree of humanity legally attributed to African American people prior to their emancipation in 1865 was "three-fifths of a person." In a compromise between northern and southern political forces, the U.S. Constitution legally defined African Americans (free and enslaved) as three-fifths of a person for purposes of determining the population represented by (white) elected officials. Beyond official law, however, there was a clear cultural assumption that "one drop of blood" from a black person was all that was necessary to make a person devoid of humanity.
- The humanness of Latinos/Hispanics and Asian Americans was considered questionable, even though not legally defined until later. The legal status of the humanity of these groups did not become an issue until after the middle of the nineteenth century. When the question was raised in everyday cultural life, however, it was usually resolved with their being grouped together with Native Americans and African Americans in the "nonwhite" (and therefore "not human") category.

White Power at the Heart of Every Institution

In any society the end-purpose of systems and institutions is to serve human beings. In our society, if none other than white people were considered to be human, there would be no reason to create systems and institutions for anyone but white people. By the mid-1800s, nearly all of our national systems (economic, educational, religious, health-care, governmental and military, and so forth) were all in place. All of them were created legally and intentionally with the purpose of serving the humans—the white people. This was our national policy and practice, and it was carried out openly, overtly, and legally.

Thus, we can see that white power was established a long time ago. The devastating truth is that *every system and every institution in the United States was created originally and structured legally and intentionally to serve white people exclusively.* (This does not refer, of course, to organizations created specifically to resist racism.) As I will argue more clearly in the discussion on institutional racism in chapter 5, this original manifestation of white power is still in the DNA of every one of our systems and institutions.

Every system and every institution in the United States was created originally and structured legally and intentionally to serve white people exclusively.

At the same time, we need to be clear that white power has not always looked the same at every stage of history. As noted in chapter 1, in the mid-1800s the passage of the Thirteenth, Fourteenth, and Fifteenth Amendments to the Constitution marked a major shift in this story of intentional development of white power. When slavery was abolished, the humanness of all people was declared, and civil rights for all people were theoretically recognized. However, this theory was not put into practice. New legal methods of restriction quickly took the place of the old, and there were no changes whatsoever in the intentional design of our societal structures. White power remained the unchanged official policy of the United States until the mid-1950s. Until that time, every system and every institution in the United States was still structured legally and intentionally to serve white people exclusively.

White Power Suffers a Serious Defeat (But Recovers)

Fifty years ago, there was a dramatic and fundamental change in the structures of white power. For those who had eyes to see and ears to hear, the fraying of the edges of white power was discernable for decades before the advent of the civil rights movement. However, it was in the 1950s and 1960s that the walls came crashing down, however, and the legal foundations for white power suffered a serious defeat. The beginning of the end of the U.S. system of apartheid was announced by the Supreme Court decision of *Brown v. the Board of Education of Topeka, Kansas*, when it reversed *Plessey v. Fergusson*. Then, as a product of both the nonviolent marches and demonstrations and the violence of police brutality and assassinations, the Civil Rights and Voting Rights Acts of 1964, 1965, and 1968 emerged. The Thirteenth, Fourteenth, and Fifteenth Amendments were finally being given their due. In many ways, the events of the 1950s and the 1960s were the beginning of a "second American revolution," a revolution that today in the twenty-first century still has not reached its end.

Tragically, white power was still not ended in the 1960s. The "second American revolution" has thus far only been a "revolution of intentions." We *said* we were going to do it differently, but we haven't really done it yet. It is extremely important for our analysis of racism to recognize that while white power is supposedly no longer approved or openly supported by law, it continues not only to exist, but to thrive. The evidence? The U.S. Congress and our state legislatures are still mostly white. The CEOs and boards of directors of most of our major corporations are still mostly white. The presidents and faculties of most of our universities are still mostly white. And even far worse, the underlying mission, purpose, values, structure, and culture of most of these institutional structures are still defined in the same terms as they were when they were legally serving only white people.

White Power Lives On

Legally, all the institutions in our society were directed to conform to the new expectations that they should function differently then they did in the days of legalized white power. Yet every measuring device available indicates that even in those cases where serious efforts are being made to do it differently, the results being produced are not very different. There is a reason for this: changing the law changes neither the structure nor the heart of an institution. Institutions do what they are designed to do, and our institutions have the same designs they had from the beginning, a design to perpetuate white power. If white power is part of the DNA of all our societal structures, then changing the law may be the beginning of change, but it does not yet get to the heart of the matter. As we shall see in chapters 5 and 6 in the discussion of institutional and cultural racism, in order for white power to be eradicated there needs to be fundamental transformation in the foundational structures of every system and institution in our country. The change has begun, but it is a very long way from being completed.

If the years prior to the civil rights movement represent 90 percent of our history, then the years since the civil rights movement represent only 10 percent of our history. Fifty years after the civil rights movement, it is time for us to become aware that this new revolution needs more than good intentions. If 90 percent of our history was given to the intentional creation and maintenance of white power, and 10 percent of our history has been given to addressing our intention to change, and we are only now discovering how difficult that is, then the true revolution has yet to take place. The true revolution is the transformation of the underlying fundamental assumptions built into all of our systems and institutions. Until then, our systems and institutions will just keep on doing what they were designed to do: create and perpetuate white power. And the product of white power will continue to be white privilege.

A Closer Look at White Privilege

White power produces white privilege—specific and identifiable individual benefits and rewards that are delivered exclusively to white people simply because we are white. The next step in our exploration of Power^2 is to examine and understand this privilege that white power produces, and to develop the skill of discerning the privileges in our personal experience of everyday life.

To begin this discussion, I believe there can be no denying the facts and the basic statistics of white privilege: white people still get a better education, better jobs, better housing, better health care, better police protection, better almost everything than people of color. Most white people are more accepted, trusted, and believed, are more encouraged, made more welcome, and given more respect in our society than are most people of color.

Unfortunately, there is a fairly standard response and explanation of all this by many white people: "I have what I have because I worked hard for it. And if people of color worked as hard as I do, they would get the same things that I do."

I am suggesting here an alternative and far more believable explanation: that these privileges come to white people as a product of the intentional design of white power, and they come to us automatically, whether we ask for them or not. We may have even worked hard for our privileges, but if they are restricted to being rewards for the hard work of white people, then they are still privileges. In this section on white privilege, I invite white readers to test whether it is in fact a reality in our society today that white people are still getting more and better services than people of color, and that the explanation of this is that these are white privileges delivered to white people by systems of white power.

In this section we need to get as practical and personal as possible. In a few pages from now, white readers will be invited to participate in several exercises to identify our privileges, including the writing of an autobiographical sketch. The premise behind these exercises is that we who are white need to take responsibility for our own lives and learn for ourselves what it means to be white. If you are a white reader, you are asked to consider this invitation as a helpful way to study yourself and to learn more about your life as a white person.

Defining White Privilege

There is no dictionary definition of white privilege, but a definition can be derived from a more generic dictionary definition of the word *privilege*. Using this method, Kendall Clark, an antiracism writer, has produced a helpful definition of white privilege. The dictionary definition of privilege that Clark uses is from the *Oxford English Dictionary*. Based on this definition, Clark derives the following definition of white privilege:

> 1. *a.* A right, advantage, or immunity granted to or enjoyed by white persons beyond the common advantage of all others; an exemption in many particular cases from certain burdens or liabilities.
>
> *b.* A special advantage or benefit of white persons; with reference to divine dispensations, natural advantages, gifts of fortune, genetic endowments, social relations, etc.
>
> 2. A privileged position; the possession of an advantage white persons enjoy over non-white persons.
>
> 3. *a.* The special right or immunity attaching to white persons as a social relation; prerogative.
>
> *b. display of white privilege*, a social expression of a white person or persons demanding to be treated as a member or members of the socially privileged class.
>
> 4. *a.* To invest white persons with a privilege or privileges; to grant to white persons a particular right or immunity; to benefit or favor specially white persons; to invest white persons with special honorable distinctions.
>
> *b.* To avail oneself of a privilege owing to one as a white person.
>
> 5. To authorize or license of white person or persons what is forbidden or wrong for non-whites; to justify, excuse.
>
> 6. To give to white persons special freedom or immunity *from* some liability or burden to which non-white persons are subject; to exempt.

Commenting on this definition, Clark writes:

> Why is it important to define "white privilege" so carefully? Because, in part, many people want to deny that it exists at all, especially in

response to other people's assertions that it is at work in some particular situation, that it exists unjustly and so should be dismantled. This pattern of assertion and denial is itself racialized: for the most part, people of color say white people enjoy white privilege, while white people for the most part deny not only that they have it, but that such a thing even exists. I have been assured countless times by white people that there is no such thing as white privilege and that the very idea is nonsensical.[7]

What do you, the reader, think of Clark's definition of white privilege? Does it communicate? Do you think you can use it to communicate with others? Continue to test this definition as we try to use it as a tool to help increase our awareness of white privilege.

Human Rights vs. White Privilege

One additional clarification in defining white privilege is the distinction that needs to be made between a "right" and a "privilege." In our society we theoretically recognize basic human and civil rights, beginning with those unalienable rights of "life, liberty, and the pursuit of happiness" that are declared as endowed by the Creator in the introduction to the Declaration of Independence. The great majority of items that might be listed as white privileges could also be seen as rights that should belong to everyone. The question is: What is the difference between a right and a privilege? And when does a human right become a white privilege, or a privilege become a right? I want to suggest that when a human or civil right is theoretically intended for everyone, but is still reserved for less than everyone, then that right has become a privilege. From this perspective, the rights supposedly guaranteed by the U.S. Constitution are still merely privileges for some.

A right is for everyone, is guaranteed by and enforced by law, and all people experience it in similar or identical ways. A privilege is not for everyone, however, and can either be granted or withdrawn at the discretion of the one who has granted the privilege. Some rights in our society are theoretically quite evident: for example, the right to equal education for all, the right to a fair trial, equal voting rights, freedom of religion, and so forth. For centuries these matters were in fact never "rights," but were privileges for white people that were not available to most people of color in the United States. Still today, even though they have now legally been recognized as rights for all people, they are quite obviously still not being implemented equally for all people.

When does a privilege once again become a right? Only when there is evidence that they are finally and fully extended for everyone. As stated in chapter 1, the results are what counts; intentionality, legality, and opportunity are not enough. Although the civil rights acts that were passed as a result of the civil rights movement extended legal recognition and the requirement that white privilege should finally become human rights for everyone, until these legal acts are implemented, until systems of white power are dismantled and replaced, the human rights that are meant for all are still white privileges.

Discerning and Naming Our Privileges: A Starter List

Now let us get practical and personal, and begin to name and count the white privileges that are all around us, but are, until now, for the most part nameless and countless. Using Clark's definition as our guide, what are the "rights, advantages, or immunities granted to or enjoyed by white persons beyond the common advantage of all others"? What are our "exemptions from certain burdens or liabilities"? Following is a starter list. The question is whether you the white reader begin to recognize yourself on this list.

Let's start with a few of the big ones—our large-scale rewards and privileges. At the top of our list are the higher salaries and other economic benefits received by white people. Of course, some white people earn a whole lot more than other white people, and some people of color earn more than some white people, but the vast majority of white people earn more than the vast majority of people of color. In addition, we receive the rewards of better and more accessible education and jobs. And then there are, of course, our better homes and living conditions, our better health and health care, our better treatment by the criminal justice system, and our better representation in the legislative halls of nation, states, cities, counties, and so forth.

Alongside these large-scale items, there are also the multitude of smaller, day-to-day "white skin privileges" that are so easily accepted, taken for granted, and generally unnoticed by us. A list of these might include the greater ease we have in opening a bank account, cashing a check, or getting a loan. It is much easier for us to have our ideas accepted or our contributions recognized in a discussion. We can shop without suspicion in a department store or food market. And these very same department stores and food markets are organized so that most of the merchandise is more oriented to people from our race and culture, with a small separate part of an aisle reserved for "ethnic" items.

White people occupy the central places in our history books, with people of color being relegated to footnotes, elective classes, and occasional recognition on holidays. The images of white people, when compared with people of color in the media, are far more positive. The values and ethics of white people are those most reflected in public life. Because of our white skin privilege, we can also be confident that our racial identity will not be used against us in applying for a job, looking for a house, relating to public authorities, or using public accommodations.

This is only a starter list. Do you agree with this list? Are any of the items surprising? Can you add to the list? Even if you knew you were receiving most or all of these things in your life, have you ever seen them as white privileges? You are invited to expand on this list in the exercises below by naming your own privileges as you become more conscious of your own rewards and benefits based on white skin privilege.

Getting Personal: My Awareness of My Own White Privileges

Even if we fully accept and are truly open to the principle of white privilege, getting in touch with them on a personal level is not a simple task. We need to know our own privileges, not just in an academic way of knowing, but to be aware deep within ourselves that we are receiving them at the moment they take place.

Following are three exercises designed to help us as white people to deepen our awareness and expand our list of white privileges. We who are white are not used to doing this. It tends to feel a little strange and awkward at first. As we move into the first of these exercises, I need to acknowledge that this will be a difficult task, and there may be a sense of being pushed unrelentingly into places we do not readily want to go. It may be helpful to keep in mind that our goal, at the end of this chapter, and by the end of this book, is to discover as much joy and freedom for white people as there is for people of color in the contemplation of strategies to dismantle and eliminate racism.

Before actually beginning to do these exercises, read through them a couple of times. Ask yourself what you need to know in order to begin doing them. If you are willing to do these exercises, it will be a serious and difficult commitment. As a way of doing these exercises, readers should set aside particular times, and perhaps even invite friends to participate with them. Another suggestion might be to keep a written journal of your feelings and thoughts as you participate in the suggested exercises.

Exercise One: Tracing Your Family History

Most white people, with a few adjustments for time and location, can identify themselves in the following words from Robert Jensen, a professor at the University of Texas:

> All through my life, I have soaked up benefits for being white. I grew up in fertile farm country taken by force from non-white indigenous people. I was educated in a well-funded, virtually all-white public school system in which I learned that white people like me made this country great. There I also was taught a variety of skills, including how to take standardized tests written by and for white people.

All my life I have been hired for jobs by white people. I was accepted for graduate school by white people. And I was hired for a teaching position at the predominantly white University of Texas, which had a white president, in a college headed by a white dean and in a department with a white chairman that at the time had one non-white tenured professor.

There certainly is individual variation in experience. Some white people have had it easier than me, probably because they came from wealthy families that gave them even more privilege. Some white people have had it tougher than me because they came from poorer families. White women face discrimination I will never know. But, in the end, white people all have drawn on white privilege somewhere in their lives.[8]

When we read the above quote, the reality of white privilege seems fairly clear. However, it needs to be just as clear when we look at the particularities of our own lives. The goal of this first exercise is to identify and explore some of the inheritances of the past that established the foundations of the lives of each one of us.

White power and privilege are inherited. They are passed down from generation to generation. Racism is a multigenerational conspiracy. This is one of the main reasons overcoming racism and its effects is so difficult. There is an enormous momentum that can be seen and felt behind the earlier statement that during 90 percent of U.S. history, every system and every institution in the United States was created originally and structured legally and intentionally to serve white people exclusively. The collective wealth and power of our nation has been passed on as a white inheritance from generation to generation. And each of us is a personal recipient of the benefits from this collective white wealth and power.

When we as white people are not aware of this inheritance, or are in denial of it, it creates strange and sometimes bizarre behavior among us. We claim credit, often with great nationalistic pride, for earning our ill-gotten inheritance. And the very slightest sense of loss of our white privilege is interpreted as an unjust attack on us by people of color. We use the term "reverse racism" to describe our having to forfeit a tiny piece of our white privilege.

This exercise is designed to help white people get in touch with the benefits and advantages we are still receiving as a result of the momentum of history. Chances are, whatever you and I have in life—our educational achievements, our economic class, our social position, our community status, our professional competence, our attitude toward life, and our self-esteem—are all tremendously influenced by our inheritance of white power and privilege.

For many people, this exercise is not overly difficult. There is a direct correspondence between what their parents and grandparents had and did and what they as the inheritors have received and what they have been able to do. For such people, white inheritance is easily seen.

Other people are not able to see this correspondence quite as directly. They have made great advancements in educational, economic, or societal achievements far beyond those of their parents and grandparents. For those people, it is easy to deny the white inheritance. They may say things like, "I pulled myself up by my own bootstraps," or "I earned everything I have in life by hard work and personal initiative." Even if such direct inheritance is not obvious, we need to see that collective power and privilege has made possible these great strides forward over the last generation.

There are three sets of questions in this exercise:

1. The first set of questions is based on your family's history and status in life. How far back can you trace your family history? Choose from the following scenarios the one that most fits your reality and answer the questions connected with it:

- You have inherited wealth and position because your forebearers arrived in this country as rich immigrants, or they became well-to-do long ago in past generations. If this describes your history, here are some questions: If they arrived rich, how did they use and pass down their wealth? If they arrived poor, how many generations did it take before their descendents achieved greater status in life? Did anyone in your family ever have slaves? Did they take advantage of westward expansion and homesteading on Indian lands? What other historical factors in their lives have brought you advantages in your life?
- Your family is relatively well-off, but it was only in this generation or in recent generations that they escaped from lower-class status or from poverty. If this describes your history, here are some questions for you: How did that escape take place? What advantage did being white play in these achievements? Did they get housing through the G.I. Bill? Did they move into white suburbs that were designed to exclude people of color legally? Did they enter professions that discriminated against people of color and in favor of white people? Are there other advantages designed primarily for white people that helped your family in this recent entrance into greater security and stability?
- You are among those white families in this country who are still either poor or relatively poor and whose lives are insecure and unstable. If your history fits this description, here are some questions for you to work on:

On whom does your family blame their condition? Who are the models that provide images for their aspirations to be other than poor or lower class? How do they relate to people of color who are also in struggle against the same forces of poverty and oppression? Even in their insecure setting, what advantages does your family have over families of color?

2. The second set of questions in this exercise is designed to trace your family's direct or indirect involvement in matters of racial conflict. Can you discover whether and where in your family history they took stands either for or against racism, or whether and how they avoided taking stands? If you can trace back that far, on whose side was your family in the Civil War? Were members of your family involved in struggles for women's suffrage or in the labor movement, and if so, did they object to the white exclusiveness of those movements? Did members of your family participate in the civil rights movement or in antiwar movements? It may be rare to find white relatives who participated in struggles against racism, but it is a rich treasure to discover. Remember, a positive response to these questions should not be seen as a means to deny white power and privilege in your family's history, but to discover other positive influences that you have also inherited.

3. The third set of questions is about your own personal history. Read again the earlier quote from Robert Jensen, describing his life of advantages as he grew up in Texas. With adjustments for time, place, and circumstances, write a description of your own advantages as a white person growing up in your family home, of your educational accomplishments, of your jobs and leisure life?

These three sets of questions may also stimulate a number of other questions about past generations in your family, your inheritance of white power and privilege, or a tradition of struggles for justice. This exercise is best carried out collectively with other members of your family, if they are open to it. Family history and memories are preserved in such a way that recall is better if it is not done individualistically. It is also helpful to have a genealogical chart of your family as far back as you can trace it. It can also be useful to create a family-history chart, showing influences of white power and privilege, as well as instances of familial participation in resistance to racism.

Exercise Two: Investigating Your Daily Environment

Every day each of us experiences white privilege in our daily lives, while we are at work, shopping in stores, watching television, going to church, or traveling. We may not be conscious of our receiving privileges, however, or know how to interpret what is happening. This exercise provides two sets of activities to help us develop the skill of observing our personal white privilege in our daily lives.

1. Ask a friend of color to accompany you into various settings in your city, town, or neighborhood, and observe how similarly or differently you and your friend are treated. Be sure this friend has an understanding of racism that is compatible with this exercise and with the analysis of this book. Also, be sure you have talked about the exercise in depth and your friend is not feeling unfairly used by doing the exercise with you. Go to a restaurant together and watch how the waiter or waitress treats you. Go to a bank and observe in the background while each of you has separate conversations with a loan officer. Shop in a department store and watch how the clerk or store security officers relate to each of you. Shop separately for the same car in a car lot and see if you are offered the same price and the same terms of payment.

As you conduct these tests together, there are two things to watch for. First, compare attitude and human relationships in the way you are treated. Observe body language, demeanor, and things like eye contact. Watch who gets the most attention, who is addressed as the person in charge, who is expected to pay, who receives service first. Second, what are the final outcomes of your transactions? Who is offered a loan? Who gets the best price? Who is followed by security people? Who is the satisfied customer?

Be aware that this will not be a totally scientific experiment with guaranteed accuracy. When professional discrimination testers conduct their investigations, they are trained extensively, and they are always paired in such a way that the only difference between them is the color of their skin. They are of similar age, gender, and class, they dress similarly, and so forth. You and your friend will not likely have the same level of skills or be the same in all other ways. If you make allowance for these differences, however, you can also learn a great deal from such an experiential investigation.

It is also important to be clear that people of color are not always treated badly, and white people are not always treated better than people of color. Perhaps you will see or feel the contrast only once or twice out of every ten times you make an attempt to do the comparison. But ask yourself how it would feel if you were pretty certain that you would be treated badly 10 or 15 percent of the time. You would probably be tense all of the time and would not even be able to enjoy the times when you were treated well.

A word of caution: the purpose of this exercise is to observe behavior, not to change those persons whose behavior you are observing. If you give in to the temptation to confront the people you are observing, you may find out how difficult it is to change people, but you also will not have the documentation that you are looking for. Also, it is important that you not place your partner or yourself in harm's way by challenging people who are not ready to be challenged. If you wish to attempt to do something about the behavior you observe, do that at another time after you have carefully planned to do so.

2. A second set of activities is for you and a friend of color to conduct a media survey. Read a newspaper together, watch the evening news together on television, or see a movie together. Our newspapers, magazines, radio, and television are constantly portraying or reporting about people of color, and especially about racial injustice. They are becoming increasingly fine-tuned and detailed in their stories and commentaries about situations and conditions in communities of color. Oftentimes the media give extremely distorted views of communities of color. However, increasingly the media are becoming more accurate and even quite sophisticated in uncovering and unveiling the continuation of increasingly subtle and sophisticated discrimination against people of color.

Even when they are doing their best, however, they usually report on Power[1] and avoid focusing on Power[2]. The media's best pieces help us to learn about the way racism hurts people of color. But often, in very subtle ways, they also help us avoid looking at ourselves. They help us look at the manifestations of racism, but not at its end-purpose of providing power and privilege for the white society. By addressing issues of people of color and not revealing the results of white power and privilege, they are contributing to the cover-up of racism. Like almost everyone else, they may be intent upon ending racism, but they are exposing the conditions of the wrong people and trying to solve the wrong problem.

While you and your friend are reading or observing together, look for this contrasting approach. How much is portrayed or reported about Power[1], and what is said or avoided being said about Power[2]? There are literally thousands of ways in which the media leads us to understand the reality of racial injustice in the daily lives of people of color. It is very important to be able to turn their message around and to see white privilege operating behind their reports of racial injustice. We need to train our eyes and our ears to see and hear the media differently.

Interpreting the Exercises. The goal of these two sets of activities is to learn by comparison and contrast. At first, this is the only way that many of us who are white can see our privileges, by contrasting them with the lack of privileges of others. These activities are aimed toward reinterpretation of what we experience every day. Our eyes and ears are trained to look and listen for Power[1], the way racism hurts people of color. Our assignment in this exercise is see and hear what is happening to white people. Usually we can see Power[1], the ways in which people of color are treated badly, before we can see Power[2], the ways in which white people are treated well. By making these contrasts, however, we are able to see and feel our white privilege. Eventually, we need to be able to reach the point that we don't need the contrasting experience of Power[1] to know we are experiencing Power[2]. Rather, we will become instinctively aware each time we are receiving rewards and services because we are white.

In the box below (fig. 3.1) is a sample list that suggests that for every experience of bias and discrimination by people of color, there is a comparable experience of privilege for white people. What we learn about Power[1] can be turned around into a new learning about Power.[2]

Power[1]: Disadvantage for People of Color	Power[2]: Advantage/Privilege for White People
• Poor service and attention	• Instant service and attention
• Lack of respect and trust	• Respect and trust
• No sense of welcomeness	• Sense of welcomeness
• Lied to	• Told the truth
• Physical and emotional danger	• Physical and emotional safety
• Limited availability of jobs	• Availability of jobs
• Limited availability of housing	• Availability of housing
• Limited freedom of movement	• Freedom of movement
• Police control and suspicion	• Police protect and serve
• Financial disadvantage	• Financial advantage
• Exclusion/segregation by race	• Inclusion by race
• Mistrust/disrespect based on race	• Trust/respect based on race
• Negative racial profiling	• Positive racial profiling
• Made to feel uncomfortable	• Made to feel comfortable
• Loss of time and great stress	• Save time and less stress
• Financial/economic disadvantage	• Financial/economic advantage
• Limited access to products and services	• Access to products and services

Fig. 3.1.

Exercise Three: A Personal Inventory of Your Daily Life

The aim of this exercise is to help an individual white person to personalize the results of our systems and institutions being designed historically and presently to function in favor of all white people. Each of us needs to be clear that in a myriad of ways we receive a daily influx of white privilege in our lives.

This exercise is simply to make a list as long as possible of our white privileges that we can recognize, and to keep on adding to the list as often as possible. This exercise was originally created by Peggy McIntosh, whose research and articles on white privilege I referred to earlier. Although the following list of white privileges is derived from Crossroads Ministry workshops, it is based on the original model of such a list created by Dr. McIntosh.[9] Study the following list, and then see how many other illustrations you can identify in your own personal life.

Power²: A Personal Inventory of White Privilege

As a White person,
. . . I am able to find positive role models depicted on TV, in the newspaper, and celebrated as heroes in most of our national holidays.
. . . in my college or professional school I find most professors look like me and talk like me, and most of the curriculum reflects my culture, history, and background.
. . . I am able to shop in most stores and not be followed by a security guard on suspicion that I might be shoplifting.
. . . when I am late for a meeting it is not attributed to my race.
. . . I can easily find artists' depictions of God, Jesus, and other biblical figures that match my skin color and facial characteristics.
. . . when I was looking for a house I did not have to worry that the realtor might not show me all available houses in my price range.
. . . no one thinks I got my job because of racial quotas.
. . . I will not be stopped by the police because of my race.

What else can you add?

Paradigm Shift: The Answer Is: "Everything." Perhaps your list will not be very long at first, but as you practice and develop your discernment skills, your personal list will grow longer and longer. It will become increasingly natural for you to perceive your privileges. Eventually, however, there is another realization, a paradigm shift that each of us needs to experience: that the question is far deeper than how long we can make our list of privileges. The answers are not, in fact, quantitative, but qualitative. The reality is that *everything* needs to be on the list. *Everything* goes better with whiteness.

When we have explored white power and privilege long enough and deeply enough, we will know and be aware that at any given moment of our lives racism is giving us something we neither earned nor deserve: white privilege. And we will know and be aware that in everything we do in our homes, and in everything we do when we leave our homes to work and shop and play and pray, we are benefiting from white privilege.

Responses to White Power and Privilege

As a white person, what are your immediate reactions to this chapter on white privilege, and especially to these exercises? What new awareness do you have? Is it beginning to make sense that instead of solving the problems of people of color that are caused by systemic racism, we need to be studying the systems of racism that are designed to favor white people, and to be strategizing how to change them? How does it feel to be "breaking the silence" of past generations and looking at ourselves in a mirror that reveals our white power and privilege? The following list of responses may serve to stimulate your own thinking and feeling about these questions.

We're Just Getting Started

The first response for many white people is that we have only scratched the surface, that this is only the beginning of digging into a part of our life we have not seen before. And if we have only just gotten started, then we need to plan carefully our next steps in order to keep on expanding on this important task. This is hard work, but it is also important work. Like any skill, we will only get good at it through constant practice.

The hoped-for long-term outcome of this work is that we will become more instinctively and automatically aware of our white power and privilege, that we will eventually be as aware of them as people of color are already aware of our receiving them, as well as of their not receiving them. It may be a little embarrassing to realize that people of color know us better than we know ourselves. But it is also important that we do not slip into the tempting trap of asking people of color to do our work for us. Although they can assist us in achieving a far more complete understanding of our white power and privilege, we dare not make that a substitute for the work we need to do ourselves. It is our responsibility to become clear about our white power and privilege.

A Good Start at Truth-Telling

A second response might be that although we are just getting started, it is a good start, and it feels good to be seeing and telling the truth about ourselves. It is not that we have been telling deliberate lies so much as that in our unawareness we have certainly been living with a lie. Many people of color believe we are telling outright lies when we say we do not see our white power and privilege. But that which we are facing here is something quite different and far more destructive than an intentional lie; we really have not been able to see it. We have allowed the truth about ourselves to be covered up; our eyes have been blinded to our own reality, and we have been living in denial.

In the language of addiction recovery, our white power and privilege is the "elephant in the room." There is a big elephant in the room, and most of us are pretending it is not there. It is not a little, cute, and cuddly elephant; it is big and ugly and it stinks. You have to look around it to see or talk to the person on the other side of the room. You have to squeeze by it to come into and leave the room. And yet, we pretend it is not there.

This elephant of white power and privilege not only impedes our lives as white people. It also gets in the way of our relationships with people of color. Again and again I have heard from colleagues of color that it is impossible to have authentic cross-racial relationships so long as this elephant in the room is not recognized. It is probably an accurate assumption that white readers of this book deeply value the cross-racial relationships in their lives. Think of your deepest and most cherished cross-racial relationship with a person of color, and ask yourself whether white power and privilege is acknowledged as a reality within that relationship. If the white person in that relationship is in denial and does not acknowledge this elephant in the room, it is unlikely that the person of color will either, even though it is very painful for them. As long as we won't see it, believe it, or express a desire to do something about it, the person of color will not risk the inevitable rejection that comes from raising the issue.

On the other hand, authentic cross-racial relationships do become possible when the elephant of white power and privilege is acknowledged. Such relations can become deep and profound when the truth is finally told. There are, in fact, few human relationships more authentic and more powerful than when white people and people of color join together in the task of addressing and seeking to eliminate white power and privilege. We must be clear that it is not only for the sake of people of color, nor for the sake of our cross-racial relationships, but also and especially for our own sake, that this truth-telling is so valuable.

Not Shame, but Anger

A third response white people are likely to be feeling is one of guilt and shame. It is virtually impossible to explore our power and privilege without such feelings. However, it needs to be recognized and doubly emphasized that the reason for doing these exercises is not to take people on guilt trips. Guilt is the least useful and least effective motivation for working against racism. Ultimately, guilt is debilitating and incapacitating. Religious leaders and psychologists tell us that the only useful response to guilt is to go to the forgiveness table and be restored, set free to struggle against that which caused us to feel guilty.

We need to exchange our guilt and shame for anger at racism, anger at the structures of systems and institutions that are set up to favor us. It is important to keep going back to our definition of racism. We are studying the misuse of power by systems and institutions. Our goal in studying Power^2 has been to explore the connection between our personal privileges and the systems and institutions of power that bestow these privileges on us. We must become absolutely clear that these privileges and rewards come to us automatically, whether we ask for them or not, whether we agree with having them or not. Our privileges are not individually generated by each of us, but come to us automatically from the systems and institutions in which we take part. The purpose of our becoming aware of our privileges is not to make us feel bad, but to become more aware of that which we are struggling to change. As we have been seeing with increasing clarity, the systems and institutions that bestow and control these privileges must be changed, and not simply our individual desire to receive them.

Several years ago, Citibank in Chicago displayed an advertisement on the side of city buses. The advertisement said: "You were born pre-approved." When I saw that sign, it was clear to me who the audience was that Citibank was addressing. To be born white in our society is to be born preapproved. Our systems and institutions know quite well how to identify and provide services for select audiences, and one of the clearest and most consistent audience of our systems and institutions has always been white people. Studying white power and privilege will help us understand how we were born pre-approved.

Schizophrenia: We Hate It and Love It

A fourth response is one of which we may not be immediately aware. It is based on an underlying reality that is likely to be present deep in the hearts of any and all white people. If we are honest, I believe we will admit that there is something inside each one of us that really loves our white power and privilege. Even while we are learning to be aware of Power^2, learning to dislike it, and learning to be angry about receiving it, we need to be in touch with this other part of us that loves it and grieves the possibility of its passing.

It is a very human thing to want to gain status and use it as a crutch in life. It is normal for us to use those aspects of our identity that societal structures will favor—whiteness, maleness, middle- and upper-class status, and positions of power. And even while we are growing in understanding that using these crutches furthers societal oppression, we need to also be clear how much we are dependent on them, and how much this dependency keeps us from helping to change it. Even though our privileges are automatically provided for us, we cooperate and either consciously or unconsciously accept this special treatment because we are white.

Conclusion: You Can't Take It Off

There is one final conclusion that needs to be stated before moving to the next step in chapter 4. This conclusion can also help lead us to through a door to explore in the next chapter the third level of racism, Power³, the worst and most serious expression of racism—racism's ultimate power to control and destroy everyone.

The final conclusion is this: if you are white, there is absolutely no way you can stop receiving your white privileges. So long as our systems and institutions are structured on the basis of white power, they will continue to provide white privileges for all white people automatically. It is impossible for anyone individually to decide to walk away.

Remember Peggy McIntosh and her concept of an "invisible knapsack" that is placed on the back of every white person when they are born? In the language of addiction therapy, that knapsack is a "monkey on our backs." You can't take it off. It was placed there on the day you were born, and it will be there until the day you die. You can't just simply say, "I'm not going to be privileged anymore." As long as the institutions are designed to do so, they will give us our privileges. It is not a matter of choosing whether or not to be a part of the racist system that benefits all white people. If you are white, your privileges will keep on coming to you, whether you want them or not.

There is no private escape from racism, no individual walking away from white power and privilege. But please do not hear this as a message of despair; rather, it is a message that can equip us to deal with reality. Together there is a great deal we can do to change our institutions. Collectively, we can transform white power and privilege. But first, before getting to solutions, we still need to be even more deeply in touch with racism's hold on us. If you as a white person are beginning to be aware that white privilege is a monkey on your back, then you are ready to move to the next step of exploring our definition of racism—the devastating power of Power³ to take us all prisoner and to destroy us all.

INDIVIDUAL RACISM

THE MAKING OF A RACIST

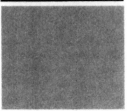

The same fetters that bind the captive bind the captor.
—C. Eric Lincoln

As long as one person is not free, none of us are free.
—Dr. Martin Luther King Jr.

Every one of us is born with a clean heart. Our babies know nothing about hate or racism. But soon they begin to learn—and only from us. We keep racism alive. We pass it on to our children. We owe it to our children to help them keep their clean start.
—Ruby Bridges

Power³: Racism at Its Worst

Now we have reached the heart of the matter. The central issue of this book is that we who are white are prisoners of our own racism. We may hold the power of racism in our hands, but we are unable to let go. Not only do we receive power and privilege from racism, but in doing so, racism gains power and control over us. All the good will in the world and all the good intentions of not being racist do not change the reality that white power and privilege is a monkey on our backs, and each of us is made—willingly or unwillingly—into an instrument of the daily and ongoing construct of white racism.

Thus far, I have presented a description of racism as a systemic problem that harms people of color (Power[1]) and benefits the white society (Power[2]). The third component of racism's system of power, which is designated *Power[3]*, now takes us to the very roots of racism. As we look at racism from the perspective of Power[3], we will confront a self-perpetuating force with the capacity to control and ultimately to destroy us all—white people and people of color alike.

At the core of racism is not simply the way it promotes inequality by taking from some and giving to others, but rather its capacity to crush the humanity of everyone it touches, to tear apart the very fabric of society. As I stated earlier, if you cut a living body in half, both parts of the body will die. White racism has cut the body of human society in half, and now both parts are bleeding to death. This is Power[3]—racism in its most devastating form.

The more we learn about Power[3], the more we will understand that racism is our common enemy that seeks to destroy not only people of color, but white people also. Racism possesses and controls oppressor and oppressed alike. It is capable of making all of us into compliant and willing prisoners, who accept, conform, and cooperate with the forces that imprison us. Racism not only subjugates people of color, but it also subjugates the white society that is doing the subjugating. The wardens are prisoners in their own prison.

"Go Home and Free Your Own People"

As a way of making myself clear about this, I would like to tell a story and share a personal experience from more than fifty years ago when I was working as a community organizer in an African American community in Chicago.

It was the time of the civil rights movement—the summer of 1966. A band of black marchers, led by Stokely Carmichael (later known as Kwame Ture), executive director of the Student Nonviolent Coordinating Committee (SNCC), carried out demonstrations across the state of Mississippi. The civil rights movement had become very strong, and this march could have been just another of the hundreds of marches and demonstrations taking place that summer. Yet it was a turning point. As the group marched, a new demand came in the form of a chant from the demonstrators, a controversial and insistent demand that had not been heard before. The chant, the demand, was:

"BLACK POWER! BLACK POWER! BLACK POWER!"

The chant was quickly taken up by others, and by the end of the summer the demand for black power was repeated in towns and cities throughout the country. The black power movement was born, and as a result the direction and strategies of the civil rights movement were significantly and dramatically altered.

There was another demand that emerged from the black power movement in that summer of 1966. The general public did not hear this second demand, but to its limited audience it was just as insistent and unsettling as the demand for black power. It was directed specifically at the relatively small number of white people like me who were living and working in black communities throughout the South and in the northern cities of the United States. We were white people working for black people's freedom; but we found ourselves suddenly faced with an ultimatum from the black power movement:

"WHITE MAN, GO HOME AND FREE YOUR OWN PEOPLE!"

The demand for "Black Power, Black Power, Black Power" not only altered the direction of the civil rights movement. In addition, the second demand for white people to "go home and free our own people" dramatically changed my life and the lives of many other white civil rights workers. Looking back to that moment in the summer of 1966 from the perspective of a half-century later, I can now see that the changes brought about by this demand were both redemptive and liberating. But at that moment, it certainly did not feel that way to me or my white colleagues!

What we felt then was rejection and confusion. We were shocked and angry. We had never before experienced tension like this between ourselves and our black colleagues in the movement. We thought there was a special, privileged relationship between us and our black friends. We were not the Klan or the White Citizens Council. We were different from the police and the white people throwing bricks at civil rights marchers. We were those white people working the hardest for change. We were the white people holding hands with blacks and singing, "Black and white together." We were willing to face the taunts and the violence against us by other white people. We were the ones who had dedicated our lives to working for freedom in the South and in the urban ghettos of the North.

And now we felt as if we were being told we were in the way and that we were not wanted. "White man, go home and free your own people." And we were being identified with other white people, lumped together with those who were obviously racist. We felt that we were being forced out of the black community, and we didn't like it. We felt hurt, angry, and rejected because we thought we were unceremoniously being pushed out of the movement.

What we didn't realize until later is that we weren't being pushed out. Rather, we were being pushed into the right direction—in a direction few of us would voluntarily have taken. The new direction was to work with white people and to work for change in the white community. For me personally, and for many others, it was the beginning of new discoveries and a new life.

Lumped Together with Racists

Being "lumped together with racists" was the best thing that could have happened to me. I began to understand for the first time my own identity as a racist. More importantly, I began to accept my identity as a white person and the need to identify with my own white people. Not only was I becoming more aware of the need for change in the white society before people of color could be free; I was also learning to see the destructive results that racism also has on white people and the white society. I began to understand what change and liberation could mean to us.

"Going home to free my own people" meant facing for the first time the reality that *my people* are not free. I had heard the words and teaching from Dr. King that "so long as one person is not free, none of us are free," but I had not really understood the meaning of these words. I thought Dr. King was teaching us that we should help free those other people who were not yet free so that the rest of us could relax and enjoy the freedom we already had. I had not yet learned that a people whose privileges, status, and accomplishments are built on a foundation of oppression of others and on a belief in their own superiority is a sick people. I had not yet begun to understand that a society that takes away the freedom of others is itself not free.

I had it all turned around: the problem is not that white people are not free because people of color are not free. Rather, it is the opposite: people of color are not free because white people are not free.

Racist and Not Free

"*Go home and free your own people.*" Behind this admonition lies an assumption that is very difficult for white people to grasp—that we are not free. Racism is a prison not only for people of color, but also for us. In a sophisticated process of incorporation, every white person in the United States is willingly or unwillingly made into a participant in our nation's system of white racism. The major thesis that underlies the analysis of racism presented in this book is based on this assumption: that individually and corporately, white Americans—all of us—are enslaved in racism and need to be set free.

At one time I thought it was possible to separate white Americans into two camps: racist and righteous. I, of course, was in the righteous camp. I also assumed that the occupants of each camp were there by choice. I believed that my friends and I had wisely chosen to be nonracists, and those in the other camp had unwisely chosen to be racists. Now I know differently. I now know there is no such thing as a nonracist camp. I know that, along with every other white American, I am a racist and a member of the racist camp. I also know that most of us are not in this camp by choice. Against our own will, we have all been made into racists. We are prisoners in our own communities, prisoners of racism.

I never wanted to be a racist. I still don't. For a long time, I even thought I wasn't. But now I know I am. And I know how I got that way. Whenever I think about it, even today I still become enraged and feel hurt deep inside myself. It is not guilt I feel—not anymore—just burning pain and anger over the fact that I was made into a racist. It happened to you too, if you are white. Whether you like it or not, you were made into a racist. I still am one and so are you. It should make you angry. Perhaps you share my anger, perhaps you don't. But I hope that by the time you finish reading this book, you will.

What and Who Is a Racist?

In chapter 2, I introduced the definition of racism that is the basis for this book: "race prejudice plus the misuse of power by systems and institutions." It is now time to go one step further and apply this definition to individual persons, and by doing so, to define what and who is an individual racist. It should be obvious by now that what I mean by a racist is quite different from the popular or common understanding of a racist. Usually when we call someone a racist in our society, we mean someone who is intentionally prejudiced or bigoted, or who feels animosity or hatred toward people of another race. We think of a racist as someone who uses the "N-word," or who talks disparagingly about "those people." By contrast, we think a nonracist is someone who has shed himself or herself of the influence of past prejudices, a person who is accepting and caring of all people and who is comfortable in cross-racial relationships.

Based on this common understanding, an individual can freely choose to be either a racist or a nonracist. It is an identity attained by a person's intentional decision and commitment. By this understanding, most people reading this book could call themselves nonracists, or at the very least, persons who were well on the way to becoming nonracist.

I am using the term "individual racist" quite differently, however. Here is the definition of an individual racist from my perspective:

> A racist is any white person who *willingly or unwillingly, wittingly or unwittingly* participates in and benefits from white power and privilege (Power²).

Read the definition and pause for a moment to reflect on its meaning. The definition does not answer the question of who *wants* to be a racist; rather, it answers the question of who *is* a racist whether they want to be or not. As you can see, this definition of a racist is quite different from our common understanding of what or who is a racist. Once again, I ask you to try this on and see if it makes sense to you.

To begin with, according to the definition, I myself am a racist. Although I am not a conscious bigot, and I value many deep cross-racial relationships and participate in efforts for racial justice and freedom, nevertheless, according to the definition of a racist that I am presenting here, I am quite clearly a racist.

And I am also suggesting that although you may be a white reader who is likewise relatively prejudice-free, quite friendly with people of color, and opposed to the poverty, discrimination, and powerlessness of anyone on the basis of race—despite your good intentions—you are also, according to the definition of a racist that I am presenting here, a racist.

I believe that many, perhaps most, white Americans do not want to be racist. I most certainly do not want to be a racist, and I assume that you do not want to be a racist either. I want to be seen as a nonracist, especially by people of color. I want to be innocent of any charges of prejudice, bigotry, or feelings of superiority. I have worked very hard and for a very long time to divest myself of any of these negative beliefs and feelings, and I have dedicated myself for many years to be part of the struggle for racial justice. But just because I do not want to be a racist, it does not mean that I am not a racist. I am a racist, and if you are white, I believe you are also a racist, whether you want to be one or not.

Against My Will

"Willingly or unwillingly, wittingly or unwittingly." Whether or not it is with personal racist intent, every white person in the United States is made to be a part of our society's racist structure and system. As we saw in the previous chapter, all of us who are white in the United States participate in and benefit from the system of white power and privilege even if it is against our will. At one time, most of us didn't even realize it was true. But now, the fact of knowing it is true still doesn't change the reality. Our white power and our white privilege continue whether we want them or not, whether we are comfortable with them or not, whether we are opposed to them or not. Our power and privilege are part of an invisible knapsack that has become a monkey on our backs. We cannot take it off. So long as the systems and institutions of the society are structured to serve white people better than people of color, we are participants in and beneficiaries of white racism.

As we shall see in the following pages, the crucial issue is that although most of us have been quite unaware of all this, we have been cooperating, compliant, and willing participants. All of us who are white have been made to participate in and benefit from systemic racism whether we have chosen it or not, and in such a way that it is not possible to extricate ourselves and choose to no longer be a racist. If you are white, I am suggesting that you are a racist because you are part of a racial group in which everyone participates and benefits from white power and privilege. Your imprisonment is that you have no power to stop being a beneficiary of racism. *Your imprisonment is that you have no power not to be a racist.*

Having said that, there are still many questions to be answered. Following is a list of some of these questions, accompanied by very brief responses. As we continue to explore Power³, most of these questions will be dealt with more deeply.

- *Does this mean that, without exception, every white person is racist?* Yes, because every white person is part of the problem, whether or not it is with personal racist intent. All of us in the United States participate in and benefit from the system of racism, even if it is against our will. All of us, willingly or unwillingly, are racists because we all participate in and benefit from white power and privilege.

- *But aren't many white people just as poor and powerless as many people of color?* It is true that many white people face issues of powerlessness on other grounds than racism, such as classism, sexism, heterosexism, and so forth. Because of these issues, many white people face problems of powerlessness quite similar to those of people of color. But because of racism, as we have seen in the previous chapter, even the most powerless of white people benefit from whiteness. And because of the division and separateness brought about by racism, white people who are oppressed by other injustices are still separated and alienated from people of color.

- *But what about people of color? Aren't they racists too?* No, people of color cannot be racist because they lack the collective and systemic power to enforce their prejudices. Of course, people of color can be just as racially prejudiced, bigoted, nasty, and unkind as white people. But in the United States, there is no such thing as black power and privilege, red power and privilege, brown power and privilege, or yellow power and privilege. And so long as power in America is distributed in an unequal and unjust manner that favors white people, there can be no such thing as red racism, black racism, yellow racism, or brown racism, or any form of "reverse racism." Racism in the United States is the exclusive property of the white community.

As will be seen more clearly before this chapter is completed, the prison for people of color is not that they are made into racists, but that they are made into *casualties of racism, victims of racism.* And the deepest level of this imprisonment is experienced when people of color are actually formed into compliant and cooperating victims who willingly support white racism.

• *Does this mean that in other parts of the world there is only white racism?* No, but in this book we are dealing only with racial justice issues in the United States. In many other nations, white people are also in control of all the systems and resources. However, in other nations other racial groups may be dominant in the society and use their power to victimize other races.

• *Isn't this just a guilt trip for white people?* No, exactly the opposite. Of course, if you have chosen to be a racist, then as far as I'm concerned, the more guilt you feel, the better. But if you are an individual who is racist against your will and are unable to escape, then guilt is your least appropriate response. If it is against our will, then the central issue is not guilt and shame, but rather the question, How were we tricked and misled into becoming someone we don't want to be? The question is not, How do we get forgiven? but, How are we imprisoned, and how do we get out? As we shall continue to explore in the following pages, a far more useful response than guilt is anger at our unwilling captivity, and determination to join the struggle to free our own people, along with everyone else.

The Two Prisons of Racism

Racism, then, creates two prisons, not just one. The first is the prison of oppressed people of color in the United States. The inmates are Native Americans, African Americans, Latinos/Hispanics, Asian Americans, and Arab Americans. Unless we have been deaf and blind, or in total denial during these unending years of social turmoil and racial conflict, we are at least aware of this prison's existence, even though all of us still need to learn a great deal more about its reality and its implications.

The other prison that racism creates is for us, the white people of the United States. Although we are in a prison, we are often deceived and don't believe it, for our prison is deceptively comfortable and disarmingly warm and friendly. But it is a prison nonetheless. You and I are its inmates, and it exists wherever we live, learn, work, and play. The walls of this prison are the residential, cultural, relational, and institutional boundaries that separate white America from the rest of America. Its bars may not be visible, but they evoke as much frustration, loneliness, fear, and anxiety as the bars of any penitentiary.

Tragically, as inmates of our white prison, we have a desperate need to pretend that the prison does not exist. An intricate web of deception disguises its reality. The bars on the windows are hidden by expensive curtains. There is thick carpeting instead of institutional flooring. Flowers and vines hide the steel plate doors. In place of a meager cot, there is a luxurious bed. The disguise is complete; the lie is convincing. Many, perhaps most, of us who are inmates firmly believe the myth that there is no prison, and pretend we live in total freedom. We repeat endlessly that we are the free ones, and we offer to others a mythic opportunity to be "free like us."

Whenever we do become aware of the confining and dehumanizing walls that surround us, we are quickly assured that we are not looking at the inside walls of our prison, but at the outside walls of the other prison—the prison for people of color. Despite our intricately spun national myths about freedom, however, the continuation of racism in America signifies that white people are no more free than people of color. It is not possible for racism to end, and it is not possible for people of color to become free if we do not go home and free our own people.

How Does Racism Do That?

Where does racism get its ability to imprison everyone? How does it get all of us—white people and people of color alike—to cooperate and conform to its will? How does it make me and every other white person in the United States—willingly or unwillingly, wittingly or unwittingly—into a racist and confine us in this racist prison? Likewise, how are people of color made to conform and cooperate with racism even while it is so painful and destructive to them? Where does racism get its incredible power to divide humanity into two groups—white people and people of color—and then make the former into compliant racists and the latter into compliant victims of racism? How does it do that? The rest of this chapter will seek to answer this question.

Let us first of all be clear that racism *does* do that. Even though many people of color and many white people heroically resist and use every opportunity to expose and confront racism, all of us must ultimately function at least in some ways that conform to societal norms dictated by racism. All of us to one degree or another end up doing what racism wants us to do in order to survive in this society. All of us, by our very participation in the systems and institutions of this society, willingly or unwillingly support the perpetuation of white power and privilege. And most of us conform to such an extent that we even feel natural and normal in doing so. White people obediently act out roles of superiority and dominance, and people of color obediently act out roles of inferiority and submission.

In order to comprehend this terrible power of racism, we must realize that racism could not exist without getting cooperation and conformity from white people and people of color alike. It is the very first and highest priority of the system of racism to ensure that this cooperation and conformity continues from year to year and from generation to generation. Racism stays strong and flourishes by creating and maintaining a continuing supply of well-trained and compliant racists and victims who carry out predetermined identities and roles.

"Racialization":
The Mass Production of Racists and Victims

This is one of racism's fundamental and essential activities: to mass-produce racists and victims of racism who "willingly or unwillingly, wittingly or unwittingly" participate in systems of white power and privilege. Through a process of systematic socialization, racism perpetuates itself by ensuring that each one of us will accept and conform to our racial identities:

- *White People*: Every white person born in the United States is "racialized" and "socialized" to accept a racial identity and membership in a racial group with superior characteristics and powerful rights and privileges. If you are white, your racial identity, along with the power and privilege that automatically go along with it, was instilled within you very early in life in a way that requires a disciplined and intense effort even to begin to disassociate yourself from it.

- *People of Color*: Every person of color born in the United States is "racialized" and "socialized" to accept a racial identity and membership in a racial group with inferior characteristics and restricted rights and privileges. If you are a person of color, your racial identity, along with the strict limitations to your power and privilege that automatically go along with it, was instilled within you very early in life, in a way that requires a disciplined and intense effort even to begin to disassociate yourself from it.

This is Power[3], racism's third and most destructive misuse of power. It shapes our racial identities and manipulates us into being compliant and cooperative—even comfortable—in carrying out our racially determined roles. In so doing, racism fulfills its underlying purpose: to imprison, control, and ultimately to destroy us all.

How Identity Formation Takes Place
In order to explore further these deepest roots of racism's power, we need to recall for a moment a bit of what we already know about the process of human identity formation. Identity formation is the process of becoming who we are. It begins the moment we are born. Our home, school, church, and

many other societal influences shape our identity, imparting a sense of who we are. In the process of growing up, different aspects of our identity—our gender, nationality, culture, class, race, and religion—are clearly and strongly implanted within us. Through a complex process of socialization, we internalize a conscious and unconscious identity, which becomes the foundation and basis for who we are.[1]

Educational experts and psychologists tell us that the foundations of individual identity become internalized within us by the time we are three or four years old—before the time of effective cognition, with the result of greatly determining who we are and what we will do with the rest of our lives. After that time, as we develop our cognitive skills, we build our conscious lives on these foundations in both overt and in subtle and hidden ways that conform to these identities.

In order to search for a deeper understanding of racism's imprisoning Power[3], we need to be aware of this socializing process all of us go through, a process that teaches us to participate in and cooperate with the social order. Our personalities and our behaviors are shaped to conform to the norms of society, to "fit in" and to become "proper" members of our group. We are taught and shaped by our families, our peers, our educational systems, and the media. Our spirituality and our religious practices also contribute in a profound way to this identity formation, as they lead us into fundamental human understandings of who we are and whose we are.

The Good and Bad Results of Socialization. When it is well intended and when it works the way it should, this social and spiritual identity formation is a positive process that results in our becoming creative persons with high self-esteem. However, there can also be negative aspects of identity formation that put undesirable ideas and feelings inside of us and have the effect of distorting our identities.

When the socializing is positive, we call it "education" and accept it as part of normal human growth. But when negative or unacceptable ideas or feelings get socialized within us, we use more descriptive words such as "brainwashing," "programming," and "conditioning." For example, we often use these words to describe the ideas taught by an enemy nation, a religious cult, or even an opposing political party.

It happens to all of us. Consciously and unconsciously, we absorb the fears, hatreds, prejudices, and unhealthy beliefs of those around us. As a result of negative socialization, small and large cracks appear in the foundation of human personality, giving rise to identity problems, insecurities, and undesirable behavior. Even if a person works diligently to defy and resist these negative aspects of identity formation, their effects remain present and continue to influence us, both consciously and unconsciously, for the rest of our lives. For some people there may even be a realization later in life that these foundations were so poorly constructed that it is necessary to spend a great deal of the rest of their lives in therapy, rebuilding the foundations.

Negative Messages of Superiority and Inferiority

One clear example of this negative socialization can be seen in the messages that lead to feelings of superiority and inferiority. There is a built-in vulnerability or susceptibility in every human being that makes us open us to receive two kinds of negative messages in our early socialization. The first is our vulnerability to the negative message of superiority. The second is our vulnerability to the negative message of inferiority. We sometimes refer to these as a "superiority complex" and an "inferiority complex."

- All of us are vulnerable to negative *superior* messages, which can create in us feelings of being better than others, or the desire to have advantages, positions, and rewards that others do not have. When we are socialized to become excessively competitive and to judge our worth and status by our achievements, we can be driven by the desire to be above everyone else.

- Likewise, all of us are vulnerable to negative *inferior* messages, which can create in us feelings of having less worth than others, to have low self-esteem, and to have diminished ability to function as individuals or as part of social groups. When we are socialized to be excessively passive and submissive, we can become overly subject to the will of others.

It is important to recognize that all of us have received some of each of these negative messages—both inferior and superior. Most of us can identify within ourselves ways in which superior messages have created in us a sense of overly high self-importance and pretentiousness. Likewise, we can identify within ourselves ways in which inferior messages have created a sense of low self-esteem and self-doubt.

Group Conditioning

This negative programming and conditioning does not only happen to individuals. It also happens to groups of people in a society. We all receive messages containing the underlying deception that some groups of people are inherently better than other groups of people. We are taught that there are upper and lower classes, superior and inferior genders, greater and lesser nations, true and false religions, good-looking and ugly people. Even if we don't consciously believe these messages, we learn to fit into the world based on this premise. And we are taught to believe this whether we are part of the better group or not. For example, the poorest person in the world is taught to believe that rich people are better than poor people.

The negative messages of superiority and inferiority come from the government, the media, schools, social and cultural organizations, the church, peers, and family. These socializing messages then become the basis for nations dominating other nations, or different groups of people setting themselves against each other to demonstrate their supremacy and to dominate over those who are lesser and inferior. And, as we shall see, these same socializing messages about superior and inferior races perpetuate systemic racism.

An Illustration of Negative Programming and Conditioning

In April 1968, shortly after the assassination of Martin Luther King Jr., Jane Elliot, a schoolteacher in Riceville, Iowa, led her all-white third-grade class in a two-day experiment. She separated the blue-eyed children from the brown-eyed children. On the first day she taught them that blue-eyed children were superior to brown-eyed children and instituted rules that gave the blue-eyed children more power and privileges than the brown-eyed children.

The results were almost immediate and overwhelming. The blue-eyed students delighted in their new status, and adapted easily to a role of superiority. They were self-confident and did exceptionally well in their class work. They also became dominant and oppressive in their relationships to the inferior brown-eyed students. The brown-eyed students were docile in adapting to their new and inferior identity and subjugated role. They accepted their new station in life with little resistance and adjusted their behavior accordingly. Their learning ability and test scores took an immediate plunge.

The next day, the roles were reversed. So also—instantly—were the behavior patterns. The brown-eyed students became superior and dominant, and the blue-eyed students accepted and lived out inferior identities and roles. Three years later, in 1970, the third time Elliot carried out this experiment in her classroom, it was recorded on film and shown on public television networks. A documentary on this experience is widely used in antiracism education programs.[2] Jane Elliot has repeated this experiment hundreds of times with both children and adults since then. Each time it demonstrates how susceptible human beings are to indoctrination into superior and inferior roles.

Racial Identity Formation:
The Shaping of Superior and Inferior Races

This same process of group identity formation describes the racialization of white people and people of color in our society. As stated in chapter 2, race is a racist concept created to support racism. To this day, we are all racialized into one or another category of races. Racial identity formation is a socializing process that takes place in every person in this country. When each of us is assigned a racial identity and is socialized to conform to the roles assigned with that racial identity, its effect is to misshape our identity. Our racial identities are a distortion of our human personalities, a psychological and a spiritual imprisonment that results in the creation and perpetuation of two groups, with each of us being made a member of one of the groups: either a superior racist or an inferior victim of racism.

Tragically, in the United States, this misshaping of our racial identities is still accepted as part of our normal educational and socializing processes. We need to be clear that, rather than "normal education," it is far more accurate to speak of our being "brainwashed, programmed, and conditioned" to accept the reality of race and racism.

All people in the United States are socialized from birth to participate in the social construct of race. As we described in chapter 2, race is a legal category in the United States, a concept that has remained basically unchanged since its formation when white was legally defined as superior and all other races as inferior. Still today, every person is assigned a race. At the time of our birth, each of us is given a racial identity, and then, in both conscious and unconscious ways, our behavior is carefully shaped to conform to the role associated with that identity. White people are shaped to conform to a superior identity and role, and people of color are shaped to conform to an inferior identity and role.

Through a process of systematic socialization, racism perpetuates itself by the mass production of compliant racists and compliant victims of racism. As stated earlier in this chapter, in order to comprehend the terrible power of racism, we must realize that racism could not exist without getting this cooperation and conformity from all of us—white people and people of color alike. It is the very first and highest priority of the system of racism to ensure that this cooperation and conformity continues from year to year and from generation to generation. Racism stays strong and flourishes by creating and maintaining a continuing supply of well-trained and compliant racists and victims who are carrying out predetermined identities and roles.

Internalizing the Lies of Racial Superiority and Inferiority

"I am superior." "I am inferior." All people are vulnerable to both messages, as Jane Elliot's "brown eyes/blue eyes" story demonstrates by reversing the roles on successive days. If I am consciously and unconsciously taught from the moment of my birth that I am superior and a member of a superior race, I will believe and act according to this message. If I am consciously and unconsciously taught from the moment of my birth that I am inferior and a member of an inferior race, I will believe and act according to this message.

As with other socialized lies, it is not even necessary to believe these lies consciously. All that is required is early conditioning and a later willingness to live *unprotestingly* in a society that functions on these premises. Once the fundamental lie about racial superiority and inferiority is internalized, all the other subsequent racist deceptions become believable and believed.

And the worst part is that it is done to each of us before we can be aware of or resist its happening. The foundations for our racial identities and the status of superiority and inferiority attendant to these identities become internalized within us before we are three or four years old—before the time of effective cognition. After that time, as we develop our cognitive skills, one of two things happens to us. Either we develop our lives in ways that consent, cooperate, and conform to our imposed racial identities or we reach the point of realization that these foundations are wrong, and we then spend the rest of our lives learning to live in contradiction to these negative foundations.

- *"Internalization of Racist Superiority"* is the term that is often used to name the racialization and socialization of white people. This socialization takes advantage of the human vulnerability to superior messages and the desire to be "better than." The message that is consciously and unconsciously inculcated within the white society is, "We are superior because are white." With great effectiveness and efficiency, every white person is shaped with an identity that conforms to the role of a member of a superior group that receives power and privileges. A formal definition of this internalization has been created by Crossroads Ministry as follows:

  A complex multi-generational socialization process that teaches White people to believe, accept and live out superior societal definitions of self and to fit into and live out superior societal roles. These behaviors define and normalize the race construct and its outcome—White supremacy.[3]

- *"Internalization of Racist Oppression"* is the contrasting term that is often used to name the racialization and socialization of people of color. This socialization of people of color takes advantage of the human vulnerability to inferior messages and the tendency toward feeling "less than." The message that is consciously and unconsciously received and believed within communities of color is, "We are inferior because we are people of color." With the same effectiveness and the same efficiency, every person of color is shaped with an identity that conforms to the role of a member of an inferior group with less power and fewer privileges, and that exists primarily to serve the needs of the white society. Crossroads Ministry's formal definition of this internalization is:

A complex multi-generational socialization process that teaches People of Color to believe, accept and live out negative societal definitions of self and to fit into and live out inferior societal roles. These behaviors support and help maintain the race construct.[4]

Even though we need to study and understand these two conditioning processes separately, we need to also see that they are closely related to each other, as well as interdependent. In the words of Crossroads, "These socialization processes support and reinforce each other in a 'dance' that helps maintain the race construct."[5]

Of course, no one individual receives and acts out these messages in the same way. In some persons it may even be extremely difficult to perceive symptoms of this internalization. Each of us is inseparably a member of a racial group, however, and it is in our group behavior that these patterns of racial conditioning can clearly be seen. In the white community, the messages of superiority are internalized, believed, and acted out in behaviors that not only reflect high self-esteem and achievement, but the meanness of racial superiority and dominance as well. Alternatively, in communities of color, the messages of inferiority are internalized, believed, and acted out in behavior patterns that not only reflect low self-esteem and lower achievement, but acceptance of roles that reflect racial inferiority and powerlessness as well.

This is Power[3] at work. It is the power of racism to "racialize" the identities of each one of us by making us part of a racial group, and to "socialize" each one of us to conform to racialized patterns of inferiority and superiority.

There are, of course, many people of color and many white people whose lives are powerful witnesses to the task of defying, rebelling against, and resisting these socializing influences. Such bold and courageous people fill the pages of history, and they are all around us in our present world. My best guess is that if you are reading this book, it is also true about you. But it is crucial to recognize that it is because these negative socializing influences are present in the first place that such defiance, rebellion, and resistance are required. Challenging and contradicting these assigned roles and behaviors requires an almost superhuman effort, because it requires resisting at the deepest levels of our consciousness the assigned roles given to us in our racial group.

The Making of a White Racist

In the rest of this chapter I will explore in greater depth the process of internalizing racial superiority in white people. While I will not further examine its counterpart, the internalization of racist oppression, this should not be understood as a statement of its relative unimportance. Quite the opposite. It is in fact such an important subject that a white person cannot and should not attempt to tackle it. As I have written in other parts of this book, the history of racism is filled with the erroneous assumption that it is the responsibility of white people to diagnose and solve the issues that white racism causes for people of color. More often than not, this conviction is one that distracts white people from seeing that racism is our problem, that we are the problem that needs to be solved, and that we have a responsibility for working on solutions to our white racism.

This section is intended to lead toward a deeper personal understanding of the effects of Power[3] on the lives of white people. In the last chapter, the exploration of white power and privilege included the assertion that all white people willingly or unwillingly receive these privileges, even though most of us are not even aware of them. Now, in this chapter, I have been suggesting that the reason we are not aware of our white power and privilege is that we have all been subjected to a process of socialization that shapes our identity as white people. This socialization conditions us to be unaware of the benefits that come with whiteness, but at the same time to receive them as a meritorious reward. Our goal now is to understand better how this socializing process takes place within each one of us as effectively as it does. It is important for each of us to be able to describe the step-by-step process, as well as the events and people who made it happen.

Breaking the Silence: Exposing the Comfortable Prison

I have suggested that we, as white people, live in a comfortable prison that is disguised not to look like a prison, either to its inmates or when viewed from the outside. An intricate web of deception disguises its reality. The disguise is complete; the lie is convincing. Most of the inmates have a firm belief that there is no prison; that they exist in total freedom.

The comfortable prison maintains itself by a conspiracy of silence. Now the silence must be broken, the disguise revealed, the curtains lifted. We need to be able to expose our own imprisonment and tell our own stories of how it came to be. We need to explore the duplicitous process that makes us ready receptacles and at the same time unaware of our receiving. In telling our stories to each other, I believe we will discover that we all have a version of the same story, and that our individual racism is a part of a collective conspiracy.

But we must begin on a personal level. Are you aware of learning the lie—either explicitly or with subtlety—that some people are better than others, and that white people are better than people of color? Even if you never consciously believed it, are you aware that you learned to accept and live comfortably in a world shaped on this belief? What can you remember about your socialization as a white person? What can you remember about what you were taught about people of color? What made you a ready receptacle to accept white power and privilege? What made you able to pretend we are all equal and then live comfortably with the reality that we are not? As we progress through a more detailed examination of the prison of white racism, try to identify yourself living within it and to remember how you were taught to be a part of its collective life.

The Prison's Foundation — Laid at Birth

Racists are made, not born. There is not a natural propensity toward racism in white people that predetermines our racism before we are born. Our identity as racists cannot be determined in our DNA. But if we are to be in touch with our earliest infection with this deadly virus called racism, we will become aware that we contracted it at the moment of our birth.

As I stated earlier, all people are born with a natural vulnerability to both messages of inferiority and superiority. But the system of racism directs its messages of superiority to white people and its messages of inferiority to people of color. As white people begin to receive messages of superiority from the time we are born, these messages become the conduit that connects our individual identities to the power of societal systems. Remember our definition of racism: *prejudice plus systemic power.* Without this linkage to systems and institutions of power controlled by and for white people there can be no racists. Because of this linkage, however, an individual white person whose sense of superiority might otherwise be limited to hurtful and ugly behavior in his or her private encounters becomes a violent and destructive instrument with far-greater scope.

Racists are made, not born—but the making of a racist begins the moment we are born. Our socialization as superior people began the moment we took our first breath (or perhaps even at the moment we were conceived). As white people, we received an uncountable number of messages of racial superiority as our families and peers gave us our orientation to life (along with other messages about gender, class, nationality, and so forth). The starting place to examine our socialization is at our birth.

Because the white society is isolated, unaware, and anesthetized into believing that the prison does not exist, making racists out of each of us is a relatively simple task. From earliest childhood each of us goes through either a subtle or not-so-subtle socializing process. Consciously and unconsciously, intellectually and emotionally, a racist mentality is created in each of us. To the stimulus of whiteness we are taught to respond with pride and identity, a sense of ease and respect. To the stimulus of African American, Latino/Hispanic, Native American, Asian American, and Arab American we are taught to respond with some combination of fear, hate, and suspicion, or with paternalistic concern and pity, or with a color blindness that pretends that difference is not there. So deeply are these responses embedded in us that no matter how much we consciously seek to reject them, they still control our lives. The very core of our being is permeated with racist assumptions and values that make us able to accept our superior position in society. Surrounding that core are many layers of insulation that muffle our feeling, our vision, and our memory, making racism appear to be subtle, elusive, and difficult to perceive.

Most of this conditioning takes place before we are old enough to understand. If we knew what was happening, some of us might have objected and rebelled. But how could we know at such an early age that growing up in an almost totally white environment is a forced and unnatural existence in a country that has a large population of people of color? How could we know that the values passed on to us are based on white control and the unspoken assumption of white superiority? How could we know that what we learned about the achievements of white people and the failures of people of color is twisted and untruthful? And even if our environment is partly multiracial and multicultural, our orientation and interpretation to these experiences is also white-directed. In our isolated and carefully protected white environment, we have no opportunity to doubt, let alone challenge, the orientation to life that we were given. White power, white control, and white superiority are presented to us as natural, the way things are, and the way things ought to be.

Within a very few years, the foundation is complete. It is important to emphasize that this means that at the beginning of our socialization none of us personally chose to become racist. The system of racism shaped each of us to be a part of the dominant, superior, white collective. We simply didn't have a choice. By the time we are three or four, the socialization has taken place that makes us adopt and adapt to a segregated, racist, and white-dominated world. Before the time of effective cognition, we have accepted our superior position in society as part of the natural world.

In the continuing years of growth and development, this socialization is either reinforced by experience, or if we are fortunate, we will begin to see its contradictions and to work at its dismantling and dissolution. If you are a white person reading this book, you have already identified yourself as one of the fortunate few who are beginning to see the prison bars and are helping to prepare a prison break.

The Four Walls of Racism's Prison

If it happened early in our lives and without our consent, can we identify the specific mechanisms by which this conditioning takes place? How do we become so completely imprisoned that most of us are not even aware of it, and often do not even feel its restrictions and limitations? There are four powerful forces that are brought to bear on every white individual, each of which contributes to this imprisonment. They define the four walls of our prison: the wall of *separation and isolation*, the wall of *illusion and delusion*, the wall of *amnesia and anesthesia*, and the wall of *power and privilege*. These forces comprise the four walls of our comfortable prison, and are the primary marks or identifying symptoms that indicate devastating damage at the level of our inscribed identity.

The Wall of Separation and Isolation

Our prison of racism is a white ghetto. The prison is maintained by keeping white inmates separate from people of color, while at the same time providing a secondhand, vividly distorted picture of people of color and the world in which they live. Fifty years after the end of legal segregation, even though a few holes have been punched in the walls of separation, the vast majority of us are still living in racial isolation from each other.

We are still a nation that lives racially apart. The product of years of segregation is two kinds of ghettos, not one. Just as most people of color are isolated from us, so also are most of us isolated from them. Even if, from within our white communities, we have contact with a few African Americans, Native Americans, Latino/Hispanics, Asian Americans, or Arab Americans, the majority of them are somewhere out there, in another part of town or in another part of the country. Through the media, we experience their virtual reality, but we seldom experience their actual reality. Everything we know about them is secondhand information filled with distortions.

It is true that there is token integration, and information about other racial groups does now flow a bit more readily. We know somewhat more about each other than we used to know. We may have a friend or two of another race or culture. But, for the vast majority of us, that is as far as it goes. It is also true that many of us attend school, work, and play in the same places as people of color. While we may be in the same rooms together doing the same things, however, we seldom actually do these things together. We do them in the same place and in each other's presence, but we still do them separately. In desegregated schools, workplaces, and recreation areas, a strict, but informal, segregation still exists. True integration in such groups is extremely rare. As Beverly Daniels Tatum has testified, we may be in the same cafeteria, but we are still sitting at separate tables.[6] And, as soon as school, work, or play is completed, white people and people of color still go home to their segregated communities knowing for the most part very little or nothing of each others' lives.

Suburbia has become a familiar symbol of our isolation and separation. It is still touted by the advertising world as an escape—the fulfillment of a person's dreams. But its distance from the city, at the end of a freeway, surrounded by six-foot fences, helps reinforce the image of a prison rather than an escape. The English author and theologian C. S. Lewis, in his book *The Great Divorce*, describes a vision of hell as a place where people perpetually move away from one another because of their inability to get along with each other. They leave houses and entire blocks and neighborhoods empty and build new houses at the edge of hell, thereby creating an ever-expanding circle with occupied houses at the edge, and with the abandoned center left behind them.[7]

Lewis's description of hell could be a description of white flight from the city after World War II and the emergence of suburbs in the United States. The development of suburbs not only created a greater gulf between suburban whites and people of color in the inner cities; it also led to a sense of great isolation for many suburbanites. Anyone who has spent several hours every day on the freeway or commuter train understands the need for tranquilizers and alcohol in order to survive and still insist with a smile, "It really isn't so bad."

The newest symbol of isolation—and the power to create and maintain it—is the trend toward moving from suburbia back into the city. It is a process called "gentrification" or "regentrification," meaning that the "landed gentry" have taken over once more. Unfortunately, gentrification is not a move away from isolating imprisonment of the suburbs; rather, it is a swapping of prisons. Moving back into the central city means moving people of color out. The poor ghettos and the high-rise public housing units are being torn down to provide a place for the returning suburbanites to build their condominiums. People of color are being dispersed to the outer rings of the city or suburbs, where new ghettos are being created. And the wall of separation and isolation between the two prisons is perpetuated, even strengthened.

The Wall of Lies and Illusions

Behind the second wall of this comfortable white prison that separates us from the rest of world, reality becomes a figment of the imagination. Alone in our prison we can lie and be lied to without fear of contradiction. Our lies are about ourselves and about people of color. And these lies define our existence. An enormous list of myths and lies has been created to control the impressions and perceptions of white people as we relate to people of color. These myths and lies are handed down from generation to generation of white people. Although they vary somewhat from one generation to another, they basically come in two kinds. The first kind can be seen in the "old" lies that are the most blatant and crude. The second kind is a more subtle and sophisticated version of the same myths and lies.

The Old Myths and Lies. In generations past, almost all white people believed the old lies. Even today, a significant portion of white Americans still maintains them. These are the unwhitewashed lies that blatantly describe people of color in terms of inferiority, ignorance, laziness, and violence. Those who still accept these blatant and ugly lies believe them to be fundamental truths. Younger readers may have heard about them, but the majority of older readers will clearly recognize and remember them. Are you old enough to remember Amos and Andy, Aunt Jemima, the Lone Ranger and loyal Tonto, the Cisco Kid and stupid Pancho? What about Stepin Fetchit or the Stephen Foster songs and minstrel shows? How about cowboy and Indian movies, still continuing to be made and seen today? Has a nation ever before celebrated the genocide of an indigenous people with such joy and pride? How could we be anything but callous in our feelings toward Native Americans when we can still turn on the television and watch John Wayne and his compatriots wiping out yet another horde of red savages so that America could belong to the civilized white man?

To this day, the influences of blatant racist indoctrination infiltrate our daily language and cultural symbols. To us, the color black still symbolizes evil, sin, death; white stands for purity, virtue, and joy. Good guys still wear white hats and ride white horses; bad guys wear black hats and ride black horses.

The New Myths and Lies. Although there are no shortages of white people perpetuating the old lies and illusions, new illusions have also been prepared to take their place. In the post–1960s years the new illusion is created by producing racism in softer terms. Racism is defined simply in terms of personal prejudice and individual bigotry, thus making it easier to believe that the problem is being solved and racism is being eliminated. Such an illusory picture of racism does not begin to explain racism's incredible power; yet, as long as this illusion is maintained, the energy for change will be focused only on improving individual attitudes and actions, and the actual power of racism that is lodged in society's systems and institutions will be untouched.

With new illusions, we convince ourselves that we are on the right track toward fairly sharing the resources. We assure ourselves that not only are we no longer racist, but we are now treating the victims of racism well and there is no need to change. Our illusions reassure us that if change is still necessary, it is people of color who need to change and we are glad to help them with that task. We are fooled by these illusions because we do not actually feel as though we are exercising the power that results in our receiving privilege.

A Kinder, Gentler "Colorblind" Lie. Younger readers may have been spared the blatant lies of the past, but not the far more dangerous softer lies of the present. These new myths and lies are more subtle and sophisticated. They are designed for the post–civil rights movement generations. These new generations consider the old lies archaic and obscene. They have been taught to be kind and respectful to people of color, and even "not to see color."

Proof positive of the overcoming of racism is demonstrated by the acceptance of Black History Month, the Martin Luther King Jr. birthday holiday, and other days, weeks, or months celebrating the cultures and histories of people of color. And our history about ourselves as white people is taught in ways that affirm the image that whatever bad that happened was in the past, and is no longer relevant in the present.

The old stereotypical images or people of color have been replaced by new stereotypical images of successful, well-educated professionals of color who are in most ways just like you and me. They have the same joys and the same heartaches, the same strengths and the same foibles. They are like us. Like us, they do not suffer from poverty, injustice, or inequality. And, most importantly, they are no longer victims of racism. These are the false images the media creates that perpetuate today's myths and lies and prevent us from understanding the realities with which most people of color live. In a study of race and racial politics, *Racial Formation in the United States*, Michael Omi and Howard Winant assert that these myths and lies are so tightly woven into the fabric of our culture that they are virtually impossible to remove:

> The continuing persistence of racial ideology suggests that these racial myths and stereotypes cannot be exposed as such in the popular imagination. They are, we think, too essential, too integral, to the maintenance of the U.S. social order. Of course, particular meanings, stereotypes and myths can change, but the presence of a system of racial meanings and stereotypes, of racial ideology, seems to be a permanent feature of U.S. culture.[8]

Make no mistake—in this new situation the old myths and lies are still present, but with a more sophisticated disguise, and they come in more acceptably packaged academic concepts and language. No matter how softly it is stated, the white community still accepts the basic message that people of color are intellectually inferior, responsible for their own oppressed condition, deserving of our fear, mistrust, and occasional charity, and to be avoided in more than token numbers.

"Little White Lies" about White People. Alongside the lies about people of color, there are just as many lies and illusions about ourselves that have an even greater effect on our racism. And we find them so attractive to believe! However easy we may find it to accept the negative stereotypes of inferiority regarding people of color, it is even more seductive to believe that the opposing positive

and superior qualities belong to us. Even when faced with their illusory nature, we think of them as "little white lies."

For centuries, we have been taught that our European forebearers demonstrated great physical and mental strength and superiority in winning American independence, taming the wild frontier, overcoming odds as immigrants, and, through that most admirable of all qualities, private initiative, amassing great fortunes and building a great economy. All of this is generally presented as something we achieved by ourselves without help or assistance, and in stark contrast to the lesser achievements of people of color.

Add to these myths the liberal lies about our generosity, philanthropy, and willingness to share our freedom. We believe in nothing more strongly than our ideology of liberty for all and charity toward the poor and needy, without comprehending that charity is a poor substitute for justice, and that the ultimate consequence of charity without justice is the loss of liberty for giver and receiver alike.

Perhaps the most difficult and most embarrassing area of our imprisonment is our continuing commitment to defend and preserve our white way of life as a source of pride and a mark of freedom. There is a powerful voice at work inside white people that keeps restating the lie that we are the free ones and our prison is not a prison at all, but a fortress we need to defend.

Old lies, new lies, color-blind lies, little white lies: the point is, we have internalized and still believe them. Even when they are repudiated and ostensibly rejected, they are still controlling our collective beliefs and behaviors. The wall of illusion and delusion continues to dominate and define our reality. Racism, from the point of view of the comfortable white prison, either pretends to no longer exist, or images itself as well on its way to extinction. And, therefore, the prison pretends also not to exist.

The Wall of Denial: Amnesia and Anesthesia

The third wall of our comfortable white prison is the wall of denial. It is composed of the amnesia and anesthesia that are fundamental conditioning tools in the process of internalizing white supremacy. Amnesia keeps us from remembering the past, and anesthesia keeps us from feeling the present. Their combined effect is to help us to live in denial, and even to deny our being in denial about racism. With the help of anesthesia and amnesia, our socialized conformity to white racist behavior is seen as unintentional. By "unintentional," I do not mean "accidental," but a socialized form of denial that enables us to act as if reality is not really happening.

With amnesia, we are programmed not to remember the past. It is quite like the hypnotist whose last instruction is, "When you awake, you will not remember anything that happened." Martin Luther King Jr. often referred to the United States as an "amnesiac country." It takes about two weeks, he remarked, to have a racial tragedy move from the front-page headlines to a small back-page article, and then to disappear from our memories. Who then can remember the names of James Byrd, Vincent Chen, Amadou Diallo, Sean Bell, or the many other persons and events that still regularly make their tragic brief appearances on the front page of the daily newspaper?

The companion to amnesia is anesthesia. Anesthesiologists prescribe drugs to reduce or eliminate pain during surgery and convalescence. From aspirin to morphine, from slight loss of sensation to total unconsciousness, the medical profession can seal us off from our feelings. On a psychological level also, an anesthetizing process takes place when a person becomes trapped in painful human predicaments from which there seem to be no escape. Slum dwellers, for example, become less aware of their crowded conditions and of the debris and waste that surround them. Prison inmates anesthetize themselves into indifference to the claustrophobic effects of their confinement. Soldiers on patrol learn to prevent the fear of ambush from driving them insane. Unhappily married partners who no longer work at the marriage seal themselves off from each other's hostility.

Anesthesia can be useful when a person is hopelessly and unalterably in pain. But it can also serve evil purposes by concealing a reality that needs to be seen. It can encourage the pretense that pain is not real and, therefore, that there is no need to diagnose the cause. Throughout history, when tyrants have sought to enslave fellow human beings, a primary technique has been to anesthetize them to the effects of their bondage by removing their hope of ever returning to freedom.

White people also use anesthesia to deaden our feelings in the comfortable prison. The most severe marks of our conditioned racism are not the bigotry and fear that have been brainwashed into us. Rather, they are the placid acceptance of our ghettoized condition, and the permission implied by our silence and our nonresistance to continued segregation from reality. The anesthetizing forces make it possible for us to go about our normal lives as though we were not being held in bondage; as though there were no alternatives to our present way of life.

There are hundreds of ways to be in denial: racist socialization didn't happen to me. Or, it did happen to me but it didn't have an effect on me. My parents taught me to love everyone. I didn't see a person of color until I was sixteen so I didn't get prejudice. Or, I grew up with people of color so I didn't get prejudice. I don't even see color. I got all the negative influences but I never believed them. I managed to avoid racism. Or, racism did infect me but I fought it and got over it. The third wall of our white prison keeps our nation believing that racism is being effectively eliminated, and the job is almost done.

The Addictive Wall of White Privilege

The fourth wall of our white prison is made of candy. It is composed of the privileges we receive as white people, to which we have become addicted and are afraid we may have to give up if racism goes away. We have already explored and exposed the reality of white power and privilege in the previous chapter when we studied Power^2. Now we need to see the insidious function that our power and privilege play in our captivity in racism. Our privileges are the bait that hooks us and makes us prisoners of racism. The delicious temptations of Power^2 become the means by which we lose our freedom to Power^3.

There are two factors involved in creating and maintaining this fourth wall of privilege. The first is that our power and privilege is inescapable. We must be absolutely clear that these privileges come to us automatically—whether we ask for them or not, whether we agree with having them or not. The very same institutions that are responsible for our socialization into racist beliefs and values also create and bestow the advantages of white skin privileges. Not only do they come to us automatically, but the socialization process make us oblivious to their existence. Even when we are directly confronted with the reality of racism's rewards, our first instinct is not to believe in their existence and especially to deny our possession of them.

The second factor, beneath the automatic imposition of these privileges, is our willing participation by accepting these addictive rewards. Let us be honest. Although our initial imprisonment in racism took place before we had a choice and although the systems of our society provide us with white privilege whether we want it or not, at the same time our continued presence in this prison is not completely against our will. Even though the symbolism of a prison assumes involuntary confinement and we can clearly see the forces that construct the prison around us, it is also true that each of us participates to a great degree in our own incarceration. We cooperate, consent, and willingly contribute to our own captivity. This is nowhere more evident than in our willingness to accept the rewards and benefits, the payoffs of racism.

We have exchanged our humanity for racism's tempting and addictive rewards of white privilege. Once our socialization is complete, we accept the benefits of racism that come to us almost automatically. We join in the pretense that we earn these privileges through our own efforts, initiative, and superior intelligence. We do not acknowledge that these gifts really fall into our laps, nor do we often admit that those who do not share the benefits are no less deserving than we are. But, if we are honest with ourselves, we will admit that we remain under the control of our jailers because we wish to protect the benefits we have "worked so hard" to achieve. Bluntly put, it is our fear of loss of privilege that keeps us attached to our chains, loyal to the wardens of the prison.

The Finished Product: Varieties of White People in the White Prison

The prison is complete. Its foundation is secure. Its four walls surround us: the wall of separation and isolation, the wall of illusion and delusion, the wall of amnesia and anesthesia, and the wall of white privilege. Not only do the walls seem impenetrable, they are defended from the inside by those who have convinced themselves that they are living in a fortress rather than a prison. When the socialization of each of the prisoners is finished and the internalization of racist superiority has taken place, the identity formation of a white person is complete.

As white people, what we all have in common is that we all, to one degree or another, consciously or unconsciously conform to the social construct of white supremacy. We all have been misshaped into "someone who believes, accepts, and lives out superior societal definitions of self" and who "willingly or unwillingly, wittingly or unwittingly participates in and benefits from the structures of white power and privilege."

Even if all the prisoners have been made into "white people," however, it is also important to recognize that the prisoners do not all look or act alike. We are each very different from one another. When the task is completed, even though we all share the same identity, we are not cloned to be identical. There are as many varieties of racists as there are white people in the white prison. Some of us are overt, extreme, and proud racists who brag about our identity even while hiding under the cover of a sheet. Others of us might privately think the thoughts of hatred, even though we would never express them out loud. Others are ashamed and humiliated by the awareness of what white racism has done, but are not prepared to speak our minds. Still others staunchly believe racism has disappeared, color is no longer important, and the walls of separation no longer exist. And others of us regularly leave the white prison for visitation of the other prison—the uncomfortable prison of people of color—for purposes of charity to help the people over there deal with their maladies caused by racism; and then we return to our comfortable home with no awareness that we are moving back and forth from one prison to another.

Even though there are multiple variations of white racists, it may be helpful to see that there are, roughly speaking, two main types of racists. I characterize these as "intentional racists" and "unintentional racists." You might recognize one or both of these inside yourself. Most of us have some of each type inside of us. If the reader remembers an earlier discussion that named the two ways that racism expresses itself as the "iron fist" and the "velvet glove," these two kinds of racists fit into those two expressions of racism. The intentional racist is a servant of the iron fist, and the "unintentional" racist is a servant of the velvet glove. (I will continue to write the word "unintentional" with quotes around it, because there is only a limited degree of unintentionality behind this socialized repression and denial.) As a final descriptive exercise of the internalization process, let us take a brief look at each of these two primary varieties of racists:

The Intentional Racist. As a result of the socialization process, some white people are overt, conscious, and intentional racists, and they really love it; many are even "damned proud of it." Those of us in this category of racist have a deliberate, intentional belief in white supremacy and in the inferiority of all other races. We learn the lies of white supremacy, believe the lies of white supremacy, act out the lies of white supremacy, tell jokes about the lies of white supremacy, and take great satisfaction in our identity as superior white people. The intentional racist will sometimes become a member of an organized hate group such as the Ku Klux Klan, the Militia, Aryan Nations, the Church of the World Creator, or the Minutemen on our southern border.

However, the vast majority of intentional racists are hate-filled supportive spectators cheering from the sidelines whenever racism has a victory, or expressing anger and discontent whenever racism suffers a defeat. The intentional racist may be a lone actor, but more often finds collegial community with others who share the ideology of white supremacy in the institutions and organizations of daily life—in school, within law enforcement agencies and other expressions of the criminal justice system, on the Internet and in reactionary radio and TV programs and other forms of media, or in ultraconservative political and religious circles, and so forth.

Before we become too self-righteous in our description of these appallingly unpleasant intentional racists, let us be clear that at least some manifestation of this kind of racist is inside of almost every one of us—especially the older readers of this book. Nearly all of us learned some of the language of overt racism—even if we also quickly learned that it was wrong to use it publicly. And we learned the myths and the lies, along with the songs and the jokes. Perhaps above all, we learned fear—the fear that keeps us from going into certain parts of town, makes us lock the car doors in certain areas, clutch our purses or not go into elevators when strange people of color approach. Some of this conscious belief in our supremacy or in the inferiority of others, and the fear that accompanies it got inside almost all of us, even if there are great variations of how much, how influential it was in our identity formation, how well we have gotten rid of it, or how well we have repressed it in our subconscious minds.

Although the power and the presence of the extreme racists is still strongly felt in our country, it can also probably be safely said that during the past forty or fifty years, their number and influence has been significantly decreasing.

The parallel reality is that the number of the second category—the "unintentional" racists—appears to be rapidly increasing. And the great illusion is that it is better to be the second than the first.

The "Unintentional," or Liberal Racist. If, as a result of our socialization, we didn't become an intentional racist, then we became an "unintentional" or a liberal racist. As I have suggested earlier, "unintentional" does not mean "accidental" or "contrary to intentions." Rather, it is a mixture of socialized repression and denial that helps us pretend we are not doing what we are doing. Since most readers of this book will probably fall into this second category of racists, it may come as a shock to realize that the "unintentional" racist is considered by many people of color to be far more dangerous than the intentional racist.

By "unintentional" racists I mean people who, by contrasting themselves with the hatefulness of the intentional racists, manage to declare themselves innocent, or relatively innocent, of racism. Even though many of us will admit that we were at one time influenced by intentional racism in our early identity formation, we are grateful that we have now come to the realization of the wrongness and falseness of these understandings. Unfortunately, the overcoming of these early influences often results in many of us saying that we are now no longer racist or at least that we have very little racism left inside us. The statement such persons often make is, "I'm not a racist, but. . . ."

"Unintentional" racists do not see themselves as racists, but as "nonracists" or "ex-racists." Keep in mind that this book suggests that all white people are made into racists by our participation in and benefiting from white power and privilege. This being true, then for a white person to deny their racism is as revealing of their captivity in racism's comfortable prison then any statement that could be made by the most extreme of racists.

Those of us who fit the category of "unintentional" racist quite often claim that racism no longer exists or that it has been greatly reduced and it is on its way to nonexistence. We believe that all or most of the barriers to the advancement of people of color have been removed, and it is only a matter of time and greater effort on the part of people of color to catch up with the rest of us. To the extent that we do acknowledge that racism continues, it is usually limited to personal bigotry and hatefulness, and we also believe that people of color are as capable of being racist as white people.

"Unintentional" racists usually profess great love for people of color. We refer often to "some of our best friends" who are people of color, and we are quite often involved in activities of charity or advocacy, aiming to help people of color on their path toward greater freedom. Oftentimes we are involved in professions that are aimed toward defending, rescuing, protecting, or empowering people of color. More often than not we have an analysis of racism that is limited to an understanding of what has been referred to in this book as "Power[1]," the power of racism to hurt people of color, and does not include an understanding of white power and privilege. Our solution to the problem of racism is based on efforts to fix or heal people of color.

Another expression of "unintentional" racism can be seen in the ideology of "color blindness," which I have referred to several times in this chapter and in earlier chapters. Proponents of this ideology do not "see color," because they believe the removal of racism requires the removal of color distinctions and racial recognition. Race is no longer seen as a factor in human relationships; color is no longer important.

Identifying Your Socialization

So, which kind of racist were you made to be? Or, how much of each of the two kinds of racism—the intentional racist and the "unintentional" racist—were part of your socialization? Although some of each of these have found their way into most or all of us, it should be emphasized once again that older generations who were born before the 1960s received a significantly greater socialization as intentional racists, and younger generations, especially the generations of the new millennium, have been increasingly influenced by socialization as "unintentional" racists.

Many of us from earlier generations have made a transition from intentional racist to "unintentional" racist. My own personal experience of this transition is very clear to me. All the forces of my socialization—including family, peers, school, and church—led me to an unchallenged position of an intentional racist. I was taught to believe in white supremacy and to blame all issues of racial problems and tension on people of color. Even past my teenage years, if I thought about matters of race at all, it was in terms of the superiority of white people and the inferiority of people of color.

My transformation from intentional to "unintentional" racist began gradually, and then came to a dramatic conclusion when I was doing postgraduate studies in Germany, and my exposure to the reality of the Jewish Holocaust resulted in my also coming to awareness of the American holocaust, and of the explosive issue of the civil rights movement that was taking place at that time. I returned from Germany to the United States a fully converted "unintentional" racist. I "discovered" racism and racial injustice. I was shocked by the victimization of people of color and ashamed of the racism of white people. Although I still had no real understanding of racism, it was clear to me that people of color were subjected to cruel and tragic evil, and I dedicated myself to the struggle for racial justice. It would still be a long time before I progressed to the point of understanding that the real purpose of racism was to provide and maintain power and privilege for the white society; it would still be a number of years more before I could accept responsibility for my own racism as part of the racism of my people, and before I would understand what it means to "go home and free my own people."

Summary and Conclusion:
None of Us Are Free

In this chapter we have explored how everyone is imprisoned in a system of racism that ghettoizes white people as well as people of color. We have seen how racism's Power[3] shapes a racist identity in individual white persons, as well as a victim identity in individual persons of color. We have seen that individual white racism is an imprisoning power over all white people that makes us into participants in systemic racism—whether we want to be or not.

If it is clear to you, the white reader, that racism does not just hurt and imprison people of color, but that it also hurts and imprisons you; if you understand that you too have been misshaped by racism, that you too have been dragged into its prison and socialized into a person that you don't want to be, then you know that none of us are winners and all of us are losers so long as racism's destructive power is not dismantled.

The critical point to understanding Power[3] is that in the final outcome, racism will never result in the victory of one racial group over another. The structure and system of racism is designed to control and destroy everyone—the oppressor as well as the oppressed. Racism makes puppets out of white people *and* people of color. None of us are free to not be a part of the racist system.

Motivation to Read On

The next step, in the context of acknowledging the reality that each of us has been imprisoned by racism, is to look at the systems and institutions that do the imprisoning. The next two chapters will closely examine the systems of racism in which everyone is either a willing or an unwilling participant. Specifically, chapter 5 will explore the structures of institutional racism, and chapter 6 will examine cultural racism.

There is an important reason for the order in which we are looking at these three manifestations of racism: first individual racism and then institutional and cultural racism. As human beings, we are generally motivated to act when we understand how we are directly involved. When we are clear that racism has had a destructive affect on each one of us personally, then we will be more highly motivated to explore the deeper sources of this destructive power.

I am suggesting that in order to explore the next steps in this analysis, each of us needs to be in touch with our personal "self-interest" for doing so. If this chapter has been successful in convincing you, the white reader, that you have been misshaped into "someone who to one degree or another believes, accepts and lives out superior societal definitions of self" and who "willingly or unwillingly, wittingly or unwittingly participates in and benefits from white power and privilege," then it is likely that your personal self-interest has been tapped and your motivation will be increased to proceed to the next question: How does racism systemically do that to me, as well as to everyone else in this society?

In my own personal experience, it was only when I began to know that racism was also destroying me, along with everyone else, only when I began to know how deeply racism also had a destructive and lasting effect on me and was preventing me from being the kind of person I want to be, that my deepest self-interest began to be touched and my lasting commitment to dismantling racism began to be reached. If you recognize that this is also true for you, then your self-interest has been established to look deeper and to come to a better understanding of how this destructive power works. You are ready to look at institutional and cultural racism.

INSTITUTIONALIZED RACISM

There are, after all, no significant formal institutions in American life—not the government, not the national economy, not the church, and not education—that are not controlled by Whites.
—Benjamin Bowser and Raymond Hunt

The face of racism has changed; the systemic and pervasive character of racism in the United States has not.
—Manning Marable

The Misuse of Power by Systems and Institutions

The distinctive mark of racism is power—collective, systemic, societal power. Not simply the power of one individual over another, but shared power expressed through political, economic, educational, cultural, religious, and other societal systems and institutions. Systemic racism is legalized, institutionalized, and self-perpetuating, resulting in the victimization of entire racial groups for the purpose of maintaining the benefits and privileges of a dominant racial group. This, then, is the key to understanding racism in the United States: that it became legalized, institutionalized, and self-perpetuating for the purpose of maintaining benefits and privileges for the white society.

Racism therefore cannot be ended without fundamental transformation of the systems and institutions in which it is institutionalized. The central argument in this book is that although significant changes were initiated in the laws that ended segregation and discrimination in the 1960s, these changes did not go to sufficient depth to transform the systems and institutional structures that are responsible for the misuse of power. Our systems and institutions are still structured to ensure their control by white people and to provide far greater access to their benefits by white people than by people of color. Conversely, they have not yet been restructured to ensure equal control and equal access for people of color.

In order to understand why the misuse of power by systems and institutions is as firmly in place as ever, our exploration must take us deeper than our society has been willing to go until now. Buried within the systems and institutions of our society are the mechanisms for racism's power. Our goal now is to look at these systems and institutions to ask the question, "How does racism do what it does so effectively, so efficiently, and in such a way that it continues to perpetuate itself in every aspect of our lives?"

Taking an X-Ray of the Happiness Machine

Let's return once again to the image of the Happiness Machine in the fable in the introduction to this book. We have been looking at the Happiness Machine from different perspectives in every chapter of the book:

- In chapter 1, when we looked at the continuing painful results of racism on people of color, we were examining the "dross," or the leftover waste of the Happiness Machine as it produces unhappiness for those who do not benefit from racism.
- In chapter 2, when we defined racism, the identity of the Happiness Machine was revealed as the systems and institutions of our country that are designed to misuse power for the benefit of white society.
- In chapter 3, we looked at the white power that controls the Happiness Machine, and at white privilege, which is the main product of the Happiness Machine.
- In chapter 4, we explored the mesmerizing and anesthetizing effects of the Happiness Machine on white people with its intoxicating "happiness," while at the same time people of color are conditioned to "adjust" to the machine's existence and passively accept its painful results.

Now, in the next three chapters we are ready to look at the inner workings of the Happiness Machine itself. We need to carefully measure its dimensions, figure out how it works. We will take an X-ray of the machine so that we can see its inner parts. We need to ask how racism got to be a part of every institution in our country and how it continues to be a part of every institution in our country. And, we need to ask whether and how it is possible to bring about the institutional transformation that will make our institutions function differently in a way that makes them able to truly and fairly serve all people in our nation.

In this chapter, we will concern ourselves specifically with the task of understanding how institutional racism exists and functions in the United States. There are five sections in this examination of institutional racism:

- The Nature and Purpose of Institutions
- Defining Institutionalized Racism
- How It Got That Way: A History of Institutionalized Racism
- How It Stayed That Way: New Forms of Institutionalized Racism
- How to "See," Identify, and Analyze Institutionalized Racism

The Nature and Purpose of Institutions

Institutions and Their Constituencies

A society is composed of a great number of institutions. As stated earlier, the purpose of these institutions is to create, produce, manage, and distribute the resources of a society. They may be private or public, secular or religious, for-profit or nonprofit, but all institutions are interconnected through their common task of helping a society to function. Institutions give expression to the organized activities of a community and serve its various needs. In a representative democracy like the United States, public institutions theoretically express the will of the democracy's citizens, and are supposed to serve their needs in a fair and egalitarian manner.

The institutions in our society are innumerable, yet each has a specific purpose of serving a particular and identifiable clientele or constituency. For example, governmental institutions claim as their constituency the citizens within their jurisdiction. The House of Representatives is a separate institution, as well as the Senate, and all their committees and offices; the Supreme Court and the separate and intricate units of the judicial system; the Executive branch of government, the White House, and the hundreds upon hundreds of departments and bureaucratic offices of government. Each of the fifty states mirrors the federal image with multiple governmental institutions, together with offices and agencies, all serving constituencies within that particular state. Every city, town, and county does likewise; each city hall, library, police department, hospital, and museum is an institution.

Each and every business and industry, factory, office, or retail store in our nation, large and small, are institutions, and they are serving their identified constituencies. Within the communications industry and the media, there are almost innumerable institutions—each newspaper, radio and TV station, magazine, and computer network is an institution. In the medical arena, each doctor's office, hospital, pharmaceutical company, and drugstore is an institution. In the religious community, every religion, denomination, diocese, and district, every synagogue, temple, parish, and congregation is an institution. Every school, college, and university, every sports team, every art gallery, dance studio, band, and orchestra, and a thousand, thousand more are institutions. The list of institutions seems almost as numerous as the stars and galaxies.

Systems and Institutions

All institutions in a society are interrelated and interconnected. Each institution is part of a larger group of similar institutions called a "system." For example:

- The *economic system* probably the most familiar of these systems, with all its banks, savings-and-loan offices, financial investment markets, and so forth;
- The *health-care and medical system* with all its doctor's offices, hospitals, pharmaceutical companies, drugstores, and research laboratories;
- The *education system*, composed of an almost uncountable number of individual public and private schools, colleges, and universities;
- The *corporate system*, composed of the nation's immense collection of businesses and industry;
- The *religious system*, including every church, temple, synagogue, mosque;
- The *political system*, consisting of every governmental office, agency, legislative unit and judiciary;
- The *communications and media system*, and its almost innumerable newspapers, books, radio and TV stations, magazines, and computer networks and related systems.

And so on. Each system is composed of hundreds of thousands of subsystems and institutions, all of which are interwoven and interdependent. Because of the way systems function, we can live almost unconscious of their existence, even while they function on our behalf. At certain times we become vividly aware of the, however. For example, the educational system is at work when a fourth-grader in a California school can transfer to a fourth-grade class in Illinois or New York without missing hardly a beat; and the health-care system is carrying out its function when our health records are transferred from one doctor to another, or our prescriptions from one pharmacy to another, either in the same town or across the nation.

Systemic and Institutional Racism

These are the systems and institutions that function as a powerful and complex machine to provide for the needs of our society. And these are also the systems and institutions of which we speak when we address the question of institutional racism. These are the structures that are functioning in ways that serve the white society exclusively or in ways that are qualitatively better than the way they serve communities of color. Through these systems and intuitions, the production of white power and privilege and the subordination and exploitation of our nation's people of color take place. Our definition of racism—"race prejudice plus the misuse of power by systems and institutions"—will become even clearer as we move now to analyzing how systemic racism takes place.

As we proceed further into this discussion of institutional racism and institutional change, I suggest that you, the reader, in addition to focusing on this giant galaxy of systems and institutions, also keep in mind those specific institutions of which you are most intimately a part. Each of us needs to stay focused on the places where we are personally involved and can have a specific impact as a result of doing this analysis of racism. As a result of this chapter, you should be able to better understand how your church, your school, your place of employment, your local government, or even your sewing club, bowling club, or Internet chat room is an instrument of racism, as well as a setting where transformation can take place.

Our approach in analyzing racism in systemic and institutional structures will not be just theoretical and academic. Rather, it will be a more practical approach aimed toward the end-goal of providing practical answers for bringing about institutional change. The result of this exploration ultimately needs to be organized action aimed toward exposing, confronting, and eradicating institutional racism at the place of our personal involvement. Through this process, you and I need to become better equipped to join with others in collective action to transform our institutions.

The Good and the Bad in Every Institution

Once again it is important to state that institutions exist for a good purpose—to create, produce, manage, and distribute the resources of a society. Systems and institutions are crucial to the fabric of a society; they enable us to live together cooperatively and have our needs taken care of. Institutions make it possible for us to buy produce in the stores, send our children to school, receive news and communication, belong to churches and clubs, and have all the public utilities that provide our gas, electricity, sewers, and transportation. We could not live together in community without institutions. And we could not begin to accomplish individually all that they do for us.

At the same time, institutions can be very difficult to deal with. Most of us do not always have the best of feelings about institutions. We frequently find them distant, unfriendly, and frustrating, and we can tell lengthy stories about our bad experiences with them. One of our favorite pastimes is to complain about the Internal Revenue Service, the department of motor vehicles, the telephone company, the government, or any other institution that intersects our lives.

To put it mildly, not every institution functions as well as we expect, and we do not have the highest trust in the way they function. We complain that they are all too often impersonal and unaccountable; they are at times riddled with dishonesty and corruption. And, worst of all, they are so difficult and slow to change.

There is good reason for our frustration with the way some institutions function. The simple reality is that the institutions with which we deal in our daily lives often misuse power and do not treat people in a fair and equal way. Although this book deals with the subject of racism, that is only one among many ways in which institutions can be dysfunctional.

Institutions are wonderful. Institutions are awful. These opposing and seemingly contradictory points of view are both true. Institutions are good and essential; institutions are frustrating and difficult. Let's explore these contrasting realities further. Better understanding of these positive and negative experiences with institutions will equip us better to understand the negative experiences people of color have with institutional racism.

In Theory, Institutions Are Accountable to the People They Serve

Every institution has a constituency or community it exists to serve. The government's constituency are the citizens in a given district. The school's constituency is its students. Doctors and hospitals serve patients. Business and industry serve customers and clients. Churches and social clubs serve their membership. Each of us has an awareness of the institutions to which we belong, or that view us as receivers of its services.

In theory, an institution exists not only to serve, but also to be accountable to its constituency and to the geographical community in which it is located. Speaking from the perspective of a white, middle-class male in our society, I have a basic assumption that an institution exists both to serve me and to be accountable to me, along with the rest of its constituency and community. I believe that most of us—at least those of us who are white, middle- and upper-class people—expect an institution to provide what we need, and expect it to treat us well, with respect and friendliness. And if an institution does not do this, if it is not accountable to us, we either try to change the way the institution treats us or we leave it to find another.

Now, I realize this is good theory, and it often is not true in reality. An institution is *supposed* to exist to serve and be accountable to us. But in fact, this does not always happen. How often do we walk through the doors of an institution, expecting friendliness, service, and respect, but the receptionist or the clerk treats us with disdain and disrespect and the whole atmosphere of the place gives us the impression that we exist for the sake of the institution rather than the institution existing for us. Or, in trying to communicate with an institution, we dial a telephone number and are greeted by a series of recordings that keep telling us how important we are while keeping us waiting for fifteen to thirty minutes before they get around to talking to us.

Our response to such treatment may be passive anger or active protest. We may return our mistreatment in kind by releasing our rage upon the institutional representative with whom we are dealing. Or we may insist on talking to a supervisor or write a letter to customer service. Or, if there is an alternative source for the product or service, we may resolve to never go back to deal with this institution again. No matter how we respond, it is patently obvious to us when a particular institution is not doing what it is supposed to do, when it is not being accountable to the constituency or community it exists to serve. And while we are constantly evaluating our options to deal with a particular situation or a particular institution, no matter how many experiences we might have to the contrary, one certain conviction within us does not change—the conviction that the institutions in this nation are supposed to exist for the purpose of serving us and are *supposed* to be accountable to us. Of course, we know institutions are also accountable to their boards of directors, their CEOs, or their stockholders; but we also want them to act accountably to us, the people they exist to serve. And when they don't do that, we are indignant in insisting they are violating their very reason for existence.

The Racial Difference

Now, I know the picture I just painted very much reflects the experience of a white person, and especially of a middle-class or upper-class male white person. And I am also aware that the experience in communities of color with institutions is as different as night and day from our experience in white communities. There is a quantitative and qualitative difference—in fact, an enormous chasm—between the way our nation's institutions serve white people and people of color. In addition, if persons of color have the added factors of class, gender, or sexual orientation working against them, then their experience is doubly and triply horrendous. We may have our gripes about the way *some* institutions function *some* of the time, but in communities of color, institutional unresponsiveness and negligence is not an occasional experience, but an everyday problem with virtually *all* of the intuitions virtually *all* of the time.

To understand this reality, we need to be aware of who controls our institutions and whom they are designed to serve. The reality is that virtually all of our institutions are controlled by white people and are more easily accessed by white people. They are designed to serve and be accountable to white people. If the purpose of institutions is to create, produce, manage, and distribute the resources of our society, we must be clear that they are creating, producing, managing, and distributing resources in ways that primarily serve the interests of white power and privilege.

We can understand this better if we compare our experiences as white people with the experiences of people of color on the receiving end of educational, housing, welfare, police, labor, political, and economic institutional activity. Then we will see that racism is far more than the occasional actions of an individual teacher, real estate agent, social worker, police officer, ward leader, or bank loan officer. Rather, it is the product of the structure, organization, policies, and practices of the institutions that these individual people represent. People of color have almost no power in comparison with white people to direct and control these institutions. Moreover, most institutions have virtually no accountability relationship to people of color. And when institutions have no accountability relationship to their constituency, they can do as they please without fear of the consequences.

When new laws are enacted that affect people of color differently than white people; when public housing is torn down in order to build condominiums so that white people can move back into the city from the suburbs; when decisions are made to lower welfare benefits or not to raise the minimum wage; when any of a thousand such decisions are made within institutions that negatively affect the daily lives of people of color and ignore their needs, then it is more than obvious who runs an institution and to whom they are accountable.

When real estate and housing industries continue to build, sell, and rent in patterns of residential segregation; when business, industry, and labor persist in discriminatory hiring and promotions either by outright rejection of people of color or by playing games with standards and qualifications; when schools continue to be racially unbalanced, with quality education withheld from students of color; when the media continues to project images of African Americans, Latinos/Hispanics, Native Americans, Asian Americans and Arab Americans that fulfill our most biased expectations and reinforce our prejudices, then it is clear that people of color and white people have totally different power relationships to our systems and institutions

It is important to also point out that most of us who are white actually are involved in one or more of these institutions and actually help them carry out their actions. As teachers, doctors, lawyers, police, clergy, social workers, business executives, real estate agents, and bankers, or even as assistants, secretaries, file clerks, and line workers, as voting members of our organizations and as voting citizens in society, or in whatever other way we are involved in institutional life, whether we like it or not, we, willingly or unwillingly, wittingly or unwittingly, share in the administration of institutional racism. As we turn to a more detailed examination of institutional racism, let us maintain our awareness of the power these organizations wield, not only over people of color who are the target of institutional racism, but also over us, who are simultaneously its beneficiaries, its functionaries, and its prisoners.

Defining Institutionalized Racism

"Institutionalized" — Built into an Institution

Almost nothing an institution does is accidental. Whatever an institution does is a result of its purpose, design, and structure. The function and behavior of institutions are built in—they are "institutionalized." To institutionalize something means to make a long-term and enduring arrangement. When something is institutionalized, it is intended to be a permanent and normal part of an institution. Institutionalization comes about as a result of careful consideration and a thoroughly planned process of initiation. For example, a new staff position or a new department in an organizational structure cannot be just added by whim one day and made to disappear the next day; they are created by intentional design, and must be "built into" the institution.

As a result of this institutionalizing process, an institution's ongoing life is made to be self-perpetuating. Without having to rethink or reinvent the process each time, an institution does the same thing over and over again, and gets the same results over and over again. There are fresh eggs in the supermarket every day, and each automobile that is mass-produced by the same factory will function like all the others. An institution will keep on doing whatever it is designed to do until it is designed to do something differently. There is no way of getting different results in a permanent and ongoing way without redesigning the way something is "institutionalized" within an institution.

It is important to note, therefore, that in this chapter I have begun to use the phrase "institutionalized racism" in place of the phrase "institutional racism." It indicates that racism is institutionalized and is self-perpetuating. Whereas "institutional racism" simply implies that racism is happening inside an institution, "institutionalized racism" emphasizes it is part of an institutional arrangement that has been built into an institution's purpose, design, and structure.

Racism was "institutionalized," that is, built into our institutions, from the very beginning. And the fact that our institutions are still practicing institutional racism is because the basic institutional design and structure have not changed. It was part of the original design and is still part of the continuing structure of our nation's institutions to benefit white Americans, to have the power to control the lives of people of color, and to be accountable to white people and not accountable to people of color. If an institution is designed to favor white people over people of color, it will continue to act that way until the design is changed.

Hence, if racism has been institutionalized, then the solution to racism must also be institutionalized. It is not enough to pass a law that an institution should act differently, because it will not act differently until the difference is built in, until it has a new institutional design. Likewise, since the problem is deeper than individual intentionality, then the solution cannot simply be improved intentionality. I want to be especially clear that this understanding of institutionalized racism excludes the possibility of a solution that allows white people to stay in control of an institution with a simple pledge that they "intend" to act more equally and fairly toward people of color. Rather, it insists on institutionalizing a solution that dramatically changes who has the power of control, access, and accountability.

Defining Accountability

Throughout the rest of this book the concept of accountability will have a central place in our conversation. With almost equal importance, the "use and misuse of accountability" joins the "use and misuse of power" in defining and discerning the presence or absence of racism. Therefore, before going on to a definition of institutionalized racism, I want to offer a definition of accountability.

> *Accountability* is an arrangement that determines whether and how individuals or groups are responsible and answerable for their actions to other individuals or groups.

Although accountability tends to be less formally defined in our personal lives, in almost every area of our public lives accountability is intentionally and legally defined in order to measure whether individuals or institutions are functioning with effectiveness and integrity. For example, accountability is clearly defined in the guarantee of every product we purchase and in many of our formalized personal relationships. When accountability is clearly defined and enforced, it becomes more possible to function in society with a sense of confidence and trust.

With regards to race relations and racism in the United States, the absence of clearly defined accountability of white people and white institutions to people of color has allowed persistent inequality and misuse of power and has resulted in the absence of the means to build confidence and trust between white people and people of color. In the rest of this chapter and embedded in institutional and cultural racism. More importantly, in the final chapter on dismantling racism, I will try to make it clear that the institutionalizing of anti-racism requires the intentional establishment of accountability of white people and white structures to people of color, with an ultimate goal of establishing institutional structures in which "mutual accountability" is a fundamentally accepted concept and practice.

A Definition of Institutionalized Racism

Now let's try out a formal definition of institutionalized racism. The simplest definition is, of course, with the original definition of racism we have been using since the beginning of this book: *Racism is race prejudice plus the misuse of power by systems and institutions.* This definition already makes it clear that the formidable power of racism is the product of systems and institutions as they transform individual prejudice into collective racist action. The basic reality reflected in this definition is that the systems and institutions in our society, which are supposed to represent all citizens, members, or clientele in a fair and equal way, in fact do not do so. And in not doing so, their inherent power is being misused, and that which is intended to be good has become a force for evil. The result of this "misuse of power by systems and institutions" is that these structures are functioning in ways that serve the white society exclusively or in ways that are qualitatively and quantitatively better than the way they serve communities of color.

In order to explore the breadth and depth of institutionalized racism, however, we need a definition that is more specific. We need an expanded definition that provides more information about what it is about an institution that makes it act differently toward people of color than the way it acts toward white people. Such a definition might look like this:

> *Institutionalized racism* is the intentional shaping and structuring of an institution so that it effectively serves and is accountable to one racial group and does not effectively serve nor is accountable to other racial groups.[1]

Note that while this definition emphasizes intentionality, it focuses on the intentionality of institutional purpose, design, and structure, rather than simply on the intentionality of individual institutional representatives. Although racism may be heightened and amplified by intentionally racist institutional personnel, the depth of the power of institutionalized racism is in its structural capacity to be self-perpetuating as though an institution has a life of its own. It is this structural reality that we must comprehend if we wish to reach the roots of institutionalized racism.

Institutionalized racism exists because of intentional structural design. It is not an accident or an oversight or simply the result of scheming by a few bigoted individuals. We must be absolutely clear that the difference between the way white people and people of color are treated by our institutions is because our institutions are designed and structured to do it that way.

It is also quite important—in fact, *critically* important to our analysis of racism—to understand that these institutional designs and structures were intentionally created in the past, and that they still remain part of virtually all of our systems and institutions today. This is the primary point that I will be seeking to document in the rest of this chapter: that racism was institutionalized in the original designing and structuring of our nation's systems and institutions, and despite all the changes that have been made in our nation with regard to racial injustice, the basic design and structure to serve white people have been left untouched. Our nation's systems and institutions are still waiting to be redesigned and restructured to serve and be accountable to people of color.

The painful realities of the present are rooted firmly in the past. It is impossible to understand the "after" picture of today's institutionalized racism without first understanding the "before" picture of institutionalized racism as it existed originally. In order to understand how new forms of institutionalized racism function today and especially what needs to be changed in our institutions, we need to take a step back and examine the evolution of institutionalized racism, briefly reviewing the historical forms of institutionalized racism and how they came into being. We need to comprehend how institutionalized racism was derived, what it looked like, and what there is about it that has evolved into the disguised forms of today. In doing this, we need to establish direct continuity between today's more hidden practices and public intentional decisions of the past.

How It Got That Way:
A History of Institutionalized Racism

The next step in exploring institutionalized racism is to take a historical snapshot of how it has functioned in the past. Much of the discussion in this section is derived from documentation and illustrations that have already been provided in earlier chapters. In order to avoid repetition, where it is appropriate I will summarize material that is already written in previous chapters and suggest the reader return to those pervious chapters to review that material in greater depth as necessary.

Our Colonial Mission and Purpose
Institutionalized racism began in the earliest days of our country's history and continued remorselessly for more than 450 years—which is approximately

90 percent of our nation's history. During this entire period, all legally recognized institutions, whether public or private, were exclusively controlled by white people and fully excluded all people of color. In chapter 1, I described and illustrated two primary ideological principles that Europeans held from the earliest colonial days:

- The first principle was white supremacy
- The second principle was the role of people of color to serve white people

These two colonizing principles laid the foundations of all the forms of racism that followed, and became the basis for an overt, clearly stated, and indelibly written racist mission and purpose for the American colonies (as well as for all other European colonies throughout the world): to preserve the land and its resources for European colonists, and to keep all people of color in service to the European colonists. These ideological principles were embedded in every aspect of colonial life in the American colonies from 1492 until independence was won and the U.S. Constitution was ratified in 1789. They guided and justified the appropriation of land and the expansion of European colonial outposts; they guided and justified the official policy of genocide of Indians; they guided and justified the legal system of enslavement of Africans; and they became the basis for the design and structure of every system and institution in the colonies.

Our National Mission and Purpose

Following the American Revolution, when the United States was giving shape to a new nation and formulating and ratifying its constitution, a moment of decision arrived when it was necessary to choose whether these two foundational principles—white supremacy and the serving/servant role of people of color—would be passed on from colony to nationhood.

They were. These two fundamental principles of racism were intentionally institutionalized in every aspect of national life, and the dominant white population in the United States clearly subscribed to them until the middle of the twentieth century. Preserving the land and its resources for white people and keeping people of color in service to the white society became a clearly stated central part of the mission and purpose of the United States of America, even to the point, in the Naturalization Act of 1790, of making "whiteness" a primary component in defining who is an "American," and allowing only white immigrants to become naturalized as citizens. From that moment on, institutionalized racism increased in complexity and intensity, reaching a point where, in 1896, a nationalized and legalized apartheid system was legally implemented in the United States, quite similar to the apartheid system that was later developed in South Africa.

Over the years, thousands upon thousands of laws were created for effective separation, segregation, and control of people of color in urban and rural ghettos and on reservations. African Americans and Native Americans were the chief targets, but increasingly Latinos/Hispanics, Asian Americans, and Arab Americans were also largely excluded from eating, sleeping, residing, walking, riding, working, playing, worshiping, voting, or doing virtually anything at the same time or place in which white people were doing these same things.

The principles of white supremacy and people of color subservience were embedded within the organizational design and structure of every institution in the United States. The reader may wish to review the information in chapter 3 that describes this devastating conclusion: *every system and every institution in the United States was created originally and structured legally and intentionally to serve white people exclusively.*

Institutionalized: Intentional, Legal, and Overt

Thus, from the very beginning and in very specific ways, every system and every institution of the United States was designed and structured to ensure that all its resources, economic control, and governmental power would exist for white people. In addition, every system and every institution was designed and structured in very specific ways to ensure that people of color would not benefit from these institutions, but would rather function as instruments of service to the white society.

In its original designs, institutionalized racism was public and was practiced unapologetically. It was *intentional*. It was *legal*. It was *overt*. Until the 1960s, intentional, legal, and overt institutionalized racism was the only form of institutional racism that existed in the United States, because it was the only kind of racism that was needed. Let's look at each of these aspects a bit more closely.

- *Intentional.* Again and again it must be stated: the institutionalization of racism was no accident. It was a product of a conscious and intentional mission and purpose. For more than 450 years, it was given overwhelming approval by the vast majority of white people. One of the hardest things today for many white people to realize and accept is the intentionality of the racism that infected and infiltrated every aspect of our history.

  The genocide of Native Americans and the taking of their land, along with the making and breaking of all the treaties, *was conscious and intentional.* Establishing a system of African slavery and creating the intricate laws that guided it *was conscious and intentional.* Enacting the complex and ever-changing laws of immigration and naturalization so as to favor Europeans and disfavor immigrants from all other parts of the world, while at the same time ensuring their availability as immigrant laborers, *was conscious and intentional.* Creating separate racial identities for Native Americans, African Americans, Latinos/Hispanics, Asian Americans, and Arab Americans and subjecting each of them to degrading and oppressive roles in our society *was conscious and intentional.* And most importantly, creating a white racial identity and establishing systems and institutions of white power and privilege *was conscious and intentional.*

- *Legal.* Institutionalized racism was fully backed by clearly written bodies of law. Every imaginable law was created in the original thirteen colonies, and then, following independence, an even-greater body of law was created by the national, state, and local governing bodies to define white institutionalized power and privilege and to define institutionalized serving/servant roles for people of color. As has already been explored in greater depth in chapter 1, thousands upon thousands of laws were passed; layer upon layer of legal structure was created. And each time a crack or a leak in the legal system of racism appeared, another layer was added to patch it. The highest courts of the nation were given the responsibility of interpreting these laws, and the criminal justice system was given the responsibility of enforcing them. It became a legal requirement of every person in the society to be racist. It was a crime not to practice racism. White people and people of color were subject to arrest, trial, and imprisonment for disobeying the laws of racism.

- *Overt.* Institutionalized racism was practiced not only intentionally and legally, but with blatant openness. It never needed to be hidden. It was never seriously endangered by societal disapproval. In fact, it was a matter of national pride. Only in the mid-twentieth century, as the movements for change were emerging, were there more than a relatively few signs of shame about its existence. And it must be clearly stated that the religious establishment of the society, including all but a few of the white church denominations, gave their blessings to the intentional, legal, and overt practice of racism.

How It Stayed That Way:
New Forms of Institutionalized Racism

The End of One Form and the Beginning of Another

Thankfully, there has always been resistance to institutionalized racism—formidable and unrelenting resistance, led by African Americans, Native Americans,

Latinos/Hispanics, Asian Americans, and Arab Americans, and supported by a significant minority of the white community. In fact, as is documented in chapter 1, it was this powerful resistance that ultimately resulted in the significant changes that have taken place. We need to acknowledge and affirm these positive accomplishments before turning once again to the negative side of this continuing saga.

It was less than a half-century ago that a significant step toward the dismantling of our nation's system of intentional, legal, and overt institutionalized racism took place. It marked the beginning of the end of institutionalized racism. After more than 450 years of resistance and struggle, the legal foundations that supported the system of segregation and discrimination were uprooted. As stated earlier, it was a momentous event of global significance comparable only to other momentous global events such as the falling of the Berlin Wall or the ending of the apartheid system in South Africa.

With the passing of civil rights legislation of the 1960s, legalized racial segregation and discrimination in the United States was abolished. At least according to the law, people of color could now eat, sleep, work, play, worship, vote, own property, and do anything at the same time and the same place as white people. In a deeply significant way, the long struggle had finally paid off. Throughout the country and even throughout the world, there was great joy and celebration that the legalized system of segregation practiced for so long was so thoroughly brought to public disgrace, and so much of it dismantled.

Even though it was only the beginning of the end, the significant changes that took place as a result of the civil rights movement and civil rights laws provide a dramatic "before and after" picture that helps us understand the accomplishments of those who have struggled before us, as well as the need to understand the changing nature of institutionalized racism that we are still dealing with today.

For a Moment It Looked as if We Were Winning . . .

It seemed at first that significant institutional change was taking place in our society. On most visible levels, the doors of our nation's institutions were being opened. A standardized declaration is now posted just inside the front doors of virtually every public institution, inviting everyone to come inside and participate. It states: "This is an equal opportunity institution that does not discriminate on the basis of race, color, creed, gender, sexual orientation, age, or disability."

Equal opportunity became enforced by law and supervised by the courts. Public commitments to diversity and inclusiveness were being made by nearly every organization, corporation, and institution in our country. In many places, affirmative-action programs were enacted to compensate for historic losses of place and position by people of color. An argument was made—and is still being made by many people—that the promises made in the 1960s were gradually being kept. From the measuring standards of "equal opportunity," "legality," and "intentionality," our nation seemed to have taken a giant step forward.

. . . and Then We Looked at the Results

Unfortunately, the sense of joy was transitory and short-lived. Even before the victory could be properly celebrated, it became clear that rather than coming to an end, institutionalized racism had gone underground and was coming back in hidden ways and new disguises. The joy of victory was soon replaced by a great sense of letdown and frustration and a growing anger at the realization that racism had not died, but was even thriving with greater energy than before.

In chapter 1, I suggested that the standards of "equal opportunity," "legality," and "intentionality" are not sufficient to measure change. Change must also be measured by results. And if we look at results, we get another picture that reveals how little change has actually taken place, despite "equal opportunity," "legality," and "intentionality." The results are clear: in virtually every area of life—income, employment, education, housing, or health—the gap between white people and people of color has remained the same or increased. Naming these ever-present gaps in our society between white people and people of color provides explicit evidence of the continuation of institutionalized racism in the twenty-first century.

The results speak for themselves. In the final analysis, the continuation of institutionalized racism is perpetuating a problem that cannot be overcome with legislation that only seeks to ensure equal opportunity, but not equal results. The design of racism is so rooted in institutional structures and so imprisoned by decisions made centuries ago that it perpetuates itself despite surface efforts to bring about change.

Thus, we see the power of racism of the past still controlling the present. There is a virtually automatic adjustment within systems and institutions that keeps them focusing on two things that were built in from the beginning: white supremacy and subservience of people of color. White empowerment and people of color disempowerment are programmed to continue "systemically." To say that racism is systemic means that it is designed to continue to function whether or not it has helping hands. Moreover, as we described as the work of Power[3] in chapter 4, racism is able to create helping hands that are unaware of and anesthetized against feeling culpable participation.

Even though racial discrimination and segregation are no longer legal, the self-preserving and self-perpetuating nature of institutionalized racism has quickly found ways to get around the law and thus to continue on as before. The fundamental design of our systems and institutions has not changed; they are still functioning with the original design and structure to exclusively serve and be accountable to white people.

It is profoundly ironic that the very same institutions that are designed and structured to serve white people exclusively were legally mandated to provide "equal" services for people of color. Those who caused the problem in the first place were assigned the responsibility of solving the problem they had caused. The thief was asked to guard the treasure. The fox was assigned to protect the henhouse. No changes have been made in their institutional designs and structures, yet they are now being used to try to "serve" people of color. Is it any wonder that people of color experience these institutions as "feet" that are kicking them? The solution that was portrayed as an improvement in fact turned out to create a greater problem. It is this contradictory reality that we must now seek to comprehend.

Mutations of Racism: New Forms of a Deadly Disease

Some diseases—cancer being a clear example—are so powerful that over time they can make their intended remedies and cures ineffective. They "mutate" into an even more powerful form of the disease that is unaffected by previous treatment. Such diseases keep on perpetuating themselves in new forms so long as the foundational cause has not been discovered and eliminated.

Institutionalized racism has proven itself to be like a cancer that mutates, carrying out its original purposes despite intended remedies, and in fact becoming a far more virulent disease than it ever was. The foundational structures of institutionalized white power and privilege are still firmly in place. Institutionalized racism has not disappeared, but rather has mutated into new forms that are more devious and disguised and more difficult than ever to understand and confront.

In its newly mutated forms, racism looks quite different from the outside. It is far more covert. It is disguised, hidden, and deceptive. It is covered with a veneer of friendliness. Institutions have developed superficial welcoming looks. They advertise nondiscrimination and the good intentions of diversity. They develop programs of inclusiveness, with goals and quotas for the minimal presence of people of color. But underneath the thin veneer the same disease is eating away at the institutional foundations. And so long as the disease itself is not being treated but only its symptoms, then all of these changes become a dangerous disguise.

It has taken time—decades, in fact—to begin to understand these new forms of institutionalized racism, to figure out how they came into being and how they function. As I will try to demonstrate, so long as we continue to deal with institutionalized racism on superficial levels, and not on levels where it is most deeply embedded, the disease will keep on mutating and coming back in more virulent forms than ever.

To What Degree Is Racism Still Intentional?

Before going further into examining how these newly mutated forms of institutionalized racism continue to function in the current setting of the twenty-first century, there is a critical—albeit quite uncomfortable—question that needs to be posed: To what extent is institutionalized racism in the post–civil rights era still being intentionally perpetuated? Or alternatively, To what extent is it only an inherited problem from the past that we have not yet developed the ability to solve? For 450 years we were an intentionally racist people, a nation of white supremacists. Are the continuing results of inequality a product of our continuing intentionality, or have we simply but frustratingly been unable to reach our intended goal of a racism-free society?

Do we really want to do it differently? Do we, the white people of the United States, want to end racism? The answers to these questions will not only dramatically affect our approach to dismantling racism presented in the last chapter of this book; it will also determine the way we continue in this chapter to analyze contemporary institutions.

Most important for our immediate task, we need to focus these questions about intentionality specifically on the people who are responsible for managing our nation's institutions. Do *they* really want to end racism? To what extent do our leaders—the legislators and administrators in our government, the CEOs and managers of our businesses and industry, the superintendents and teachers in our schools, the bishops, priests, and rabbis in our religious institutions, and all the rest of the institutional leaders and managers—want to end the institutionalized racism that is embedded in the institutions they are responsible for running? And to what extent are these leaders consciously and intentionally trying to keep things the way they are?

Despite the fact that these questions are subjective and require judgments about people's motivation, we need to make an effort to answer them. Actually, if we have adequately analyzed the issues that have been raised in previous chapters, the answers to these questions should not be so difficult to find.

Commitment to Change

I believe that there are many white institutional leaders who are quite sincere in their desire for racial harmony and equality, but they are more often than not unaware and are in deep denial about the existence of continuing institutionalized racism in their institutions. They want change, but do not understand what causes racial problems, and are honestly not conscious or intentional in their racism. This is, of course, quite consistent with the analysis in the previous chapter of Power[3] and the imprisoning socialization that leaves so many of us quite oblivious to our personal racism and to the institutionalized racism we help to perpetuate.

Institutional leaders have the capacity to become aware of and to help confront and change their institution's racism. It is to such people that this book is addressed, and specifically for whom the strategies for change in the last chapter of this book are presented. Joining together with people of color, it is possible for these people to help organize powerful forces of resistance to racism and to work for transformation at institutional levels that can produce long-lasting and effective change.

Continuing Duplicity and Treachery

On the other hand, and tragically, I believe there are also a significant number of leaders who are still quite intentional in furthering institutionalized racism. These are leaders who at best support superficial changes while avoiding more profound changes in the institutions they are responsible for leading. I believe that if they spoke honestly they would state quite clearly that they have no desire to change the fundamental relationships between white people and people of color, and never intended to change the power structure of racism that provides power and privilege for white people and not for people of color. They also are committed to continue to resist institutional changes at levels that would change the racialized power structure of our society.

Although most of these leaders manage to do their work with relative secrecy and hiddenness, and with a cover of liberal concern, there are also many spokespersons for this point of view who blatantly affirm their beliefs. They can especially be heard on radio talk shows, preaching in conservative churches, and making right-wing political speeches.

We need to be as aware as possible of those who deliberately and intentionally further the continuation of institutionalized racism. It is impossible to exaggerate the extent of the duplicity and treachery still being practiced by many of our nation's leaders in order to control and exploit people of color and to maintain white power and privilege in our society. Individually and collectively, as leaders and managers of public and private institutions, they have created sophisticated methods of hiding illegal racist practices. The blame for these practices, however, must be shared by all of us who actively or passively condone them and willingly accept their benefits. This "hidden" form of racism would not be so nearly well hidden if we didn't cooperate by covering our eyes and ears so that we will not see and hear it.

Instances of continuing deliberate racism can be found in nearly every institutional arena. Some examples:

- Intentional racism within the real estate, banking, and mortgage industry is one of the primary reasons why residential segregation is greater today than it was before the enactment of civil rights laws. When it was still legal to do so, the real estate industry simply refused to show or sell property to a person of color, and the banking and mortgage companies simply refused to provide loans for mortgages. Now, however, there are within the real estate industry ingenious schemes and systems of illegally "steering" customers toward or away from locations that have been primarily designated for one particular racial group. Likewise, banks have created such strategies as "redlining" to achieve the same results. "Redlining" refers to the illegal practice of drawing a red line on a map around a community of color and designating it as a place in which service or financial investment will be reduced or eliminated. As a result, extensive studies of major U.S. cities document continuing dramatic racial disparities in mortgage lending.

- While this practice of redlining was initiated by the banking and real estate industry, it can also be seen functioning in every institution that operates in communities of color: government agencies, insurance, retail marketing, education, churches, even pizza and newspaper delivery and taxicab services. It is clear that in every one of these areas, decisions have been made to divest, to invest differently, or to provide inferior services compared to the services provided in other race-based communities. Even though the practice of redlining has been made illegal in almost every one of these areas, it continues almost universally to be practiced in covert ways.

- Secret and hidden intentional racism is practiced by many employers, despite their pledges to obey the laws of equal-employment opportunity. Prior to changes in the law, an employer could freely and openly accept or reject persons of color according to their personal racist views; now they have learned to use other methods to disqualify and exclude unwanted persons. For example, educational criteria are manipulated, residential requirements are added, together with age, height, and weight qualifications, and many other means are used to defy and refuse to comply with the law.

- Governmental elections and representative appointments are controlled by carefully concealing private decisions, changing political boundaries, and even manipulating vote counts. Of course, unlike decisions of the past, these equally deliberate decisions are rarely recorded and, therefore, seldom traceable. They are made quietly and secretly at lunch, on the golf course, and in the men's washroom.

- The problem of police brutality has been dramatically caught by video cameras in the cases of Rodney King in Los Angeles and many others in cities throughout the country. However, this is only a small part of the continued intentional racism of the criminal justice system. Police harassment, racial profiling, selective prosecution, unequal imprisonment, and racially disproportionate application of capital punishment are just a few examples of the ways in which the criminal justice system continues to be racially criminal.

The ending of intentional racist practices such as these is not just a matter of detection and prosecution by those who enforce the law. Like moles that respond to threats by burrowing deeper into the ground, people who engage in such practices develop increasingly subtle and sophisticated methods of deception. Moreover, those who are responsible for enforcing the law generally have little enthusiasm for rooting out these forms of racism. They are like spinning saucers that lose their momentum and must be set spinning again and again. It takes an almost endless process to create new energy for one more effort to correct another instance of institutional racism. It is usually sparked by a dramatic racial tragedy, followed by a news media expose, an increasing momentum of protest, then public indignation and anger, and finally, the implementation of whatever minimal changes are required until amnesia and anesthesia settle in once again.

"Correlate Racism"

An additional problem is that many of these intentional actions are still technically legal. Often they are by-products of what is perceived as necessary "good business" practices. A term I use to describe this is "correlate racism." For example, most major banks as well as many supermarket chains and other commercial businesses often close their branches in poor urban communities. These closures are usually justified on financial terms. The correlate results of such decisions, however, are that poor people, and disproportionately people of color, are once again denied the services that are found elsewhere. Should such decisions that result in correlate racism be judged simply on the basis of the financial bottom line? Or do these corporations, in their role as service industries, also have responsibilities to the society, responsibilities that require more of them than the selection of a clientele that provides them with the highest profit?

Likewise, when disinvestment and reduction of services by schools, churches, and social agencies are decided and justified by criteria other than their correlate effects on a racially identified community, the racist results are either denied or rationalized. If, however, racism is measured by results, the message is clear. Such correlate decisions deny to people of color convenient access to products and services that are available to the rest of society.

Correlate racism is also evident when corporate executives, government officials, union leaders, and other institutional representatives justify their lack of success in hiring or upgrading employees of color. "We want to," they say, "but it is not our fault if we can't find qualified people." Whereas, in the past, people of color were denied training because of their race, today they are rejected because they lack the necessary qualifications. It is like hitting people over the head and then rejecting them because they have lumps on their heads. A process of deliberate and direct racism throughout our history created the conditions that prevented people of color from becoming properly educated and well qualified for a host of occupations. Now correlate racism rejects them because they are poorly educated and ill trained. As long as we permit this situation to continue, we are responsible for the results.

The insurance industry provides a final illustration of correlate racism as a by-product of corporate practices. Most insurance companies charge different rates depending on where one lives, and usually the dividing line between higher and lower rates follows the boundaries between white communities and communities of color. A by-product of such higher rates is correlate racism. Insurance companies may not actually charge people of color higher rates because they are people of color. Rather, insurance rates are simply higher where the risk is higher. And the risk of fire, auto theft, accident, and a hundred other insurance losses is higher in communities of color. Coincidence or correlate racism? Racism is measured by results, and the results are that people of color pay more. The racism that is a consequence of the seemingly neutral practice of charging rates according to risk is perceived only by those who understand the underlying reasons why poor urban communities are high-risk areas in the first place.

Correlate racism may be perceived as unintentional and caused involuntarily, but the decisions are quite intentional, even if the rationale covers up the results. If only the practices are scrutinized and not their results, they may appear to be completely innocent of intentional racism. The results, however, are what count. If there are no significant changes in the discrimination, exclusion, or exploitation of people of color, then institutionalized racism is still at work.

How to "See," Identify, and Analyze
Institutionalized Racism

I hope the preceding pages have made it clear that, despite changes in the law and despite the good intentions of many people, new generations of intentionally designed racist structures are still perpetuating systemic inequality.

But it is much more difficult to "see" these new forms. The results make it clear that it is still present, but the new disguises make it more difficult to identify while it is at work.

As I have already acknowledged, while some institutional leaders culpably and intentionally encourage this continuing racism, other institutional leaders and managers do not intend to further racism, and are even working hard to end racial inequality in their institutions. Many of these people are frustrated by the ineffectiveness of their efforts. The final section in this chapter is aimed toward equipping such people who do want to work for institutional transformation to learn how to look at the various levels and expressions of racism within an institution, and to understand better where and how transformation needs to take place.

Five Levels of an Institution

To do this, I want to describe a cross section of a typical institution and how institutional racism affects it. One way of looking at any institution is to see a design with five distinct levels or structural layers:

The Three Most Visible Levels
1. *Personnel:* the people who represent the institution and make it function.
2. *Programs, Products, or Services:* what an institution produces for its constituency.
3. *Constituency and Community:* the people an institution exists to serve.

The Two Least Visible Levels
1. *Organizational Structure:* the way an institution is put together and is managed.
2. *Mission, Purpose, and Identity:* the "foundations" of an institution; the formally stated reason the institution exists, along with its history, traditions, and culture.

The first three of these institutional levels—Personnel, Programs, and Constituency—are quite visible from the outside. They are intended to be seen, and are "dressed up" to make the institution inviting and attractive.

The last two levels of an institution are far less visible from the outside. They reflect the inner working of an institution. Most of the information about these two levels is "insider information" and is known best by the personnel within the institution.

In order to study how racism operates in any given institution, we need to be familiar with these five institutional levels and be prepared to recognize them in any institution we are studying. It is simply not helpful or effective to suggest that an institution is racist without being prepared to describe in specific terms on what level and in what ways it is racist, and what needs to be changed on each level if the racism is to be eliminated.

The chart on the following page (fig. 5.1) portrays an institutional structure with these five levels, along with the ways that racism can affect each of them. Take a moment to become familiar with this chart, since we will be referring to it a number of times during the next pages.

Discerning Institutionalized Racism at Each Institutional Level

As we examine these five levels, it will become clear that racism may be operating at any or all of these levels, and that the degree of racism in an institution can vary from level to level. At the same time, the more deeply it exists, especially in the foundations of an institution, the more difficult it is to eradicate. The most important conclusion I will be drawing in the next few pages is that the institutionalized racism that has been inherited from the past—the design and structure to serve and be accountable to the white society but not people of color—is embedded most deeply in the last two levels of an institution.

Most institutional leaders are willing to acknowledge the existence of problems with racism on the first three levels. It is on these levels where racism is most visibly expressed and experienced and where institutions have tended to focus their efforts to fix the problems. In fact, significant changes have taken place on the three visible levels in many institutions.

However, institutional leaders tend to be far more reluctant to recognize and deal with the racism that exists on the last two levels: "Organizational Structure" and "Mission, Purpose, and Identity." It is on these bottom two levels that self-perpetuating racism is most deeply institutionalized and entrenched, and where racism is far more serious and difficult to deal with. Thus, on these last two levels, most institutions have made very little change, and as I will try to demonstrate, this is where there is great need for decades to come. Dismantling racism in the twenty-first century means transforming the deepest levels of institutionalized life.

If we focus on fixing racism on superficial levels, and not on the levels where it makes a permanent difference, the result is that it looks like change is taking place, while the most serious expressions of racism are not dealt with. In fact, change at the upper layers even helps to cover up the more complex and difficult problems below.

Let's take a closer look at each of these five levels, and what has been done or not done in our society's efforts for change, beginning with the more visible top three levels. On these upper levels, we shall see that great efforts for change have been implemented and celebrated, but there has also been continued frus-

Levels of an Institution

Levels	Explanation	Examples of Racism
Personnel	• People who work or volunteer for an institution • People who are authorized to speak, act, and implement programs in institution's name • People who act as gatekeepers for the constituency and the general public	• Racial inequality in numbers, positions, and salaries • Ineffective training on racism and race relations • Different treatment for white people and people of color • Lack of community and trust
Programs, Products, and Services	• What an institution provides for its constituency: food, clothing, technical services, entertainment, worship services, etc. • Designed to attract, nurture and retain members or customers or clients	• Different quality programs, products, and services for white people than for people of color • Programs are not designed to reflect commitments of institution regarding racism and race relations. • Policies regarding racism and race relations in personnel, finances, facility use, programs, etc., are absent, inadequate, or not enforced.
Constituency and Community	• People served by an institution • People who belong to or patronize an institution • Decisions and actions of an institution are taken in the name of and on behalf of its community and constituency.	• Constituency is not representative of community of color. • People of color community or constituency are not adequately or equally served • Outreach to community or constituency is discriminatory
Organizational Structure	• Where the power of the institution is: people in charge, board of directors, managers, etc. • Where the decisions are made, budgets are decided, people are hired and fired, programs are approved, boundaries are set, etc. • Where structures of accountability are designed and implemented	• Geographic or organizational boundaries exclude people of color or ineffectively represent people of color • People of color do not have power or authority in institution • Institutional structures are accountable to white people and not accountable to people of color
Mission, Purpose, and Identity	• What an institution is for and why it exists • Mission, purpose and identity are defined by constitution, by-laws, mission statement, belief system, worldview, history, and tradition	• The original mission, purpose, organizational structure of every institution in the United States was to serve white people exclusively. • It is still true today that the identity, values, and worldview of nearly every institution reflects its commitment to serve white people better than people of color

Fig. 5.1. ©Crossroads Ministry Used by Permission.[2]

tration in the superficiality of the changes and in their not being able to be sustained. After looking at these top three levels, we will then proceed to the deeper levels to examine what still needs to be done. My contention will be that the forces and powers of racism at the deeper levels are self-perpetuating and keep on counteracting the achievements in the upper levels of the institution.

First Institutional Level: Personnel

Personnel are the people who work inside an institution. They may be paid or they may be volunteers; however, they are all authorized by the institution to work for it and to represent it. Along with the physical facilities, personnel are the most visible part of an institution. The most visible personnel are the receptionists, the store clerks, the bank tellers, loan officers, teachers and professors, traffic cops, and thousands of people we see each day who represent the institutions we deal with. The common characteristic all personnel share is that, to one degree or another, they all have been authorized to represent the institution to the constituency or to the public officially.

Normally, an institution wants its personnel to be seen, and provides very specific instruction and training so they will be seen exactly the way the institution wants them to be seen. Their words and their actions are usually defined clearly by institutional policies, and there are formal means of holding personnel accountable to these policies. There are often dress requirements, and even at times a uniform that provides specific institutional identity, such as with the case of police, firefighters, hotel bellhops, clergy, or airplane pilots and flight attendants. An institution trains its personnel to present whatever image is desirable for the institution.

"Persons" become "Personnel." There are no purely individual actions in an institution. Personnel speak for and represent the institution, and do not speak or act as independent individuals. When individual persons are authorized to speak or act for an institution, in a very real sense they lose their individuality. A person's actions are no longer individual, but institutional.

For example, when you shop at a department store and the clerk does not treat you well, it is not just the individual clerk, but the department store that has mistreated you; conversely, if the clerk treats you well, the department store has treated you well. If you enter a restaurant, a church, or a place of public entertainment and the greeter or the receptionist snubs you, you say this is an unfriendly place, and you may have to go someplace else. But if the receptionist or the greeter treats you well, you say this is a friendly place, and you are probably going to enjoy being here.

Racism on Personnel Levels. Just as there are no purely individual actions in an institution, so also there is no such thing as purely individual racism in an institution. Racism in personnel is experienced as far more than the private attitudes or actions of an individual. An act of individual racism automatically becomes an act of institutional racism.

The racist behavior of a police officer has the effect of painting the entire police department with a racist brush. Likewise, the racist actions of a single teacher can make the entire school system racist. A bigoted court clerk or judge infects the entire legal system. A sales clerk or security officer who acts with hostility toward people of color will communicate that the entire store is racist.

Often, when a person who represents an institution commits a public act of racism, the embarrassed institution will incorrectly try to disassociate itself from that person. For example, when a police officer is caught in an act of racial harassment or brutality, there seems to always be a police chief who will stand up and say that this was an individual act by a "bad apple" and should not be seen as casting negative light on the police as a whole. The question that is almost never asked is, What tree did this bad apple grow on, and why does this tree repeatedly grow bad apples? The racist behavior of individual police officers sends an inescapable message that the police department is itself racist. There is no distinction between the blue uniform and the person inside it. The same is true with any institution; the actions of one or two individuals are all it takes to demonstrate that an entire institution is racist.

In identifying racism in institutional personnel, it is also important to understand the distinction, and oftentimes the large gap, between policy and practice. The practices of personnel may not correspond to institutional policies. Racism in practice may be the direct result of fulfilling racist policy, or it may exist in contradiction to official policy or even reflect the absence of policy.

For example, a school district may have a policy that educational materials of equal quality should be provided for every school, but in practice it may be far from fulfilling this policy. A corporation's policy may be to locate housing for personnel on an equal basis, but in practice it may place white personnel in the white suburbs and personnel of color in the inner city. Or a city police department may have a stated policy of equal protection for all neighborhoods, but its practice may be very different.

Finally, a major issue of racism in personnel is the degree to which an institution's personnel are racially diverse. Since the days of the civil rights movement, and especially since the 1980s, there has been a great emphasis on racial diversity and inclusiveness in institutional personnel. Following the publication of a study by the Hudson Institute entitled "Workforce 2000," it became obvious to the corporate world that in the twenty-first century the majority of their workforce would be people of color.[3] As a result, major efforts began to be made to carry out effectively the diversification of the U.S. workforce. Almost every other institution began to follow suit, and multicultural inclusiveness and diversity became a part of the top ten priorities in virtually every corner of the nation.

On the one hand, the diversification of personnel in most of our nation's institutions is an important sign of positive change. People of color are not only present, but even in some institutional settings are the predominant personnel. It is important to note that in many ways institutions have learned an enormous amount about dealing with diversity. Not only has virtually every institution developed hiring policies and practices to enhance staff inclusiveness and diversity; additionally, sophisticated education and training programs have been created to help multicultural staff relate better to one another. In multiple ways, institutions have been increasingly effective in projecting an image on the personnel level that racial inequality is being overcome and progress is being made in overcoming racism.

As will be discussed in greater detail in the following chapter on cultural racism, however, there are unrealistic and unjust demands for assimilation and cultural identity change that are made upon people of color before they are allowed to enter into most of our institutions as personnel. Moreover, there are serious limitations as to the higher positions of personnel to which people of color have been permitted to ascend. As will become much clearer when we examine below the organizational structure and focus on the offices of the corporate decision makers, the more powerful positions are still reserved for white people and especially for white men.

Finally, the most important critique of efforts to address racism on the level of personnel, and especially of programs aimed toward racial diversification of personnel, is that they are often the *only* institutional level where significant change is taking place. As we shall see more clearly when we examine the other levels of an institution, change on the level of personnel can all too easily be a cover for racism that is embedded in other levels of an institution.

Second Institutional Level: Programs, Products, and Services

The central function of an institution—in fact, the reason it exists—is to provide programs, products, and services for its immediate membership or constituency, or for the general public. For example, manufacturing and agricultural industries and their distributors provide products that are purchased by consumers, such as food, clothing, houses, automobiles, and so forth. Service industries provide programs and services for their clientele, such as educational programs, information technology, financial services, health care, spiritual guidance, and the like.

Just as with personnel, an institution's programs, products, and services are highly visible and intended to be seen from the outside. They are designed with an aim to attract, nurture, and retain an institution's constituency. Promotional programs and media advertisements are directed toward the public with the intent of gaining new participants in the institution's realm of activities.

The production and delivery of programs, products, and services to a constituency are guided by institutional policies, procedures, and protocols. Whether it is a product for sale or a program to be participated in, institutional policies and guidelines are intended to be strictly followed in order to present a consistent quality for the institution's constituency or consumer.

The Rules of the Market Economy Determine Quantity and Quality of Service. In order to discuss racism adequately on this institutional level of programs, products, and services, I need to deal for a moment with how economics affects the distribution of goods and services in our society. The simple fact is that white communities have historically received and still receive today more and better of almost everything than communities of color receive. The cause of this reality is obviously the relative economic power of the white community compared to communities of color. However, an even more important concern is the long-term effect of economic inequality as it perpetuates power and powerlessness in each of the communities. Power begets power and perpetuates itself, and powerlessness begets powerlessness and perpetuates itself. It is a centuries-long chain of cause and effect that has yet to be broken, and it is perhaps the largest single factor in perpetuating racism in the distribution of goods and services in our society.

To explain a bit further: in the United States, with its system of market supply and demand, the availability, quality, and cost of goods and services vary greatly from community to community. To a great extent the economic and political power of any given community, city, or geographical region determines the accessibility of institutional programs, products, and services. The most serious result of this unequal system of production and distribution is the long-term effect on communities of people. Not only is economic and political power necessary to acquire goods and services, but the long-term absence of goods and services helps to perpetuate disempowerment and the ability to acquire them.

Market-Determined Racism. The effects of this economically determined powerlessness can be seen clearly in communities of color. Despite decades of efforts to apply principles of equal opportunity, the limited availability of goods and services (government services, educational quality, adequate housing, public transportation, and so forth) in communities of color has not significantly changed. The cycle of institutionalized disempowerment continues. As I explained above, these patterns do not even have to be intentionally perpetuated. "Correlate racism" is often seen in inferior institutional programs and services in communities of color being defended on grounds of economic infeasibility, and not because of intentional racism.

Some readers might argue that the increased availability of popular consumer goods (clothing, electronics, automobiles, alcohol, and so forth) in many communities of color can be seen as a contradiction to what I have just written. Aren't these "goods and services," and isn't this a positive sign of change? It is true that the practice of massive targeting of communities of color in the marketing of popular consumer goods has escalated enormously since the 1990s. While this marketing strategy does take advantage of the greater purchasing capacity of many people of color, however, it also results mostly in the flow of money out of communities of color, rather than the building of capacity to retain and develop economic power within the community.

Nevertheless, despite these highly popularized visible signs of change, the differences are still quite dramatic with regard to essential human services and programs such as medical care, insurance, banking services, education, utilities, social services, and the like. The reason these have not changed must be understood in terms of what I have described above as the continuing effects of market-determined institutionalized disempowerment. The long-term result of preventing communities of color from receiving the society's institutional programs, products, and services before the civil rights movement was the shaping of communities of color with intrinsically less power and economic capacity. Since the rules of the market economy require economic power to attract goods and services, the result is that the presence of goods and services within communities of color is almost as limited now as it was in the days of legalized discrimination. Thus, despite the concept of equal opportunity, the laws of the market economy continue to protect unequal distribution of programs, products, and services.

The Failure of Affirmative Action

Affirmative action is one of the major solutions that have been attempted thus far in order to address this "unequal playing field." Many programs of affirmative action have been implemented with regard to government, education, and public contracts in business and industry, as well as other areas. However, it has become clear that there are two basic problems with the solution of affirmative action. The first is the reality that affirmative-action programs have increasingly been undermined, weakened, and destroyed through legislation and court decisions. The second problem is even more serious: it is the "Achilles heel" of affirmative action. Affirmative action is designed to compensate for, but not to permanently correct, the intrinsic patterns of institutionalized disempowerment that required affirmative action in the first place. As we shall further explore when we begin to discuss the deeper levels of an institution, it will take more than adjustments in the distribution of institutional programs, products, and services in order to change the power and economic capacity of people of color and communities of color.

Other Issues of Racism on the Level of Programs, Products, and Services. In addition to this central issue of institutionalized economic disempowerment, there are a myriad of other problems of racism at this level of programs, products, and services. For example, educational materials designed for the white community are still being distributed to communities of color with little or no adjustments for cultural realities in those communities. And even though history courses and special days and months are added to emphasize the realities of people of color, these superficial changes are seldom integrated into the continuingly dominant white history and reality at the center. Another example: although some "ethnic" foods, beauty aids, health-care items, and cultural specialties are provided in some stores in hidden aisles, the dominant culture is still the primary determinant of what other cultural goods and services are provided for people of color.

Of course, many corrective efforts to adjust the situation at this level of an institution are being implemented, and they certainly need to be continued. Institutional promotion of multicultural diversity on the level of programs, products, and services is often quite impressive. However, it is crucial to understand that if such changes are made without confronting the underlying structures and foundations of an institution and without confronting racism in its deepest institutional expression, the result will continue to be like using Band-Aids to cover up cancer. As we shall see more clearly when we explore institutional structure, design, and purpose, the continuing control and favoring of white power and privilege goes much deeper than an institution's programs, products, and services.

Third Institutional Level: Community and Constituency
Most institutions exist in clearly defined geographical communities, such as a neighborhood, city, region, state, and so forth. The institution may exist to serve its entire community, or it may serve a particular constituency within that community. Governmental agencies, for example, usually name as constituencies all the people of a given geographical community. Other institutions, such as business or medical offices, may consciously define a particular or limited constituency within their community.

It is important to note that even if an institution's constituency is a select group within a given community, that institution still has a relationship with and has accountability to the larger geographical community. It obeys the community's laws, pays taxes, use its utilities, and so forth. It is possible, therefore, to speak of every institution having dual accountability—to its immediately defined constituency and to the larger geographically defined community. In this section, as well as in the final chapter, I will emphasize this dual relationship and suggest that in dismantling racism it is necessary to respond to the needs of both an institution's immediate constituency as well as to the larger geographical community.

In the same way that I have described the level of *Personnel* and the level of *Programs, Products, and Services,* an institution's *Community* or *Constituency* is visible from outside the institution. We see shoppers at the mall, customers at the car sales lot, students entering and leaving the school grounds, patients entering and leaving the pharmacy or the doctor's office, churchgoers entering and leaving church, and so on. However, the constituency of an institution is only partially visible from an outside observer's perspective.

From the outside one may see only the active and current constituency, or may see a representative constituency gathering at an institutional public assembly. However, it requires an insider's perspective to get a more comprehensive picture. A more complete analysis of the constituency will include knowledge of who have been past members or customers, who are the potential future members or customers, and also intimate knowledge about which members or customers can be depended on, which must be treated with special care, and so forth.

From the inside, it is also possible to do a "power analysis" of a community or a particular constituency. For some institutions, the community or the constituency may have a great deal of power. For example, in some institutions the leadership is elected by the community as a whole or by a particular constituency, and all major decisions are made or must be confirmed by them. In other institutions the constituency has little power other than the choice to be served or not to be served.

It is also important to understand the varying degrees of power that institutions have *over* their constituencies, and how that power is exercised. For example, every decision and action in an institution is taken in the name of and on behalf of its community or constituency. Whether the decisions and actions are just and good—such as to improve its services or become more accessible—or whether the decisions and actions are unjust and unfair—such as to reduce the quality of its services or become less accessible—institutional decisions and actions not only affect the community or a particular constituency, but they also presume the community's or the constituency's assent, or at least acquiescence.

Racism on the level of Community and Constituency. As we have seen, most institutions in this country were created to serve exclusively white communities and white constituencies. When they were not exclusively white they were strictly segregated, with people of color receiving far less quality of service and having little or no power. With the passage of civil rights laws, institutions were required to desegregate and to define their community and constituency without regard to race, color, or creed. From this perspective, a great deal of progress has been made with regard to overcoming racism in institutional constituencies. There are very few institutions in the United States that have not, at least theoretically, redefined their constituency in multiracial terms.

In theory, at least, communities and constituencies are now expected to be addressed with equality. The police are now supposed to protect and serve everyone; the banks are mandated to make loans and provide mortgages for everyone; the real estate agencies, the schools, the hospitals, and the shopping malls are told they must serve everyone. Even though reality continues to be significantly different from theory, it is a step forward that the expectations of the law have redefined the racial basis for institutional communities and constituencies.

But it must be kept uppermost in our minds that this is only theory. As we have seen, despite the changes in the law, *de facto* segregation is still the predominant reality in our nation, and therefore most institutions are still serving segregated communities and constituencies. Moreover, it is also tragically true that the quality of service offered to constituencies in communities of color is still significantly inferior to service offered to constituencies in white communities. Furthermore, decisions about the quality of service within communities of color are made from outside the community and without regard for or accountability to the constituency being served.

In racially changing neighborhoods, when white residents leave and people of color are moved in, institutions such as shopping malls, restaurants, schools, and churches tend to close and move away or in other ways change the quality of service they offer, without consultation with their new constituency. The opposite experience is seen within neighborhoods that experience "regentrification," when people of color are forced out by racist economics and politics and white people return to "reclaim the community." When regentrification takes place, the shopping malls, restaurants, schools, and churches return to serve the white constituencies.

There is another phenomenon to which I referred earlier, and has been analyzed with particular clarity by Beverly Daniel Tatum in her book *Why Are All the Black Kids Sitting Together in the Cafeteria?*[4] When the constituency of a given institution is desegregated, a pattern of resegregation often takes place within the interior life of that institution. Mandating desegregation does not necessarily result in integration. No longer closing the door to people of color will not automatically result in all people feeling welcome to come through the door. How often the cry is heard: "We have opened the door for those people, but we don't know why they don't come in."

These are some of the visible marks of racism as it affects institutional constituencies that are easily seen from the outside. However, it requires an insider's perspective to get a more comprehensive picture of how racism is functioning on this level of the constituency. It is especially an insider's ability to assess the power of people of color within the constituency as compared to the white constituency. Even if there are increasing numbers of people of color in the constituency, it is still usually the case that decision-making power does not change, and how the institution cares for people of color has little relevance to how people of color in the constituency are feeling about the service they are receiving.

In chapter 7's discussion of organizing to dismantle racism, I will emphasize the importance of building new relationships with an institution's constituency and with the geographical community in which the institution is located. I will especially underscore the accountability relationship between an institution and its community and constituency. Since I have defined institutionalized racism in terms of accountability, then this is the point with which the dismantling of racism must begin.

Going Deeper Where Power Is Exercised. There can be no denying that many positive changes have been made on these first three institutional levels. And those changes have been important. The effects of these changes, however, have been quite limited. Despite manifold efforts to develop, recruit, train, and equip racially diverse personnel; despite endeavors to make programs, products, and services more multicultural and to more equally distribute them; despite serious attempts to reconstitute constituencies, the pattern created by centuries of racially determined privilege and lack of privilege continues to manifest itself in ways that are seemingly beyond the control of those working for change on these three levels. Addressing issues of race and diversity on visible and public levels, and not on the less visible levels where power is exercised, turns out to be not only superficial and ineffective; it also turns out to be a way of covering up problems rather than dealing with problems with a goal of truly solving them.

To answer the questions of why many efforts on these three visible levels of an institution seem to be failing and what keeps them from being effective, we need to examine the other two, less visible levels of an institution: the *Organizational Structure* and the institution's *Mission, Purpose, and Identity.* These are the levels of an institution where most of the power resides. We need especially to observe what usually happens when change is attempted on these two lower levels. To put it mildly, permission to enter and to make changes on these levels is not easily acquired. There is an invisible barrier that is often encountered between the first three levels and the other two levels of an institution, a barrier that creates resistance to entering these two lower levels.

In order to comprehend the inaccessibility and resistance to change on these levels, as well as the potential for deeper change when these levels do become accessible, we have to look more closely at the function they play in institutional life. Let us turn to the institution's internal organizational structure and to its underlying mission and purpose.

Fourth Institutional Level: Organizational Structure

Every institution and organization has a formal institutional structure. The formal description of the institutional structure usually includes a map that locates the personnel and their functions within the institution. The map contains a flow chart that describes how decisions are made and implemented within an institution. And it usually includes an institutional chart with boxes connected to boxes, and you are supposed to know which box you fit into and which boxes are connected to your box.

Equally important, in addition to the "formal" organizational structure, every institution also has an "informal" organizational structure that is just as important to its functioning as is the formal structure. The formal structure describes how decisions are theoretically made and implemented. The informal structure will tell you how these decisions are really made—in the hallways, by the coffeemaker, and on the golf course.

Knowledge of an institution's formal or informal organizational structure is insider information; it is not usually seen by the general public. A person has to be an insider to know its details and its complexities. However, if a person is an insider—part of an institution's personnel—knowledge about this institutional level is an imperative.

The Center of Institutional Power. The organizational structure of an institution is usually hierarchical in nature. At the peak of this organizational structure is the center of power. This is where the CEO and the board function; this is where the decision-making power lies and where the primary decisions are made, where policies are defined and implemented, and where programs are created, altered, or ended. Here is where personnel are hired and where personnel are fired. Here is where the institution's programs and products are designed, where the budgets are approved, and where the service boundaries are demarcated or changed. And finally, it is here where institutional accountability is defined and enforced.

Institutionalized racism is most deeply embedded where the power is. Our definition of racism is "*race prejudice plus the misuse of power by systems and institutions.*" If the center of power resides at the level of an institution's organizational structure (and, as we shall see in a moment, also on the level of *Mission and Purpose*), then this is also where the center of racism's misuse of power also will be found, and where it needs to be addressed. Here is where we should spend a lot of time analyzing and transforming institutional racism.

The opposite is usually the case. In fact, most institutions quite specifically avoid the center of power when issues of race relations and racial conflict are identified, analyzed, or addressed. And such decisions to avoid levels of power are made by people whose power controls those levels. In most institutions, racial issues are addressed only on levels that are visible to the outside, because the goal in addressing racial issues is to look good, to look racially just and fair.

Unfortunately—and here is the major point of our analysis of institutional racism—when efforts to deal with racism are addressed only on levels of personnel, products and services, and constituency, then institutional power structures will stay the way they were when they were originally created for purposes of serving an all-white constituency. This means that the way things were and the way things still are in the organizational structure of most institutions is that they are still virtually all white, and they are still structured to serve a white constituency. While the less powerful personnel positions may have been to one degree or another diversified, the more powerful positions of management, and especially the highest positions of decision-making power remain virtually unchanged.

Everywhere one looks in our nation, the vast majority of the seats of power are still occupied by white men: the Congress and the White House, state legislatures and governors, the financial centers, the CEOs and boardrooms of business and industry, the directors of media and communication, the leaders in technology, medicine, and space exploration, and the leadership of our mainline churches. Of course, there is a token presence of women and people of color that give it the slightest flavor of change. But positional presence of people of color does not change power; in fact, it tends to support and extend white power, and it even prevents deeper change.

Power and Accountability. As is reflected clearly in the definition of institutionalized racism, it is on this level of an institution that the issues of power and accountability become central. Just the presence of a few persons of color on this level is not enough. If we look at those few places where people of color have assumed important positions, such as mayors of many of our largest cities, it must also be noted that "position" is not necessarily the same thing as "power." As I suggested earlier, people of color who are elected or appointed to positions that were previously occupied by white people have repeatedly experienced that there is often a sharp reduction in the power of that position when they move into it. This has been particularly the experience of mayors in our large metropolitan areas, beginning with Richard Hatcher in Gary, Indiana, who was the first African American mayor of a large U.S. city, and continuing through mayors such as Coleman Young in Detroit, Harold Washington in Chicago, Henry Cisneros in San Antonio, or Antonio Villaraigosa in Los Angeles.

Moreover, one of the primary means of reducing or limiting the power of people of color in such positions is the continued absence of accountability of institutions to communities of color. No matter how many persons of color occupy leadership positions within organizational structures, the continued racism of those structures is assured if the institutions remain exclusively accountable to the white community.

Thus, the two central issues for understanding racism on this level of organizational structure are, first, the presence and power or leadership of color; and second, the accountability of the organizational structure to communities of color inside and outside the institution. Only when positions and power at the center of the organizational and institutional structures of our society are restructured in such a way as to permit our institutions to be led by people of color equally with white people, and to make institutions as formally accountable to communities of color as they are presently formally accountable to white people, will we be in a position to design and shape new anti-racist institutions in the United States. It is to these two issues we will return in chapter 7, in the discussion of dismantling racism.

Fifth Institutional Level: Mission and Purpose

We have now arrived at the foundations of an institution, where the institution's reason for existence is not only defined but defended and preserved. An institution's identity is reflected in its mission and purpose, and is preserved in formal and legal "identity documents," such as a constitution and by-laws and in ideological documents created at its inception and usually expanded and refined with time. Identity documents reflect an institution's worldview: its values, belief system, and its ideology, philosophy, or theology. Nearly every institution develops and often revises its mission statement, which is a brief summary and a reflection of what lies deeper within an institution's foundations.

Besides its formal and legal identity documents, other marks of identity are built in an institution's history and tradition. Tradition can be as powerful in determining and institution's identity as its legal documents. Most institutions also have their identity symbolized in a logo, in music, or other artistic representations.

The Origin and Source of Institutional Identity. This level of mission, purpose, and identity is the deepest expression of power in an institution. This level determines what will happen on all the other levels. Ultimately, all the other levels are accountable to this level.

In a real sense, an institution's purpose and identity are sacred and unalterable. If an institution wanders away from its purpose that is stated in its identity documents, it will ultimately be lost and face self-destruction. When an institution does find its directions needing to make substantive changes, however, as is the case with dismantling racism, those changes need to be ultimately reflected in the purpose and identity documents.

Racism in Mission, Purpose, and Identity. It is on this deepest level of an institution that racism is most securely preserved, the level where the most important transformation must take place. I hope the previous chapters have clearly established that every institution in the United States was created with a mission and purpose to serve white people exclusively. This same mission and purpose was nurtured and deepened for 450 years. It is on this level that this white racist institutionalized identity has been preserved and protected. All the identity documents, mission statements and constitutions, institutional values, belief systems, ideology, philosophy, and theology, along with traditions, symbolic logos, music, and other artistic expressions have been shaped to be consistent with this racist mission and purpose. From this racist identity, the institutionalized designs and structures were created that would serve and be accountable to the white society and ensure the subservience and powerlessness of people of color. Likewise, it was this racist identity that the constituency, programs and personnel were designed to serve.

At this level of an institution's identity, we are once again confronted by Power[3], the most destructive expression of racism's power that we described in chapter 4. Now it is crucial to see that just as Power[3] is responsible for socializing and misshaping the identity of every individual, so also has Power[3] socialized and misshaped the identity of every institution. Racism is institutionalized and self-perpetuating because it is inscribed in the identity, in the DNA of our institutions. It began centuries ago with intentionality and deliberate design. Then it was passed on to generation after generation, as all of our institutions continued to inherit this racist identity. And now in the twenty-first century, we are finally coming face to face with the responsibility and the opportunity to work for institutional transformation on this level, where true change can be initiated.

Of course, such a profoundly inscribed and embedded identity is not easily or quickly transformed. During the past fifty years, we have softened the descriptive words of our mission statements by removing offensive words about exclusion; and we have added on our intentions of desiring diversity, inclusiveness, and equality; but these words have too easily become disguises to cover up a white identity that is still present and functioning to guide our nation's institutions.

Conclusion:

The Possibility of Authentic Institutional Transformation

When specialists in systems change and institutional change describe their work, they make the distinction between "transactional change" and "transformational change," as can be seen in the following quote from Bachman Global Associates:

> Business leaders need to recognize that organizations go through two different types of change: transactional and transformational. Transactional or evolutionary changes are those in which one or more features of the organization changes, but the organization's underlying character and culture remains untouched. Transformational changes, on the other hand, are revolutionary and sweeping, in that they fundamentally alter the very nature of the organization itself. Each type of change calls for a different type of leadership.[5]

The basic distinction between these two terms is that if we are satisfied with what a system or institution is producing, we need only to make adjustments, or "transactional" changes that will improve—but not significantly change—the product or the method of production. However, if we are dissatisfied with what a system is producing, however, transactional change will have no permanent effect. Deeper change, referred to here as "transformational" change is required to obtain a different product.

A system or institution will produce what it is designed to produce. If we want it to produce something different, we have to redesign the system. In the case of institutionalized racism, an institution that is designed to produce racism will produce racism. If it is designed to produce white power and privilege, it will produce white power and privilege. And if it is designed to subordinate people of color, it will subordinate people of color. Transactional change on the three institutional levels of personnel, programs/products/services, and constituency may make racism look better or feel softer, or even make it seem like it is going away. But it will not eliminate institutionalized racism. As important as changes in laws of segregation and discrimination have been, and as important as equal opportunity and improved intentionality have been, they ultimately result only in incremental change in our systems and institutions.

The frustration that results from transactional change alone, when transformational change is also needed, is inevitable. As long as we depend upon these transactional changes alone to produce transformational results, we will not go to the levels of change that are required for true transformation. In fact, they will even temporarily cover up the need for transformational change, which can ultimately make the need for transformational change to be felt more severely. Institutionalized racism can only be eliminated if transactional change on the institutional levels of personnel, programs, and constituency is accompanied by transformational change on institutional levels of organizational design, structure, and mission and purpose.

Where once our intentionality wreaked havoc and terrifying destruction by creating racist institutions, now our intentionality must be applied to creating *antiracist* institutions. And, since it is on the level of mission and purpose that the identity of racism has been institutionalized, then it is to this level and to the level of organizational structure that we must turn for the transformative work that will shape a new antiracist identity. It is to these levels that we will return in the last chapter as we begin to face the transformative work of redesigning and restructuring institutions to serve and be accountable to people of color. Before that, however, we now turn to a chapter on cultural racism, the third manifestation of racism.

CULTURAL RACISM

America is an unfinished nation—the product of a badly bungled process of inter-group cultural fusion.
—Harold Cruse, *The Crisis of the Negro Intellectual*

In recent years, the subject of "multicultural diversity" has become tremendously important in our society. There is a growing awareness that a racially just society must be built on a "multicultural" foundation. When cultures come together, however, cultural conflict is inevitable. Eventually, these conflicts must be resolved or they will become a permanent barrier to effective and authentic diversity.

"Cultural racism" has become a major barrier in a society that prevents multicultural foundations from being built. Therefore, in addition to "individual racism" and "institutional racism"—the subjects of the past two chapters—and before finally getting to the subject of dismantling racism in the next chapter, it is important to dedicate a chapter to the subject of "cultural racism."

Let's begin by recognizing that each racial grouping in the United States has, over past centuries, developed separate and distinct cultures. There is an African American culture, a Native American culture, an Asian American culture, a Latino/Hispanic culture, an Arab American culture, and a white culture. Each of these cultures is an amalgamation of many cultures that were forced together inside the racialized and segregated walls that required each racial group to have separate identity and existence.

I will use the term "race-based cultures" to refer to these cultures, in order to identify them as cultures that are derived from the experience of race, and to distinguish them from other societal cultural expressions. The goal of this chapter is to describe these race-based cultures, along with the interaction and interrelationships among them—an interaction that has resulted in a great amount of cultural conflict and oppression called "cultural racism." By the end of this chapter, I hope it will be clear why "multicultural diversity" is so difficult to achieve, and how the task of overcoming cultural racism is so important in building a multicultural society.

Before looking more closely at "race-based culture" and "multicultural diversity," however, we first need to be clear about the general concept of "culture," which includes much more than culture that is identified with race. There are not only race-based cultures, but also national cultures, ethnic cultures, religious cultures, age-based cultures, gender-based cultures, cultures of differing sexual orientations, and so on. The terms "multicultural" or "cultural diversity" not only refer to the interrelationship and interaction among race-based cultural groups, but also among cultures of different nationalities, ethnicities, genders, sexual orientations, ages, religions, and so forth. In the interchange among any of these groups, one can speak about a far broader concept of cultural diversity.

There are also many different kinds of cultural oppression. Cultural racism is only one of them. Cultural oppression happens when the values or behaviors of any group are suppressed by another group; it might be oppression of people with different gender or sexual behaviors or different religious practices, people of different age groups, people who walk differently or talk differently, people whose songs are controversial, people who eat strange food, people with beards or different hairstyles, or any number of values or behaviors that cause other groups in society to act in oppressive or unjust ways toward them.

Cultural racism is a specific kind of cultural oppression that is acted out against people with race-based cultures. I will suggest a more specific definition of cultural racism later in this chapter, but it is important to begin by this simple distinction that places cultural racism in the context of other forms of cultural oppression. There are five sections in the discussion of cultural racism in this chapter:

1. *What Is Culture?* An introduction to the general subject of culture.
2. *The Creating of Race-Based Cultures.* An exploration of the concept of "race-based culture" as a phenomenon that evolves from the creation of distinct and separated races.

3. *Defining Cultural Racism.* A more thorough definition of cultural racism and its power to separate and oppress people of color.

4. *The Race-Based Cultures of Communities of Color.* A brief examination of why people of color maintain race-based cultures in the twenty-first century.

5. *White Cultural Identity in the Twenty-First Century.* An examination of the collective "way of life" of white people today.

Throughout this book I have gratefully acknowledged the contributions of many people, especially those in Crossroads Ministry and People's Institute for Survival and Beyond. In this chapter on cultural racism, I am particularly grateful to Anne Stewart and Victor Rodriguez who have been my closest colleagues in developing a teaching model on this subject.

What Is Culture?

Many people often think of "culture" as a narrowly defined area of life that includes things like music, art, and dance. As important as they are, we are concerned here with much, much more. Culture, as we shall discuss it here, includes nearly every aspect of life. Certainly it includes music, art, and dance; but it also includes everything else that makes one society or a group within a society distinctive from another: the values, worldview, language, literature, religion, food, clothing, rituals, holidays, and the ideas, beliefs, and behaviors that constitute a particular group's lifestyle.

Culture Is Collective

All societies or groups within a society have their own culture, their own way of doing things. The way a specific group of people eats, dresses, builds houses, raises a family, gets married, educates their children, buries their dead, celebrates rites of passage, defines good and evil, observes religious beliefs, rewards the obedient and punishes the disobedient, and a thousand other beliefs, values, attitudes, and activities—all of these define a people's culture. Culture represents that which is most valued by a people, and how those values are lived out. Culture is a people's way of life.

It is important also to emphasize that culture is about how people in a society or in a group within a society do these things together or collectively. Culture is not a person's individual choice about how to live. It is about how groups of people live life together. It is especially important to emphasize this in the United States, where individualism exerts such a distorting influence upon our thinking and our activities. In almost no other part of the world do people talk about culture and not understand that they are referencing group membership or a collective identity.

In the United States we often, and from my perspective quite wrongly, speak about "personal culture" in terms of individual preferences without referencing collective identity or group membership. Individualism allows persons to think that they can create their own individual cultural identity by combining aspects of different cultures and mixing them together. One gets the impression in our society that cultural beliefs and actions are on display in a supermarket for our personal selection and purchase. If we choose to do so, we can pick up this piece of Native American culture and make it ours; or we can adapt that piece of Eastern religion and become that; or we can decide that this part of a group's rite of passage is interesting or exciting, and we can adopt that.

Culture does not happen that way, and that is not the way we learn to live life. We do things the way we do them because we were taught by a group to which we belong to do them that way. Even our individualism is a result of group socialization.

Of course, there is such a thing as "counterculture"; any one of us can decide to rebel against aspects of our culture, and make other choices. But that is a decision to act counter to the culture that a particular group has already instilled in us. Moreover, the counterculture in which we participate is also a group action or activity.

How We Get Culture: "Socialization"

Every aspect of our culture, we learn from the group or groups of which we are a part. Culture is transmitted through a group socialization process. Very early in life we are socialized by our families, our schools, our church, our friends, and by other social and cultural institutions in which we take part.

Our socialization also takes on different shapes and forms, depending upon our geographic location: urban or rural, upstate or downstate, north, south, east, or west. And of course, our national identity carries with it a cultural identity into which we are socialized. When we cross national borders, we also cross cultural borders that dramatically demonstrate how our socialization has shaped us.

Increasingly, we are also socialized by media, particularly television and the Internet. Not only do television and the Internet take us beyond our culture and expose us to other cultures, providing us with multicultural experiences, they also tend to homogenize culture, creating a blend of many cultures that has never before been possible. Although many experts see this homogenization as a negative trend, it nevertheless inevitably exerts tremendous influence on our collective cultural self-understanding.

Culture, Subculture, and Race

Each of us participates in or is socialized by more than one cultural source. We can speak of our predominant or main culture, usually a national culture such as German culture, Chinese culture, or U.S. culture, and the like. But we can also identify many subcultures that influence our lives, even if in a more peripheral or secondary way, such as the culture of our hometown, our school culture, our work culture, or the culture of our sports club or church.

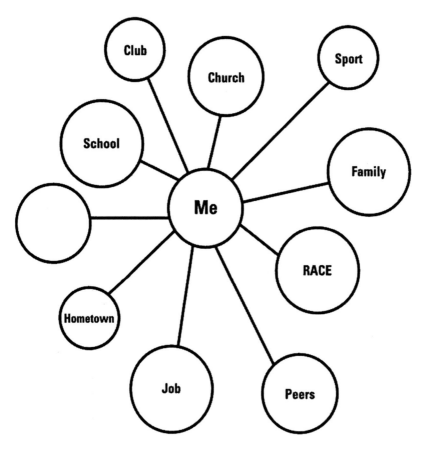

Fig. 6.1. Socialization & Identity Mapping. A chart developed by Dr. Victor M. Rodriguez[1]

Sociologist Victor Rodriguez uses a social identity mapping exercise to help students comprehend this complex socializing process. As can be seen on the chart (fig. 6.1) above, one can draw a larger circle close to the center to represent the major cultural socializing forces in a person's life—such as family, school, church, and so on—and a smaller circle farther from the center to represent the subcultures with a lesser socializing impact, such as a club or an occasional interest. We can begin to capture our total socialized identity as the sum of the circles drawn to represent the cultures and subcultures that have socialized us.

Socialization and Race

On the accompanying identity mapping chart, along with naming other cultural influences, I have placed a large circle entitled "Race" close to the center. It illustrates the importance of understanding the powerful effect of race in determining our cultural identity in the United States. The racial identity of each of us is a product of cultural socialization.

Of course, no matter what our race, there are many ways in which our cultural way of life is alike cross-racially, simply because we are born, raised, and socialized in the same nation, the same community, the same school, etc. Nevertheless, depending upon our racial identity, there is much that is different in the cultural identity of each of us, depending upon whether our predominant race-based culture is African American, Native American, Asian American, Latino/Hispanic, Arab American, or white.

It is interesting and important to note that while it is usually quite obvious to people of color that we have all been significantly and differently socialized by our racial identity, for white people this idea more often than not is new and somewhat shocking information. As white people, even though much of what we experience and receive in life is directly a result of our being part of a white racial collective, we are also socialized not to be conscious of it. We have a silently shared agreement not to be conscious of our collective racial identity, and this becomes an important factor in the perpetuation of racism. If we do not understand that we are part of a white collective, then we will never see beyond our individual race or individual racism; and if we don't see the product of our collective racial identity, we won't have to accept responsibility for it, nor deal with it. I hope the importance of racial socialization and of our being aware of our collective racial identities will become increasingly clear in the following conversation about race-based culture.

The Creating of Race-Based Cultures

The Racialization of Everyone

We have already seen in chapter 2 that our racial identities are artificial and are imposed on us without a choice. Although race is a myth, it has a tremendously real impact on all of our lives. Race, as we understand it and use it in the United States today, is a sociopolitical construct developed more than four hundred years ago during the days of European colonial expansion in order to establish and justify white supremacy and world domination. The entire world and all its peoples were not only colonized, but also racialized. Our imposed racial identities superseded and, in many places in the world including the United States, still supersede other identities of nation, culture, and ethnicity.

In a forced process of "lumping" people together, this process of "racialization" made race to be among the most predominant factors in our personal and collective identities. The first thing that happened to immigrants coming to the United States was (and still is) to be given a racial identity. Groups of people from many nations were lumped together into large racial groupings, even though their national and cultural identities were very different from each another. Through this racialization process, everyone had a racial identity imposed on them, to the extent that their racial identity gradually became paramount, while their prior national and cultural identities began to dwindle and ultimately to disappear. During the centuries of racial segregation that followed, six separate racial groupings evolved, which were also color-coded: red, yellow, black, white, and at least two shades of brown.

"Lumped" Together

The final result was that an enormous number of distinctly different national or cultural identities were lumped together into six uniquely American racial expressions:

1. Immigrants from Japan, China, Korea, Vietnam, Laos, India, Philippines, Pacific Islands, and many other Asian countries, each with a different nationality, culture, and language, and many of them also having long histories of tensions dividing them from each other, are racialized into a single group called *Asian Americans*.

2. Peoples from numerous countries and regions once colonized by Spain and Portugal such as Puerto Rico, Cuba, Dominican Republic, Mexico, Central America, and South America, all with vastly differing cultures, as immigrants in or though colonial annexation by the United States are grouped together in a race called *Latinos* or *Hispanic Americans*. Even the supposedly common bond of language among Latinos/Hispanics is false, being an unnatural merging of many dialects and accents, as well as other languages besides Spanish, such as Portuguese and many indigenous languages.

3. The racialization of *African Americans* into a single race in the United States began with European colonialization and racialization of all the tribes and nations of Africa. Then the United States continued this racialization process with the inclusion in a single group anyone who looks "African," whether

they are descendents of enslaved Africans, or arrived since the time of slavery through various paths of immigration with greatly varying national and cultural identities from Africa, the Caribbean, Central America, South America, and even Europe.

4. The indigenous people of North America, from hundreds of separate nations, each with its distinctly different cultural identity, and all who were present in North America before the colonial invasion of Europeans, were combined into a single racialized group called "Indians," or *Native Americans.*

5. *Arab and Middle Eastern* people in the United States, caught in the centuries-long conflict in their countries over religion and the more recent wars over the control of oil, have been tossed back and forth for more than a century by the Supreme Court and by popular perception as to their racial identity—at one moment white and at another moment a new shade of brown. Now, however, in the twenty-first century, especially following the 9/11 attacks, their racialization appears to be taking another step toward completion.

6. The authors of this abhorrent process of racialization have also themselves been racialized. The Europeans who immigrated into the United States, from many nations, cultures, and languages, have also been fused together in a "melting pot" from which emerged the dominant race called *white.* It is important to remember here from our discussion in chapter 3 that in the history of the United States the legal name for European immigrants has been "white," and not Caucasian or European American. The privilege and power belonging to the dominant race required a belief and acceptance of white racial identity and white racial superiority.

As a result of this long and torturous path of racialization, each of us still today is assigned with a racial identity and belongs to a racial group. No matter how recent the immigrant, designation as a member of a specific racial group is immediate. Our national and cultural heritage is still subsumed under whatever racial category to which we have been assigned: African American, Latino/Hispanic American, Asian American, Native American, Arab American, or white. Each person is placed immovably within a racial group and given an identity that is also associated with the value of "inferior" or "superior," and which determines the size of the "privilege packet" that comes on the welcome wagon. Within two or three generations, for many or perhaps most of us, it becomes increasingly difficult, no matter the depth of our longing, to look back and find our connections to a national or cultural identity in the lands from which we either voluntarily or involuntarily came.

An example of the fixed nature of these racial identities can be seen in what happens to multiracial children. Cross-racial childbearing began centuries ago with the rape of enslaved Africans by their white masters, and with other cross-racial relationships seldom recognized or legalized by the dominant white society. Now in recent decades we have seen a dramatic increase of cross-racial marriages and adoptions, which has produced significantly large numbers of multiracial families and children. Multiracial children are often inflicted with confusing and psychologically damaging efforts to deny one or the other of their multiracial identities. Despite the occasional presence of an additional category of "other" on the checklist of racial identity, multiracial children are usually required to choose, or to have assigned to them if they are unwilling to choose, a primary racial identity.

The "Birth" of Race-Based Cultures

Over the centuries this forced racialization has had a remarkable consequence—the emergence of new cultures based on race. As a result of the "lumping" together of many nations, ethnicities, and cultures into six primary racial groups, new cultures based on race have emerged. Within each of the six racialized groups, there have evolved—and are still evolving—new collective cultural identities. In our society, we can identify and name six uniquely different race-based cultures: African American culture, Asian American culture, Latino/Hispanic American culture, Native American culture, Arab American culture, and white culture.

Actually, this result should not be surprising. Throughout history, whenever different cultures come into extended contact with each other, a turbulent process of cultural interaction has taken place, with a new culture—a new way of life—eventually emerging that is derived from the strongest elements of each. For example, as the Greeks and the Romans collided several thousand years ago, a new Greco-Roman culture evolved out of the two. And when the cultures of the Angles and Saxons intermeshed in the ninth century, the Anglo-Saxon culture gradually came into being. A more recent example is in Mexico, Puerto Rico, and other lands Spain conquered in the sixteenth and seventeenth centuries, where the merging of the Spanish culture with indigenous cultures began to form new merged cultures and peoples, often popularly referred to as the *la nueva raza*—"the new race."

Not surprisingly, therefore, in the United States it was inevitable that the process of racialization that forced many cultures to merge together would also result in the shaping of new cultures. Because of the power of racism, however, it was not one new culture, but six new cultures that began to emerge. Racial segregation created an almost impenetrable "cultural curtain" that isolated each of the six racialized groups from each other and produced six separate processes of cultural development, each with a separate process and timeline, and each at different levels of completion.

In our historical survey in chapter 1, we saw how this happened. The white society acted swiftly to dominate and separate themselves from other racial groupings. By killing, enslaving, and herding into reservations and into ghettos almost all red, brown, yellow, and black people, the white dominant group prevented virtually all possibility of cultural interaction. Behind the carefully maintained and guarded cultural curtain, the racialized people of color groups lived in a state of forced isolation not only from the white population, but also from one another. Every effort was made by the white society to prevent intercommunication from happening. The result was that the cultural curtain not only forced separate race-based cultural evolution, but caused and encouraged hostility among and between each of the groups.

Behind the Cultural Curtain

With the cultural curtain in place, instead of one single process of intermeshing and intermingling of cultures, six separate and distinct processes took place. As segregation ensured that each of the racialized groups would be isolated from each other, new cultural evolution began to happen within each of them. Inside all six racialized and segregated groups—each of them composed of people from many nations and many cultures—the cultural intermeshing took place, and within each of them a new race-based culture began to emerge.

Gradually, people who once clearly had originally many different national, ethnic, and cultural identities, now forced together as a single race, began to shape common identities, lifestyles, and worldviews. The names "African American" or "black," "Latino" or "Hispanic," "Asian American," "Native American," "Arab American," and "white" were no longer simply racial identities, but also described emerging race-based cultures that formed and are still forming out of the merging of all the peoples in their racialized group.

Each group has been affected differently by this process and is still in the process of developing its own unique race-based cultural expression. Not only is the culture that emerged within people of color groups wholly different from white culture; the cultures of each of the five people of color groups and subgroups are also vastly different from each other.

Thus, the United States can be broadly viewed and described as a nation of six race-based cultures, each of them the product of the concentration, compression, and amalgamation of six racialized and segregated groups. The result is that in the United States, a significant part of every person's cultural identity is a direct product of racial identity. Each of us is socialized to accept the cultural norms that are associated with the race-based culture that is associated with our group's racial identity.

Defining Cultural Racism

Now that we have seen the origin and significance of race-based culture, let's try out a definition of cultural racism. I already stated in the introduction to this chapter that cultural racism is a specific kind of cultural oppression that is acted out by a dominant race against the ideas and behaviors of people of suppressed races. If we simply build a definition of cultural racism based on the definition of racism we have been using since the beginning of this book (race prejudice plus the misuse of systemic and institutional power), it might look like this:

CULTURAL RACISM
Is
Race-Based Cultural Prejudice
Plus the Misuse of Systemic and Institutional Power

Once again, any definition of racism needs to emphasize the issue of power. It has to include the principle factor that makes all forms of racism so devastating: the misuse of power by societal systems and institutions. Thus cultural racism is not the same thing as cultural prejudice. Practically everyone is culturally prejudiced. Even if my food or music or art does seem to me preferable to yours, however, my being culturally prejudiced does not mean that I necessarily have the power to enforce my views onto you or others. By contrast, cultural racism is about having the collective power for one racial group to claim and establish a dominant and superior way of life, as well as to impose that way of life on others.

The controlling power is the dominant white race and culture. As will be discussed in greater detail in the pages that follow, the cultural curtain not only kept the six race-based cultures separated from each other; it also demanded that the white culture be predominant and to be defined as the cultural way of life that is most associated with our national identity. In most respects, the lifestyle, language, art, music, and other aspects of national culture in the United States have developed, with little contest, in ways that favor that which is white and Western. From this dominant position, it has also been possible for the cultural contributions of the other five racial groupings to be appropriated by the white society and allowed to pass though the cultural curtain and to be made part of the dominant white culture (for example, jazz, or Indian names for football teams).

Expanding the Definition

In order to further explore cultural racism, it is helpful to have a more detailed and more comprehensive definition, as follows:

> **CULTURAL RACISM is a racially defined societal group using systemic power**
> 1. **to establish its cultural way of life as dominant and superior;**
> 2. **and to simultaneously:**
>   - **impose its cultural way of life onto oppressed groups;**
>   **destroy, distort, discount, and discredit the cultures of oppressed**
>   **race-based groups;**
>   - **while appropriating aspects of their cultures without accountability to**
>   **those groups.**[2]

This second and more detailed definition has two parts. First, it takes into account the process just described above, in which white people established themselves as a superior racial group, and then declared themselves as having a dominant and superior race-based culture.

The second half of the definition reflects the ongoing painful story of centuries of cultural imposition and cultural suppression of each of the five subjugated cultures—a carefully controlled, oppressive relationship in which the white culture destroyed, distorted, discounted, and discredited the other cultures, even while importing, adapting, and claiming as their own whatever they chose from the music, dance, clothing style, and language of other races on the other side of the cultural curtain.

This definition not only describes past history, but also applies to our twenty-first century experience. The end of enforced segregation and the enactment of civil rights laws did little to change cultural racism. The white society still dominates the lifestyle of the workplace, our communities where we play and pray, and the way we live our lives at home.

It is impossible to portray with words the painful destruction wrought by white cultural racism throughout our history in the United States. It is particularly problematical for a white person to write about or read and try to comprehend the devastation and loss of people whose identity has for centuries been stolen, maligned, and destroyed. A few pages from now, I will ask white readers to attempt to understand how our own identity has been distorted and destroyed by our own white cultural racism. However, I believe that we as white people cannot even begin to understand what has happened to our own cultural identity unless it has been at least partially mirrored by the cultural destruction we have caused in others.

In the next few pages we will attempt to look a little more closely at the reality of white cultural domination over the culture of people of color, as well as to remember the resistance of people of color as they have over the centuries courageously struggled against cultural oppression in order to maintain their sense of identity and ways of life. Following this, we want to look more closely at the white culture, and in particular to look at its underside, in order to understand better the ways in which, as a result of our own cultural racism, the white culture is being as negatively affected as are the race-based cultures of people of color.

Destroy, Distort, Discount, Discredit

The history of cultural racism in the United States is long and ugly. Looking behind the cultural curtain, there is no end to the list of ways in which the cultures of people of color have been destroyed, distorted, discounted, and discredited. The following examples are given only to indicate a few of these ways, and to encourage readers to further explore this subject.

- *Hell's Kitchen.* This name for a neighborhood in New York City is a symbol of our "initiation rites" for all immigrants into the United States, both white and people of color. However, no group of white immigrants was ever so excluded from protection by law and made into permanent communities of perpetual aliens as were enslaved Africans and imported laborers from places like China, Mexico, and the Caribbean. And no newly recognized citizens have been so completely dishonored and disgraced as were Mexicans in the U.S. Southwest following annexation in 1848, freed African slaves following emancipation in 1865, and Puerto Ricans after they were granted citizenship in 1917.
- *Native American Boarding Schools.* "Getting the Indian out of the Indian" was the goal of this shameful exercise of cultural racism, carried out by church and state throughout the last part of the nineteenth and the first half of the twentieth centuries. Not knowing what to do with the few Indians left that had not been massacred, there was a serious debate in Congress as to whether we should massacre the rest. The alternative solutions were reservations and Native American boarding schools. Systematically, young Native Americans were taken from their families, removed to a distant location, and placed in boarding schools where they had their names changed, their hair cut, their clothing replaced, their language and religion changed, and their self-identity shredded. Still today, a great number of Native Americans are a mere generation away from the destructive results in this horrific experiment in cultural destruction.
- *The Nuclear Family.* Long before the nuclear bomb became a symbol of unspeakably destructive power, the social-work schools of the early twentieth century created a weapon of destruction out of the seemingly innocent image of the nuclear family, taking it upon themselves to define the ideal human family from a white point of view, and imposing it upon the life and lifestyle of people of color. The individualism that pervades white

culture, and is inherently present in this definition of family life, became a weapon to destroy the extended family in the culture of people of color. This power of the social welfare system to narrowly define family structure was—and still is—backed up by the power to enforce its imposition on others, even to the extent of having the authority to take a child away from any family that refuses to adhere to its rules and principles.

- *Heroes and Holidays.* Almost all our national heroes are white (and for the most part white men). Moreover, our holidays focus on white history and experience, and are interpreted from a white point of view that serves the purpose of preserving white power and privilege. Obvious examples are Columbus Day and Thanksgiving, which are direct celebrations of white dominance. Most other holidays, such as Christmas, Easter, and Presidents Day, are also viewed from very white perspectives.

- Dr. Martin Luther King Jr. is one of the very few persons of color we recognize as a national hero, and his birthday is the only major holiday in the United States for a person of color. Throughout our history, there has been little recognition or crediting of the many women and men of color whose strength, ingenuity, inventiveness, and leadership have contributed to our history, nor of the collective strength and labor that people of color have contributed in building our country.

- *Linguistic Racism.* Cultural racism is reinforced and perpetuated by the language we speak. In addition to the insistence on English as the only language recognized in the United States, there are literally hundreds of ways in the English language in which the word *white* signifies goodness and purity, while the word *black* signifies evil and uncleanness. Moreover, the debates and battles that rage continuously in our country about the place of the English language and other languages in society reflect our racism and our resistance to multicultural ways of life. Proponents of a multilingual country and culture have never resisted English as the primary language, nor have they suggested that all people should not learn English. The "English-only" movements that seek to suppress Spanish and other languages promote the incredible position that a person who speaks only one language is superior to the person who can speak two or more languages.

Appropriation without Accountability

During the entire time the white culture has been discounting and destroying the cultures of people of color, it has also been, in a twisted way, "appreciating" them—enough, at least, to "borrow" a great deal from them. "Borrowing" is far too mild a word to describe the way in which cultural aspects from other racial groups have been brought into the white community. Imitation, it is often said, is the highest form of flattery. But when the imitation is done with neither permission nor acknowledgment, and for a great deal of profit for the white community, and when it is accompanied by assertions that the culture from which it is taken is inferior, then imitation becomes the lowest form of racist theft.

In white America, many aspects of our culture, such as religion, fashion, style, music, dance, and language (especially slang), have been either directly appropriated or modified from cultural forms or ideas that began in communities of color. For example, there seems to be no end to appropriating aspects of Native American and Asian religious rites and traditions, as if they were for sale in a cultural marketplace. And it is easy to trace directly to their African American origins such music and dance forms as the Charleston and the Black Bottom in the 1920s, rock 'n' roll, the twist, disco, jazz, blues, and more recently rap and hip hop. But the decision to appropriate has always been made by the dominant white culture, and credit for the source is seldom given.

Underlying the issue of cultural appropriation is the deeper concern for accountability. Once an aspect of culture is taken from people of color and transferred to the dominant white culture, control by people of color tends to be lost as it becomes the property of those who did the appropriating. Whether it is an invention for which no credit is given to the inventor, or a musical or dance style for which the income goes into the pockets of the dominant culture, there is usually neither attribution nor payment, and even less accountability to the community of color from whence it came.

Positive and Negative Change in the Twenty-First Century

In order to understand the impact of cultural racism more clearly, we need to ask if it still affects our lives in the twenty-first century as it has for the past hundreds of years. In matters of cultural interaction, our society portrays itself, especially in the media, as being far different today than fifty years ago. U.S. society has been desegregated. Integration is the law of the land, and there are no longer supposed to be boundaries that prevent the cultural intersection of our lives. A measurable portion of our population now lives and works, plays and prays together across racial and cultural lines. Many schools are now multiracial and multicultural, some even boasting student bodies that speak beyond a hundred languages. Interracial marriages and multicultural children seem to be more visibly present among us. The youth of our land are listening to the same music, speaking the same slang, dancing the same dances, some even bragging, as though it were a good thing, that they do not notice any longer that they are a different color or culture.

However, conditions may not be as different as they are portrayed. Many of these changes have only come to a relatively small percentage of us—people of color and white people alike. The cultural curtain still surrounds and separates most of us from each other. In many, perhaps most, U.S. communities, the curtain has been barely ruffled by the winds of change. The majority of white people and people of color still live in *de facto* segregated communities, and lead completely separate lives. Residential and educational separation is still the reality for the majority of the U.S. population. Even though our lives are occasionally exposed to each other—we see each other on television, pass by each other on the streets and in department stores, perhaps even have colleagues we barely know in school or workplace—the default position of our lives is still measured by separateness, and our token intimacy seldom leaves a lasting impression or relationship.

Nevertheless, it is also clear that some significant steps forward have been taken. The cultural curtain, in some parts of our society, has been parted, and in some cases large portions have even been torn down. Wherever there are improved personal relationships, deeper understanding, greater acceptance, increased cooperation, and mutual trust, these can only be reason for celebration.

But at the same time, as we examine this "progress" more closely, we need to realize that not everyone in the white community or in communities of color believes these steps forward have been all that positive. It is the judgment of many people that the removal of the cultural curtain has not resulted in significant benefits for people of color, and for many has meant a step backward rather than forward. As we have suggested in previous chapters, so long as the underlying power structures of our society are still directed toward the preservation of white power and privilege, there will be a tendency to co-opt any well-intended changes to continue to serve the purposes of the dominant culture. Let's take look at a few ways in which that tendency has played out in recent years in the realm of cultural racism.

Integration: Another Word for Assimilation. "Two, four, six, eight, we don't want to integrate!" This was the chant of white counter-demonstrators in the days of the civil rights movement. But if these counter-demonstrators had known what the results of "integration" would be, they might have changed their chant. The criteria for integration and the determination of who gets to integrate have never left the control of the white society. In our white communities we have capitulated, gradually and in token measure, to demands for integration of our neighborhoods and schools and other aspects of our lives, as long as it does not change the way we live, and as long as those who come into the community are willing to change the way they live. Entry into the dominant culture has been permitted only to those people of color who "assimilate" aspects of white culture and adapt to the white society.

Kenji Yoshino, a professor at Yale Law School, gives the name of "covering" to this forced assimilation process. There is a demand made upon people of color and other minorities to "cover" their identity and to become what the dominant culture desires. Those who are unwilling to "cover" their identity will not be permitted to enter the society.

> In recent decades, discrimination in America has undergone a generational shift. Discrimination was once aimed at entire groups, resulting in the exclusion of all racial minorities, women, gays, religious minorities, and people with disabilities. A battery of civil rights laws—like the Civil Rights Act of 1964 and the Americans with Disabilities Act of 1990—sought to combat these forms of discrimination. The triumph of American civil rights is that such categorical exclusions by the state or employers are now relatively rare.
>
> Now a subtler form of discrimination has risen to take its place. This discrimination does not aim at groups as a whole. Rather, it aims at the subset of the group that refuses to cover, that is, to assimilate to dominant norms. And for the most part, existing civil rights laws do not protect individuals against such covering demands. The question of our time is whether we should understand this new discrimination to be harmful and, if so, whether the remedy is legal or social in nature.[3]

White Cultural Dominance Is Still in Place. In our efforts toward cultural integration, the fundamental issue of power has once again failed to be addressed. The white culture still arrogantly imposes itself on people of color and dictates the interaction between the cultures. Wherever one looks, it is possible to see this cultural dominance at work; for example:

- in the English-only movement that still insists on one language and one culture in this supposedly multicultural world;
- in the unwillingness to end the use of Indian names, religious symbols, and mascots by sports teams, as well as by the military in the naming of its most vicious weaponry;
- in the imposition of forms of tribal governments on Native Americans that are culturally devastating to Indian people;
- in the siphoning of music, dance, language, and other cultural expressions from people of color into the white community for profit-making purposes, as well as for shoring up our cultural vacuum;
- and perhaps most dramatically, as we shall explore more deeply in the next paragraphs, in programs of multicultural inclusiveness and diversity that have resulted in our society and its institutions looking more colorful, even while maintaining white power and white control.

Why Multicultural Diversity Is Failing

"Multicultural Diversity and Inclusiveness" is one of the most popular names given to intentional efforts during the past few decades to bring about cultural integration throughout our society. Since the mid-1980s, almost every level of society has emphasized inclusiveness of people of color, women, and other so-called minorities. By the turn of the twenty-first century, virtually every community and institution in our nation was placing very high importance on this subject. Today it is almost impossible to name a community or an institution that hasn't placed multicultural diversity somewhere on its top-ten priority list.

In many ways, the rest of the society has been following the leadership of the corporate world in these endeavors. As I mentioned earlier, in 1987, the Hudson Institute published a landmark study, *Workforce 2000*, which accurately forecasted changes that the American workforce would encounter with the new millennium. The study predicted that by the year 2000, the majority of the workforce in the United States would be people of color.[4] The response of the corporate world to these predictions was almost immediate. "Developing diversity" and "managing diversity" in the workplace quickly became required professional skills. It was not long before nearly everyone—schools, city halls, churches, social-service agencies, the entertainment industry, the media, and so forth—was following the corporate world's example.

In the name of multicultural diversity, nearly everyone observes special months, such as Black History Month and Hispanic History Month; race and ethnic studies are standard electives in high schools, colleges, and universities; ethnic food aisles can be found in the major food markets; and significant energy continues to be given to multicultural hiring practices in order to have multicultural workforces in most of our institutions. There is a multicultural committee or "table" in many, perhaps most, of our communities and institutions, where people of diverse cultural backgrounds can come together and plan how they will celebrate multicultural history, learn from each other's diversity, and have exchanges of choirs, food, and clothing.

Yet, despite all these efforts, there is still a sense that we have barely broken through the most superficial beginnings in these multicultural diversity programs. Sadly, the highest levels of employee diversity in our institutions are at the lowest level of employee status—secretaries, administrative assistants, and maintenance and cleaning personnel. The diversity rate rapidly diminishes into tokenism as one looks higher up the ladder to managerial positions where power and control are written in the job description. And, as discussed in the previous chapter, when a person of color *is* elected or appointed to a position previously held by a white person, the power of that position usually decreases measurably, whether it is a teacher in a classroom, a pastor of a parish, the director of a program, or a mayor of a city.

Problems of mistrust and misunderstanding plague most diversity efforts. People of color go out the back door of our institutions faster than they can be brought in the front door, their exit interviews reflecting that their experience of racism is just as serious a problem today as it ever was. Rodney King's question, "Why can't we just all get along?" becomes a plaintive plea of staff supervisors who are responsible for orchestrating and harmonizing diversity programs.

In efforts to overcome these difficulties with diversity, human relations professionals have created "multicultural diversity training programs" and "cultural competency programs" to help people get along. Cross-cultural exchange programs are developed in order to foster harmony and mutual understanding, especially on Martin Luther King's birthday and Black History Month. Portrayals of harmony are created by taking advantage of "photo opportunity moments" so that pictures of the two or three people of color within an institution can be placed on every promotional piece done for the public.

But most of these diversity programs turn out to be painfully difficult and ineffective efforts to get along, as the real issues of significant power sharing and mutual accountability are avoided like the plague. The cultural curtain that divides us is still firmly in place, keeping race-based cultures separated and controlled. So long as the cultural curtain is in place, our efforts in diversity will continue to be superficial efforts that take off the pressure for real change. It will remain the kind of diversity that helps white-controlled communities and institutions look more colorful and pretend to be nonracist. It will be a form of diversity that is racist and ultimately does not work.

We are in fact still a segregated society. Integration and cultural diversity represent only a thin layer of change. School districts with multiple languages and cultures are anomalous islands in an ocean of still separate and unequal education. Neighborhoods and communities that boast of balanced diversity are highly unusual and need to be regulated and manipulated to keep them that way. Workplace diversity is tentative and teetering. We can pretend otherwise, but it will be ultimately to our own disservice if we do so. We can hold up our anomalies and our carefully crafted images of diversity and pretend we are on the path to success, but it will not change the reality that the cultural curtain is still in place and cultural racism is still waiting to be dismantled.

The Race-Based Cultures of Communities of Color

Life Behind the Cultural Curtain

The cultural curtain is still in place. Cultural racism, taking a far more sophisticated form than in the days of segregation, still maintains the walls of division that keep race-based cultures separated from each other. And white culture is still the powerfully dominant culture that is in charge of how the race-based cultures interact with each other. On one side of the cultural curtain, in separated and segregated race-based communities, the collective cultural lives of African Americans, Native Americans, Latinos/Hispanics, Asian Americans, Arab Americans, and white people continue. What is presently happening to these separated race–based cultures fifty years after they were supposed to have been desegregated? What is going on behind the cultural curtain that hides our separated lives from each other? The process of desegregation opened a few doors to allow some "day passage" from one community to another, but what happens when we go home to our own communities and life continues in our separated "ghettos"? What is happening to the cultures in each of the people of color communities? What is happening to the white culture in the white community?

Since this is a book by a white person written primarily to white people about white reality and white racism, it is the last of these questions I primarily want to address: What is happening to the white culture in the white community? That will be the subject of the final section of this chapter.

First, however, as a way of encouraging readers to read, listen, and learn from spokespersons from communities of color, it seems important to reflect briefly on race-based cultural life and strength in communities of color, and point in the direction of settings in which that listening might take place. As I have stated before, I do not speak with authority about people of color, and the reader should keep in mind that anything written here by me about people of color is subject to correction by people of color. I depend very heavily in the following pages on the descriptions developed by Crossroads colleague and co-trainer Anne Stewart. In addition, the bibliography points to other resources in which people of color report on and interpret far more extensively the status of their race-based cultures.

Survival and Strength of People of Color

Ironically and tragically, one of the most serious negative effects of desegregation on communities of color has been to weaken cultural and community-based infrastructures that had been for centuries so important for surviving and resisting racism. Prior to desegregation, the system of racism isolated communities of color, and created the necessity of building new or strengthening existing infrastructures for survival. Then when desegregation opened doors and promised rewards of equal access and mutual cultural exchange, not only was the promise not paid off, but the very doors that were opened were the same doors that previously had served as gates of self-protection from white racism. Now the gates were down and the protection was gone. The result was a new vulnerability and a further weakening of the infrastructures that had provided some protection from racism for communities of color.

In recent years, responding to the false promises of desegregation and the reality of resegregation, new efforts are once again being made within each of these communities to rebuild their cultural infrastructures. Despite the destructive influences, these communities have been regaining a new kind of strength. More and more, people of color are seeking to rediscover and rebuild cultural identity and insist that it not be lost in the superficial and inadequate efforts to foster diversity in the United States.

Many white people are shocked when they see people of color resisting integration and assimilation and instead becoming increasingly conscious and ever more proud of their own culture identities. Anne Stewart lists three clear reasons why people of color maintain and hold onto their cultures, despite the forces that pull them in the opposite direction:

1. *In order to deal with the "Big White Lie" (not one of those "little white lies")*. It has become quite clear to the majority of people of color that it is quite simply a lie that if they learn to walk right, talk right, act right, dress right, if they are willing to forfeit their language, their heritage, their values, and other aspects of their cultural identity and become "Americanized," they will be allowed to pass through the cultural curtain and be "integrated" into the dominant culture. No matter how much they "cover" their identity, no matter how much they are coerced into assimilating and acting white, they will still be marked as "less than" because of their racialized identity.

2. *In order to maintain identity.* In the face of powerful forces that seek to destroy their collective identities, the need for people of color to maintain distinct cultures as a basis for survival has become even stronger. Culture is about having a home; culture is about claiming a community of people who also claim you. Culture is a way of locating where you really belong, and indicating who your people are. The need for a sense of identity is among the strongest of human needs. Having a distinct culture gives a person the ability to say, "This is who I am, and this is my people." The cultures of African Americans, Native Americans, Latinos/Hispanics, Asian Americans, and Arab Americans provide protective homes and the means of survival for those whom racism continues to oppress.

3. *In order to resist and struggle.* Maintaining a strong cultural identity is an essential element for rebuilding the movement to resist and struggle to end

racism. In the borderlands between white culture and the cultures of people of color, the struggle for justice is still being fought—a struggle against the evil forces of racism that remain strong in the twenty-first century. Down through the centuries, people of color have consistently and persistently organized to confront and demolish the powerful forces of racism. The civil rights movement and the other movements for change in the twentieth century did not complete the task; the new movements for change that are being organized today, including the struggle to dismantle cultural racism, have the goal of finishing the job that was begun and carried out for centuries before this one.

People of Color as Bicultural People

Another strength of people of color Anne Stewart lists is the capacity to be bicultural. In a nation that demands that people of color function to meet the needs of the white society, but at the same time provides few choices between assimilation and outright dismissal, being bicultural is another survival skill that has served people of color well.

Perhaps in one sense, all of us are to one degree or another bicultural. We all have a private and a public face. And we all develop skills to be polite and conform in the face of the formal demands of society, and to be a totally different person when we let our hair down with those who a trusted part of our crowd. Moreover, many people are quite proud of their ability to move in and out of two totally different cultures, even to speak fluently the language of each culture.

The bicultural character of communities of color is based on more than individual abilities, however. Rather, it is an expression of a collective way of life that for the sake of survival consistently instills in each of its members the skill of moving in and out of another way of life, and to come back "home" and to be at home at any time. "People got to eat," someone has said, and in order to have money for survival and beyond, people of color have to cross the line and function with full capacity in the white world. But people also have to have a home, family, and a place to sleep, and for most people of color, home is not in the white community where they have to go to work.

And so, the people of color whom we who are white know at work, who follow the norms of the white society, are probably totally different persons culturally when they go home. A person of color learns to speak two languages and has a clothes closet with two wardrobes—one that is appropriate for the white society and one that is appropriate for the Arab American, African American, Asian American, Native American, or Latino/Hispanic culture of which he or she is a member. All the cultural norms of how one speaks, when one speaks, how loudly or softly one speaks, how close one stands to the person to whom one is speaking, whether you look at the eyes of the person to whom one is speaking, how you walk, how you move, how you shake hands, and a thousand other things a person does at home are different from the way they are done in the white world.

Being bicultural means being able to live simultaneously in two different cultures. People of color in this country have to be at least bicultural, and often times more than that. At the same time, one can imagine that it is not easy to live such a dual life. Despite the well-honed skills of doing so, maintaining this dichotomy on the level of identity is often very difficult, for it constantly forces people of color to choose between their own culture and assimilating into white culture.

White Cultural Identity in the Twenty-First Century

The White Side of the Cultural Curtain

In the past several pages, we who are white have been visitors in cultural lands in which most of us are strangers, places where we can at best be guests and learners about the powerful lives of survival and strength of people of color. This final section in the exploration of cultural racism takes a look at the cultural land that is "our home"—white culture and what goes on in the white community. The white community is where you and I, the white readers and the white writer of this book, live and have our being. It is where we are at home and where we have a sense of belonging. We, too, like people of color, have a race-based culture that is our way of life.

From the beginning, the purpose of this book has been to turn the subject of racism around, to insist that a clear understanding of racism cannot be achieved by studying people of color alone, but by studying us, by studying the cause and effects of racism within the white society. Earlier in this chapter, while looking at the social identity mapping chart, I suggested that most of us who are white have been socialized to be unaware of the effects of race and racialization on our identity development. Yet it is one of the most significant factors in shaping who we are. Looking into a mirror, we need to have a conversation about ourselves, and to ask, after fifty years of desegregation and resegregation: What does it mean today to speak of a white cultural identity produced by the racialization of white people? We will now take a look behind the other side of the cultural curtain—the white side—and explore what white culture looks like today.

A Group Photograph

What is white culture? I want to reemphasize that this is not a question about each of us as individual white people, but rather about how we as white people look as a group, no matter how many individual variations and exceptions we may observe. In previous chapters, we addressed the individual question of how racism has had a personal impact on each of us. We asked, for example in chapter 4, how each of us individually was socialized to accept our racialized identity and to receive privileges based on our whiteness. Now we are asking questions about the impact of these experiences in terms of our group identity, how we live and act collectively as white people.

Of course, there are also deeply personal implications behind this question because each of us individually is a part of the collective white culture. We cannot step outside the white culture and talk about "them" when we are really talking about "us." It is imperative that the pronoun *we* be used to speak about white people and the white culture. We are talking about "our people."

For some of us, asking this question about our collective white identity and culture may be the most difficult task since the beginning of this book, and the hardest part of an analysis of racism for us to deal with. While you and I may be ready to confront our identities as individual white persons, it is far more difficult to view the white community as "our people." One reason for this is that when we accept our personal relationship as part of the white culture, the last protective barrier falls away that allows us to claim personal innocence; for when we accept our identity as part of a group, then we have to also accept responsibility and be accountable for what that group does.

How We Became Culturally White

There were two steps in our becoming a "white people." First we became legally white, and then we became a part of the white culture. When white people immigrate to or are born in the United States, we are automatically classified as legally white. We join a collective group of people that has been legally white since the beginning of our nation. As readers will remember from the discussion in previous chapters, the Caucasoid race was created along with the other races back in the sixteenth and seventeenth centuries. As a part of this process, white racial identity was invented in Europe and in the United States as a means of determining and justifying dominance over the rest of the so-called races in our society and the rest of the world.

The legal term at first used to identify us was simply "European." By the time of the writing of the U.S. Constitution, however, our legal collective racial identity was designated as "white," a way of distinguishing ourselves from others who were legally "nonwhite." Each time the Supreme Court with the stroke of a pen adjusted the definition of white identity, all white people were instantly redefined. From a legal point of view, white people have been repeatedly defined and redefined as a group, and no individual who is part of that group has been able to step away from the legal designation. Of course, because of the benefits of privilege gained by this designation, very few of us have ever wanted to do so.

The second question, beyond our legal status, is to ask, When and how did we become culturally white? This was not an instant happening, but a process that took place gradually, at different speeds, and in different ways for each of the national, ethnic, and religious groups that came from Europe to the American colonies, and then later to the United States. As each group gradually lost their European cultural identity and took on American identity, they became culturally white. Group by group, they divested themselves of their past identities and joined the large and powerful race-based culture group called "white."

As we explore the history of the entry of our various groups into cultural whiteness, we need to keep in mind that this step in white racialization was not so much a struggle against people of color, but rather a competition among white people about who was "whiter" than other white people. The designation as "legally white" had already settled the question of the status of all white people with regard to those designated "nonwhite." But the struggle to attain cultural white identity was an internecine contest for status between legally white people who already had the confidence of knowing that they were not red, yellow, black, or brown.

A White Melting Pot Shaped a White Culture

The shaping of a white culture in the United States is often described as a "melting-pot experience." Recently it has become popular, even though highly inaccurate, to describe the melting pot as a multiracial phenomenon in which all races get blended and amalgamated. That is not true and has never been so. The melting pot is, and has always been, an exclusively white phenomenon. It was never meant for anybody but European immigrants; it was (and still is) a pot reserved only for those who will emerge as white people when they come out of the melting experience. In the earlier days, "white people" referred only to northern Europeans, but later southern Europeans—Italians, Spanish, and Portuguese people—also became legally recognized as white people, and qualified for entrance into the melting pot.

The exclusive whiteness of the melting pot is reflected in Israel Zangwill's play, entitled *The Melting Pot*, written in 1906 and successfully produced on Broadway. The play views America as a crucible in which ethnic groups would be blended together and emerge as the "true Americans." Zangwill's cast of characters includes only Europeans; no people of color are included. Here are the final words of the play:

America is God's Crucible, the great Melting Pot where all the races of Europe are melting and reforming! Here you stand, good folk, think I, when I see you at Ellis Island, here you stand, in your fifty groups, with your fifty languages and histories, and your fifty blood hatreds and rivalries. But you won't be long like that, brothers, for these are the fires of God. A fig for your feuds and your vendettas! German and Frenchmen, Irishmen and English, Jews and Russians, into the Crucible with you all. God is making the American!

. . . The real American has not yet arrived. . . . He will be the fusion of all the races, perhaps the coming superman. . . . Ah, what is the glory of Rome and Jerusalem, where all the races come to worship and look back, compared with the glory of America, where all nations come to labor and look forward. *[From below comes up the softened sound of voices and instruments joining in "My Country, 'tis of Thee." The curtain falls slowly.]*[5]

The transition to whiteness began first and happened most quickly for colonists from England. White culture was first defined by the growing distinctions between those who were British and those who were the colonists. It became rapidly clear that a "Yankee" was someone quite different from British. Even the English language in the United States took on significant differences as the culture of white America evolved.

Other groups of European immigrants followed different paths to become culturally white. One particularly clear example of this is the history of Irish immigrants, as has been documented in Noel Ignatiev's book, *How the Irish Became White.*[6] Because of their persecution by the English in their homeland of Ireland, the Irish were the only northern European immigrants to the United States who were considered to be of another race. Up and down the Atlantic coast, one would find signs placed in front of public establishments stating, "No colored or Irish allowed," and advertisements for employment often had the postscript, "No colored or Irish wanted." Because of this common racial oppression, Irish people had an almost instant political bond with African slaves.

Then the leaders of the Irish community made an exciting discovery: they could become white. With practice and diligence, hard work and good organizing, they could gradually qualify for the melting pot and join the white race. They broke their bond with African slaves, and especially in the northeastern cities of Boston, New York, and Philadelphia, they organized and created political power. Step by step, they worked toward acceptance as white people. Many Irish people would claim that the final step to whiteness was completed in 1960, when John Fitzgerald Kennedy was elected President of the United States.

But not only the British and the Irish; it is an interesting and enlightening exercise to explore the historical process by which each of our national, ethnic, and religious groups entered the melting pot and took on the cultural identity of whiteness. For example:

- People of German heritage became culturally white especially during the times of special effort made during World War I and World War II to divest themselves of any mark of German identity.
- The transition of people of Scandinavian heritage—Norway, Sweden, Denmark, and Finland—is part of the history of rural America, as has been popularly portrayed by Garrison Keillor.
- For people of Polish background it happened in various ways, depending upon geographic locations in the United States; there are neighborhood pockets in cities like Chicago where one gets the feeling that the transition from Polish culture has barely begun to take place.
- Other Eastern Europeans passed through enormous struggles of cultural transition as they passed through the "hell's kitchens" of our nation's cities.
- Southern Europeans—especially Italian, Spanish, and Portuguese peoples —as they became legally defined as white, also entered the slow process of becoming identified culturally as white.
- Even Jewish people, although they were also experiencing the vicious and powerful forces of anti-Semitism, have gradually found their way into white cultural identity, as Karen Brodkin describes in her book *How Jews Became White Folks and What That Says about Race in America.*[7]

I do not wish to understate the difficulties and oppressive limitations faced by southern Europeans and especially Jews in entering into the melting pot and finding gradual acceptance within white culture. As with people of color, so also for many white people, assimilation has been as much a coercive process as a willing exchange for privilege. As stated by sociologist Rachel Luft:

> During the first half of the twentieth century, from the large migration of Eastern European Jews in the first two decades until after WWII, Jews were in an ambiguous, liminal racial category in the United States, which again highlights the fluidity and politics of racial categorization. Jews were systematically excluded from residential integration and early suburbanization (housing covenants), upward mobility (university quotas), and social integration (private clubs). The fact that this happened on quasi-racial grounds also helps to highlight the fact that although certain groups have eventually been invited into whiteness, again it is a whiteness with qualifiers—it is possible to be

more white (Christian, Anglo, German, etc.) and less white (Jewish, Italian, non-Christian, etc). The transitional period of the 1950s, in which some Jews began to "pass" into whiteness—name changes, nose jobs, moving out of the city, etc.—highlights the centrality of assimilation as a racial border-crossing mechanism allowed to some groups and not to others. As we know from other contexts, border-crossing usually consists of both push and pull factors.[8]

Nevertheless, it is by and large true for all of us. When we entered the melting pot, we were Europeans of many nationalities and ethnicities. At the exit, we were all people of the same white race and the same white culture. Our European identities were, for the most part, so fused together as to become almost indistinguishable in the mainstream white American culture.

What We Gained and What We Lost in the Melting Pot

In order to understand this fusing process better, and especially our willingness to participate in it, there are two questions we need to probe a bit further:

- What did we gain in the transformation into a race called white?
- And what, if anything, did we lose by becoming white?

What Did We Gain? There are clear and obvious reasons we so readily and so willingly ran toward and jumped into the melting pot and there are very specific rewards for becoming white. As white people we gained identification with the collective power of the people who were legally declared to be the ones who deserved the resources of this land. The melting pot qualified us for everything that is reserved for white people in our society—namely white power and privilege.

What have we gained from the melting pot that made us white? What is it that we really like about being white, and would have a difficult time giving up if suddenly we were not white anymore? These questions are not all that difficult to answer. If you, the white reader, have accepted the basic argument throughout this book, then even though it is hard at first to say it out loud, then you will recognize that what we have gained is everything that white people have more of in this country than do people of color. A list of what we have gained from our whiteness would be simply to restate the white privileges that we listed in chapter 3. Although the list could go on almost forever, predominant on the list would be:

- our freedom of choices
- our economic status and advantages

- our access to and control of institutions
- our quality of education
- the safety of our children
- our better housing
- our being represented by elected officials
- our lack of being discriminated against because of our race
- our protection by the police and the courts
- our freedom of movement
- our being what is accepted as "normal"
- and a thousand other things that have become the possession of the white society just because we are white

What we have gained and still gain from white culture is a way of life that provides power and privilege for our special existence. This is what we have gained and this is what we really like about being white, and would have a hard time giving up if we were not white. Because of our socialization, we may want to deny it; we may want to say we have these things because we have worked hard and earned them. We want to say no, this is not true, but can we? Can we deny that so much of what we have as a collective group comes to us because we are white? Of course, there are great variations because of gender discrimination, economic class differences, and many other factors, but in the final analysis there can be no denying that power and privilege are the primary identifying marks of the race-based culture that was forged in the white melting pot.

And What Did We Lose? But there is a second and far more important question: What have we lost? What did we lose in the melting-pot experience of becoming a collective called "white"? Are we who are white aware that we lost anything because of the melting-pot experience that made us into white people? Are we aware of having lost anything as a result of racism? I believe there is no more important question in this book than this.

What have we lost by being white? I deeply believe that at the root of our white cultural identity, underneath our white power and privilege, is a nearly fatal cultural loss and an ultimate powerlessness.

To begin with, entering the melting pot required the renunciation of all our former cultural and national heritages. Several decades ago, the TV movie *Roots,* from Alex Haley's book of the same title, depicted the heartbreaking pain and difficulty for African Americans who, because of their enforced enslavement and subsequent cultural and identity losses, were unable to trace their heritage and the source of their African identity.[9] The response by white people to this movie was astounding. It awakened an awareness that, because of the melting-pot experience, white people also have lost former heritages and cultures. As a result, a great wave of activity began in which white people began to attempt to trace and seek to recover their memories and the values of a lost heritage.

When our foreparents came over from Europe and went through Ellis Island, they were told that if they wanted to make it here, they had to conform, they had to learn English, and they had to renounce the past and learn to be Americans. Many of our European forebearers even anglicized their names as they gave up their European cultural identity in order to be white.

As a result of the melting-pot experience, in varying degrees, we who are now white lost our languages, our previous national identities, and our ethnic heritages; we gave up our European cultures, our ways of life, our values, and the richness of the past. In many ways, we have even lost our memories of what once was. Our foreparents were called upon to reject, often with shame, the roots of the past. Then, two or three generations after their arrival, the memory of a former way of life virtually disappeared. Many of us have become hybrids who cannot even trace where we originally came from.

But something even more serious happened to our foreparents as they came through the immigration lines at Ellis Island and other points of entry into the United States. They became infected with a deadly disease called white supremacy.

There is a myth, often stated with a sense of pride, that former generations of white people arrived from Europe in a state of great destitution and, starting from the "bottom of the ladder," worked their way toward the top. Actually, that is not accurate. What they actually learned is that they would not have to start at the bottom, but only *near* the bottom, at the third or fourth rung. They quickly learned that there were others who were worth even less who would always remain at the bottom of the ladder—the nonwhite people who were below them and would always be below them. As white people fought their way up the ladder, they learned to be cruel and despising toward people of color, who would always be less than the poorest white people. The poorest of white immigrant learned to say with pride and arrogance, "I may be poor, but I ain't black." At Ellis Island, among the first lessons to be learned was the lesson of racism.

What did the melting pot take from us? In the melting pot, we lost our innocence, our sense of authenticity, and a crucial part of that which makes us human. Because we wanted the power and the privileges so desperately, we hardly even noticed the destruction and loss of all we once were, the process of grinding us up, heating us to a melting point, stripping us of everything, and spitting us out the other end with a new identity called white. And the first requirement of whiteness was a willingness to be racist.

White Culture: An Imprisoned Culture

As we look at our losses as white people, some of us might have a tendency to be defensive. During a discussion of white culture in an antiracism workshop, a white person asked, "How much longer is this attack on us white people going to take place?" My response was that we were not attacking white people, but looking at how racism and the process of racialization has hurt white people as well as people of color. I reminded the person that racism has racialized and misshaped the identity of all of us, people of color and white people alike. Rather than defend our whiteness as if it were our friend, we must learn to see our white racial identity and our white culture as an imposed and dangerously divisive social construct that is designed to alienate us from the rest of humanity and the rest of humanity from us. Attempting to understand this is not "attacking" white people, but attacking the power of racism that is destroying us all.

We need to remember from our discussion in chapter 4 that as individuals, we who are white did not choose our racial identity any more than did people of color, but it was imposed on us when we were born, and we were socialized into participation in the white collective while we were still too young to resist. In the language of our definition of racism, we are still looking at the results of Power[3] in its shaping of who we are.

We acquired our collective white identity through the same racialization or "lumping" process that happened to people of color. We came from many cultures, languages, ethnicities, and nations in Europe, all of which were replaced by a new white identity based upon the myth of race. The white identity that took the place of all these past identities is not an identity based upon nationalities, ethnicities, or cultures of the past, but rather a new identity based upon race, color, and a myth called white supremacy. We were fused together into this new identity in the melting-pot experience, and our white racial identity became our legal proof of authenticity and our source of power. More important, all other factors of our identity, including our nationality, our class, and our culture were either lost or redefined through the lens of our whiteness.

I am suggesting that our white racial identity is an imprisoning identity. When we look at our name—"white people"—we are analyzing a descriptive adjective that we did not ask for and do not need to defend. We are looking at racism's destructive power over us and its ability to define our individual and collective racial identity. The prison of racism makes us be and do things we don't want to be and do. We do not need to defend the impact of racialization upon us any more than we would want to defend a disease. When we examine white cultural identity, we are asking how whiteness has been a source of injury and harm, not only for people of color, but also for ourselves as white people. The cultural curtain has harmed not only people of color by locking them out, but has also harmed us by locking us in.

We who are white live behind a cultural curtain in a white cultural ghetto, in a separated, cut-off state of existence. Our lifestyle is dramatically affected by white racism. Almost everything about our way of life would be very different without cultural racism and our retreat behind the cultural curtain. Every aspect of our lives has been distorted by our own racial/cultural isolation. Our culture embodies a lifestyle and a set of problems that result directly from our confinement in a prison built by racism. We have been separated by our white identity. The language we speak, the food we eat, the people we marry, the songs we sing, and the organizations we belong to are all unique because of our separate residential and cultural life. And they would be very different if we did not live behind a cultural curtain.

Our cultural isolation not only prevents us from sharing in the riches of other cultures in the United States; it also drains the authenticity from our own cultural expressions, leaving behind an increased blandness and weakness. It takes only one evening of television, or one day in a public-school classroom, or a walk through a suburban shopping mall to recognize the deterioration of our values, the insipid nature of much of our self-expression, and the ugliness we often create out of our affluence. Isolated, sterile, and devoid of stimulation behind our cultural curtain, our lives are increasingly flabby, boring, dishonest, and corrupt.

Going Home to Free Our Own People
People of color often ask this question: "Why would white people want to give up racism? It has been so very good to them. It has given them all this power and privilege. Why do you think white people would want to change?" It's a good question. Why would we want to change? Is there something in it for us, or is it just an altruistic sacrifice required of us for the sake of people of color? What would make us motivated to join the struggle to end racism?

I would suggest that our ability to come out at the end of this book with a purpose and a plan of action to dismantle racism is dependent on how we deal with this question. The answer to this question depends upon what we think we lost and what we think we gained by racism. It depends on how we react to the discussion in the previous paragraphs, which suggest that we may have gained a lot of privileges from racism, but that we have also lost a great deal—our past, our heritage, our access to an authentic culture.

Furthermore, I believe the answer to this question, Why would we want to give up racism? depends on how we define what it means to be human. I would suggest that our own freedom and our own humanity are at stake in the struggle to end racism. If we understand that we are damaged and destroyed by racism and that racism strips us individually and collectively of our humanity, then we might see how much we will benefit by the end of racism. If we define life by the acquisition of the white privileges granted to us by white power, however, then we might be hard pressed to think of ending racism as anything other than a sacrifice.

Here is another place where profound honesty is required of us. I believe that in the socialization process that imposed our racial identity in us, an unconscious message was inscribed inside us individually and collectively as white people. That message is: "*With racism we gain, and with the end of racism we will lose.*"

How that message got there and how we can erase it are very important questions. But first we need to recognize that the message *is there*—written so deeply and hidden so well that we can barely perceive its presence. Even if we are committed to ending racism, the message is still there, and it is repeated subliminally and incessantly: when racism is gone the rewards of racism will be taken away. Our hesitancy in ending racism betrays us; we really believe that even though the whole of humanity may benefit from the end of racism, it will inevitably be a loss for white people. Why else would we call it a sacrifice to end racism? Why else would we invent such phrases as "reverse racism" to describe an incremental loss of our illicit white power?

Our ability to work for the ending of racism depends on our being able to turn this message around. We need to be able to say with clarity and with courage: "*With racism we lose, and with the end of racism we will gain.*"

Not only people of color, but also we who are white lose with racism. We lose our humanity, our authenticity, and our freedom. And with the end of racism we can gain back our humanity, our authenticity, and our freedom. Rather than losing power, we will gain the ability to use power rightly and to share power willingly. And instead of sacrificing private privileges, we will gain and share with equality the human rights of everyone.

Cultural racism has formed two kinds of ghettos, both suffering losses that cannot be overcome so long as they are isolated from each other. The tearing down of the cultural curtain is an urgent necessity for both sides. We must cross our segregated cultural boundaries in order to learn to be different.

But we must start with ourselves and with each other. There is no individual escape. Only as we build new relationships within the white community and with our white sisters and brothers will we be able to move forward. The cultural curtain will not be lifted, at least voluntarily, until there is a deep sense of need within the white community to come out of our isolation. It will happen only when we become aware of how much we are losing and how much there is to gain from co-participating in the creation of a truly American culture. This is the beginning of our path to freedom, as we shall explore in the next chapter on dismantling racism.

7

DISMANTLING RACISM

There is a time for everything, and a season for every activity under heaven. . . . a time to tear down and a time to build. . . .

—Ecclesiastes 3:1, 3 (NIV)

A Time to Tear Down . . . and a Time to Build

To study racism is to study walls. In every chapter of this book, we have looked at barriers and fences, restraints and limitations, ghettos and prisons, bars and curtains. We have examined a prison of racism that confines us all—people of color and white people alike. Victimizers as well as victims are in shackles. The walls of the prison forcibly separate communities of color and white communities from each other, as well as divide communities of color from each other. In our separate prisons we are all shut off from each other. The constraints imposed on people of color by subservience, powerlessness, and poverty are inhuman and unjust; but the effects of uncontrolled power, privilege, and greed that are the marks of our white prison inevitably destroy white people as well.

To dismantle racism is to tear down walls. The walls of racism can be dismantled. We are not condemned to an inexorable fate, but are offered the vision and the possibility of freedom. Brick by brick, stone by stone, the prison of individual, institutional, and cultural racism can be destroyed. It is an organizing task that can be accomplished. You and I are urgently called to join the efforts of those who know it is time to tear down, once and for all, the walls of racism.

The walls of racism must be dismantled. Facing up to these realities offers new possibilities, but refusing to face them threatens yet greater dangers. The results of centuries of national and worldwide colonial conquest and racial domination, of military buildups and violent aggression, of over-consumption and environmental destruction may be reaching a point of no return. The moment of self-destruction seems to be drawing ever more near, nationally and globally. A small and predominantly white minority of the global population derives its power and privilege from the sufferings of the vast majority of peoples of color. For the sake of the world and ourselves, we dare not allow it to continue.

Dismantling racism also means building something new. It means building an antiracist society. The bricks that were used to build the walls of the prison must now be used for a better purpose. Just as we must tear down the wall brick by brick, so also we must build new structures of power and justice. Although we still need many more reminders that we cannot build a multiracial and multicultural society without tearing down the walls of racism, this negative reminder must be turned around and stated in reverse: we cannot tear down the walls without building new antiracist structures of power in our institutions and communities. Transforming and building anti-racist institutions is the path to a racism-free society.

After six chapters of defining and analyzing racism, of remembering and reinterpreting the past, and removing the disguises that prevent us from seeing the present, we are now ready to explore this double task of dismantling racism and working toward the future by building a racism-free society.

Survival and Escape from Prison

A person in prison is faced with two persistent and burning questions. The first question is, How do I survive in here? The second question is, How do I get out? Inside a prison, a prisoner must work hard to stay alive mentally, spiritually, intellectually, and physically. At the same time, a prisoner never stops thinking about getting out, either by completing the sentence or by escaping.

Trapped inside the prison of racism, both of these questions are appropriate for all of us—people of color and white people alike. How do we survive? And how do we get out? As long as we are bound within the prison of racism, how do we endure and counteract its devastating effects on all of us? But even more important, how do we escape? How do we end racism? How do we dismantle and destroy this abominable and vicious prison that oppresses and confines all people of color and all white people in our society? These questions suggest the two sections of the discussion about dismantling racism in this final chapter.

1. *Building Antiracist Communities of Resistance.* The first part of this chapter will deal with issues of survival, freedom, and resistance within the prison of racism. It will focus on building new personal identities and new communities of people committed to resisting racism, even while surrounded by racism's forbidding walls.

2. *Planning a Jailbreak: Dismantling Institutional Racism.* The second part of the chapter is about planning a jailbreak, about dismantling the prison of systemic racism. It will focus on community and institutional transformation and on the organizing skills and organizing tasks required in order to make transformation take place.

Making a Path by Walking on It

No one has all the answers on how to end racism. There is no instant way to bring racism to a screeching halt. All of us involved in the struggle to end racism are "making a path by walking on it." What is presented here is the result of my personal experience with Crossroads Ministry and with the People's Institute for Survival and Beyond in building antiracist communities and organizing to dismantle racism. It is a report on the creating of new paths by a rather large number of people over the past several decades. I hope it can make a contribution to the thinking and action of others in the future.

Most of the discussion in this chapter is addressed to both white people and people of color and our need to be together and work together on this path toward dismantling racism. In previous chapters, major sections have been directed specifically to white people with a particular goal of understanding racism in the white community and from a white perspective. In this chapter, although there are a few places where it is still necessary to focus directly on the situation of white people, the primary focus will be upon the building of multiracial communities to resist and dismantle institutionalized racism.

Building Antiracist Communities of Resistance

Survival Inside Racism's Prison

Personal transformation and the building of communities of resistance begin inside the prison walls. It is not possible to address the question of how to break down the walls of racism's prison until we have first dealt with our own issues from within the prison. The trek toward freedom commences while we are still in chains.

There is a strange and wonderful dual nature to freedom. In a very real sense, it can be held onto even when it has been taken away. No matter what a person's situation inside a prison's walls—behind bars, in solitary confinement, bound by chains—it is possible to hold onto one's freedom. It is possible to be free inside a prison. Whether one is justly or unjustly imprisoned, it is the power of the state to do as it pleases, even take away a person's life. But, as a great many prisoners down through the centuries have demonstrated, no matter how dehumanizing or enslaving, the warden and the guards do not have ultimate control over a person's essential humanity and freedom.

Witnesses to this truth abound. St. Paul's great dissertations on freedom were written from a jail cell. Mahatma Gandhi and Martin Luther King Jr. taught and demonstrated that being in prison can even be a means of promoting freedom. Nelson Mandela, after twenty-one years in prison, emerged to demonstrate that his identity as a free person had been strengthened in prison. And during three hundred years of bondage, enslaved Africans in the United States never lost sight of freedom, and proclaimed in their spirituals that their slave masters could "kill the body but not the soul."

This amazing dual nature of freedom applies also to our imprisonment within the system of racism. For people of color and white people alike, it is possible to become a free person, though still restricted within the prison walls of systemic and institutionalized racism. It is possible to break the shackles of lies, to be no longer deceived, no longer controlled by anesthetizing and brainwashing. A person of color can break the control of the internalization of racist oppression. A white person can wake up to the reality of white power and privilege and resist the internalization of racism.

It is possible to be simultaneously imprisoned and free. It is possible to be an unwilling, uncooperative prisoner, straining against the chains, refusing any longer to be anesthetized against the pain of imprisonment, and working to rid one's self of the countless effects of racist programming in a lifelong, step-by-step process. Vibrant and alive even while still contained by racism's iron bars, we can all begin to experience freedom and transformed lives, and prepare ourselves along with our fellow prisoners to participate in the long-term struggle for freedom.

Above all it must be clear that the process of becoming free while still within the prison cannot be accomplished alone. It is not an individual or private achievement. Freedom within the prison is a relational process that calls for the building of community inside the prison, a community of fellow prisoners who support and strengthen each other, a community of resistance committed to the struggle against racism. And, as we shall see later in this chapter, the ultimate escape from and destruction of the prison is even more dependent upon united and collective antiracist organizing efforts.

Antiracism: The Opposite of Racism

Since the words *antiracism* and *antiracist* will be used extensively in this chapter, a bit of an introduction and explanation may be required. "Antiracism," in contrast to "nonracism," is used here to express the opposite, or the antithesis of racism. The language of antiracism has become very important in recent years for people at work at the task of dismantling racism.

"Antiracism" is a word that describes the work of dismantling racism, and "antiracist" describes a person or a people who are committed to the task of bringing racism to an end. Antiracism is the exciting and powerful work of tearing down the systemic and institutional barriers of injustice that divide us. Antiracism is long-term work that has been carried out by antiracist people in our society for centuries, and that needs to be continued until the prison of racism has been completely eliminated.

Of course, antiracism is not the only name associated with dismantling racism. There are other similar or comparable expressions that are used by individuals and organizations working to end racism, phrases such as "undoing racism," "resisting racism," or "erasing racism." What all these phrases have in common is they describe a process, an active task of dismantling racism. Using the words *antiracism* and *antiracist* makes it clear that dismantling racism is an active task. Racism cannot end by passive dismissal or wishful dreams; rather, dismantling racism is an active verb that calls for intentional and collective organizing action to work for its elimination.

Far too often in our society, "nonracism" is defined as the opposite of racism. Nonracism is wrongly portrayed as an easily achieved state of being by any white person who decides not to participate in racism and who simply wants everyone to get along with each other. I have attempted to show in previous chapters that trying to achieve the status of nonracist is an impossible dream of individualistic escape into innocence. So long as the systems and institutions of our society are structured and functioning to provide power and privilege for the white society, and so long as all people of color continue to be systemically subjected to racism's destructive power, there are no private escapes, no private paths to purity; there can be no claims of nonracism by white people in our society.

I have often noted that white people have difficulty using this word *antiracist*. We who are white are much more comfortable with the word *nonracist*, and we want to use it to replace *racist*. As I have already stated in earlier chapters, however, a white person claiming to be a nonracist is denying reality. If we seek to become individually nonracist as a way of escaping from racism, we are trying to separate ourselves from the problem, while doing little or nothing to end racism. So long as the prison of racism exists, everyone is inside; there can be no such thing as a nonracist, and it is a waste of time trying to become one. Trying to be seen as a nonracist by others is just another way of being racist.

For white people considering the words *antiracism* and *antiracist*, the crucial question is not whether we can escape our identity as racists but what more we can be *in addition to* being racist. Robert Terry, as one of the earliest white leaders who understood what it means for us to "go home and free our own people," put it this way:

> I am not personally offended when someone says being White in America makes me a White racist. That is true. I am offended, however, if someone says that is all I am. That is not true. I am both a racist and an antiracist, and, as an antiracist, strongly committed to the elimination of racism.[1]

White readers: reread these words, try them on, and test them. See if they are words that you can own. Yes, I am a racist; that is inescapable. But a racist is not all that I am. There is far more to my identity than that. I am a person who is also an antiracist. I am a person who is committed and dedicated to the exciting and liberating task of resisting racism and of dismantling and tearing down the system of racism that traps me in this racist identity.

Becoming an Antiracist People

Of course, the eventual objective is nonracism—a racism-free society. This vision needs to be always before us. But instead of distancing ourselves from racism and searching futilely for a place where racism does not exist, the way to get rid of racism is to plant our feet squarely in the middle of where racism exists and work for its elimination.

This is a task for antiracist people. It is the only path for people of color and white people who acknowledge their imprisonment in this diabolical state of racism. Antiracism is the long-term process of tearing down, brick by brick, the structures of white power and privilege and the systems of oppression of people of color that have been in place in our society for centuries, and of rebuilding them as structures and systems that resist racism and intentionally share power equally.

Becoming antiracist begins by taking on a new identity. Although antiracism also requires *action* against racism, it is first of all a new *identity* for individuals and for communities. As an individual, antiracist is not only something I can *do*, but it is someone I can *be*. Antiracist is a new name for a person who becomes committed to resisting racism and ultimately escaping from the prison of racism. Antiracist communities are made up of people who are antiracists working in concert with others for the prison's eventual destruction. Only antiracist individuals who are part of antiracist communities of resistance can be free people inside the prison, working for the prison's ultimate destruction, working toward the elimination of racism in people and institutions.

In previous chapters, I described the destructiveness of racism's Power[3] as a socializing influence that implants in all of us—white people and people of color alike—a racialized identity that supports the construct of racism. Now, in order to counter and overcome the identities given to us by Power[3], it is important for all of us to claim the freedom and power of this new antiracist identity.

Thus, in this chapter "antiracist" and "antiracism" are primary words that will be used to describe the identity of people who are surviving racism's imprisonment and dismantling the walls of racism's prison. And, later, "antiracist" is the word I will also use to describe the nature of the new society and its systems and institutions that we need to build. An institution needs to be permanently antiracist in its design, structure, and functions.

Antiracist Identity Is a Positive Identity

As we further reflect on our work as antiracists, it is very important to understand and affirm that antiracist is not negative, but a very positive identity. It is fairly common for people who are exposed for the first time to this concept of antiracism to ask: Why do we have to express it so negatively? Isn't there a term that is more positive? I don't want to be "anti" anything; I want to be "for" something.

There is a simple response to these questions: antiracism is positive. It is very positive to be against something as evil as racism. It is a very important affirmative activity to resist racism and to work for its demise and its deconstruction and to build something new in the place where it once stood. Being against racism is a good thing. Before we can work for additional positive expressions of relations between white people and people of color, we have to positively affirm our opposition to racism.

In our society, there is widespread acceptance of other "anti" words like *anti*biotic and *anti*war as very positive expressions. But some people find it harder to express the same feelings toward antiracism. It should be noted that this seems to be a problem particularly—or perhaps exclusively—for white people. People of color seldom or never have difficulty understanding that being against racism is a good thing. White people who are trying on this new identity and considering a long-term commitment to it need to also come to an understanding that an antiracist identity is a very positive thing.

Antiracist Communities of Resistance

Antiracists exist and work together in community. There can never be such a thing as a "lone ranger" antiracist. Individualism and antiracism are mutually contradictory. The work of dismantling racism is always the work of a collective. An antiracist responds to a call from an antiracist community, and is also called to be a builder of antiracist community.

I will use the term "antiracist community of resistance" in the following pages to refer to what is usually at first a small group of people in an institution or in a geographic area who come together in response to their experience of racism within their particular setting. Their setting may be, for example, a school, business, social-service agency, church, governmental agency, neighborhood, or city. This *ad hoc* group of people might begin to come together for mutual support, but the hope is that they will develop into an organizing group. Ultimately, the central purpose of antiracist communities of resistance is to become long-term organizers to dismantle racism and to build new structures of racial justice in the setting in which they exist.

Antiracist communities of resistance are multiracial and multicultural. They are composed of antiracist people from communities of color and from the white community. They are made up of people who have discovered they can share the same name and the same identity of "antiracist." It is especially important to remember that there have always been white people—even though few in number—who joined the company of people of color in struggles to resist racism. Even though, as we shall see in a moment, there are times when white people and people of color need to be apart in order to carry out separate responsibilities, we must all first become rooted together in a unified antiracist community.

Building communities of resistance in order to deal with racism is not new to people of color. It has been a primary means of survival for centuries. For most white people, however, it is a new idea and experience. As long as we are anesthetized and in denial about the effects of racism on us, we usually think that resisting racism is only a need for communities of color. But when we tear down the curtains of denial and expose the reality that white people are also imprisoned and controlled by racism's power, it is possible to see that survival and resistance are an urgent need for white people as well as for communities of color.

Antiracist communities of resistance are being organized in many places throughout the United States. The examples I will refer to have come into being as a result of the training and organizing work by Crossroads Ministry and People's Institute for Survival and Beyond. Many hundreds of antiracism communities of resistance have been formed throughout the United States by these two organizations. Further description of these two organizations can be found in the resource section at the end of this book. There are also other anti-racism organizations besides Crossroads and People's Institute who are building such communities, but these are the ones whose experience I draw upon in this book and especially in the following pages. Many of these antiracist communities of resistance are leadership teams that have been formed and trained within institutions. Others are community-based organizing groups in cities, towns, and rural areas in almost every state. Some have been in existence for decades. Others have more recently come into being.

Building Blocks of Antiracist Community

Building a multiracial antiracist community of resistance is not easy; it requires a great deal of intentionality and discipline. Racism has kept us separated for so long it does not come to us naturally to be together. All the forces of society still work to keep us apart. There are great difficulties in communicating with each other, trusting each other, and depending upon each other. Building multiracial antiracist community takes work.

Antiracist communities of resistance are also "laboratories of learning," developing and testing principles of antiracist community building and antiracist organizing. Their experiences are helping others to build antiracist communities. What are some of the principles derived from the experiences of these groups? What follows is a list of building blocks of antiracist communities of resistance:

1. Developing a common analysis of racism. The most important first step in building antiracist community is to agree on a common analysis of racism, which will be the lens for the antiracism community to look at racism's reality. Such an analysis of racism must be based upon the teaching and experiences of communities of color, and must include (as this book has tried to include) an understanding of historical and systemic racism as it is manifested individually, institutionally, and culturally.

A common and collective analysis of racism does not come easily. An analysis does not get created by committee and cannot be based on perceptions that are the result of past socialization. Although reading a book about racism can certainly be helpful, it is not enough to create and shape a shared analysis. The only way I know to build a common analysis of racism is through participation in antiracism training workshops—usually a two- or three-day collective experience. The purpose and function of an antiracism training workshop is not just teaching and learning, but to help a group of people understand how a shared analysis can be a powerful instrument of shaping, strengthening, and preserving the life of antiracist community.

2. Undoing internalized socialization. Building antiracist community requires working hard at developing cross-racial relationships. In chapter 4, we discussed the socializing effects of racism's Power[3], using the name of "Internalization of Racism" for white people and "Internalization of Racist Oppression" for people of color. Our socialization has caused all of us—white people and people of color alike—to have distorted self-understandings and dysfunctional relationships within and across racial lines. The ongoing process of building antiracist community must serve the function of "deprogramming" our socialization and enabling new self-understanding and new cross-racial relationships to be strengthened.

One important way of addressing this need is through a disciplined "caucusing" process in which white people and people of color dedicate time to be apart from each other, with the objective of each group helping participants identify and deal therapeutically with negative socialization and building new antiracist self-images and identities. The result of this caucusing process is that the separate groups are then prepared to come together with more effective cross-racial relationships. The experiences of Crossroads Ministry and People's Institute for Survival and Beyond with the caucusing process, along with guidance for new groups to do this work, are available from each of the organizations.[2]

Healing almost always involves pain. Recovering from the effects of internalized socialization means taking away the anesthesia and welcoming the opportunity to feel again, even if it also includes feeling pain. Antiracists must be willing to give up the anesthesia that deadens our nerves and prevents us from feeling the reality of racism's prison. When we become aware of the ways in which racism hurts and destroys us, and how it uses us to hurt and destroy others, we will increasingly be unable to tolerate the prison. Above all, I want to reemphasize that the end-goal of dealing separately with each group's internalization is to enable the building of new relationships between people of color and white people.

3. Learning to be accountable. In building antiracist communities, new relationships of power and accountability need to develop. This is another difficult task, and therefore must be an important and consistent part of the discussion, reflection, and action of an antiracist community. For white people, it is an entirely new learning to be accountable to communities of color. And for people of color, dealing with mutual power and mutual accountability are also not easy.

As discussed in previous chapters, white people are socialized to not believe, trust, or follow the leadership of people of color. This is just as true for people who care deeply about people of color as it is for hard-core bigots who openly reject people of color. White people have been conditioned throughout our history to assume that we are the natural leaders of people of color, and that their leadership cannot be as effective as ours.

By contrast, the true leaders in the struggle to combat racism are people of color. White people who participate in antiracist communities of resistance must learn to believe, trust, and follow the leadership of people of color, and above all, to be accountable to communities of color. Being accountable to communities of color does not mean passively relinquishing leadership roles and disappearing into the ranks of willing followers; rather, it means becoming different kind of leaders. It means leading with a new understanding of power and with new accountability relationships. The white community needs to be accountable to communities of color, while communities of color must have the structured capacity to hold white individuals and the white community accountable in clearly measured and enforceable ways.

Sometimes white people respond to this principle of accountability in ridiculous ways. Of course, this does not mean that white people should walk up to unknown people of color and start being accountable to them. By accountability, I do not mean that any person of color can tell any white person what do at any time of the day or night. As foolish as this may sound, there are many white people whose fear and guilt actually move them into this kind of behavior.

Equally important to this discussion of accountability is the subject of *mutual* accountability—antiracist white communities and communities of color finding clear and measurable ways in which we all become ultimately accountable to each other. Since accountability is presently so heavily weighted in a one-way direction, however, mutual accountability cannot begin until white people learn to be *as accountable* to people of color as we have expected them to be to us. And of course, a mutually accountable relationship between white people and people of color must be rooted in a shared common understanding and analysis of racism.

4. Maintaining spiritual roots. Antiracist community and action are sacred undertakings that derive from our deepest values and are expressions of our most profound spirituality. Survival in racism's prison, as well as organizing a prison escape, call for the highest of spiritual and moral values. We need not be ashamed of our spirituality, for the work of dismantling racism requires a deep understanding of spiritual freedom.

Throughout history, the ability of oppressed people to survive and resist the onslaught of racism and other forms of human cruelty and oppression has always been attributed to the sources of their spiritual or religious strength. There are many examples and models:

- The strength given to Jewish people by their religious faith has led them to resist anti-Semitism and survive pogroms and holocausts for centuries;
- Native Americans survived genocidal oppression and resisted obliteration through the power of their religion and spirituality;
- Enslaved Africans attributed their ability to survive and resist to the religion of their ancestors, as well as to their transforming the version of Christianity their slave masters gave to them into a religion of survival and freedom;
- For more than five hundred years, colonized peoples throughout the world have called upon their sacred religious and spiritual roots in order to resist, survive, and overcome the effects of their colonization.

The list of illustrations could go on and on. For all who build antiracist community, our work must begin by transforming and redefining our spirituality. Racism has defiled all that is holy and sacred to us. Racism has all too often been publicly supported by our religious faiths. Our sense of morality, our ethics and values, and our deepest expressions of religious life have been taken captive, distorted, and misshaped by the powerful evil of racism. We must take them back. We must reclaim all that is sacred to us and redefine it from an antiracist perspective. We must rediscover a spirituality that can sustain us in our antiracist life.

5. Learning to organize. Above all, an antiracist community of resistance needs to learn the skills of organizing to dismantle systemic and institutional racism. Although it is important to survive as anti-racists within racism's prison, it is even more essential to be learning to organize to dismantle the prison itself, to destroy the imprisoning power of racism that is entrenched in the policies, practices, structures, and foundations of our institutions.

Racism will not go away simply by wishing it to be so. Only by implementing concrete step-by-step strategies will racism be dismantled. As we will see more clearly, organizing is a learned skill. Antiracist communities of resistance need to place a high priority on the collective process of learning this skill of organizing.

This brings us to the second half of this chapter, which is dedicated to further exploration of this task of developing organizing strategies to dismantle racism. Earlier chapters of this book have already described the institutional walls that form our prison of racism, revealing their nature and their dimensions with new clarity and understanding. Now we will describe the task of tearing down these walls, as well as the skills and ability required to accomplish this task. We must not talk about wonderful dreams of freedom without addressing the practical questions of how we attain these dreams. We need to know not only the kind of change that is needed, but we also need to know how we go about organizing to make this change happen. We turn now to the task of confronting and dismantling these formidable walls of systemic and institutionalized racism.

Planning a Jailbreak:
Organizing to Dismantle Racism

Tearing Down the Prison Walls of Racism

Working within the prison walls for personal transformation and to build antiracist communities of resistance is only the first half of freedom's path. The second and primary focus of the work of antiracism is about planning a jailbreak. As an antiracist community, the central mission and goal must be to break out, to escape, and to destroy the imprisoning and dehumanizing power of systemic and institutional racism. Until the prison of racism is destroyed once and for all, none of us is truly free.

Since racism is the misuse of power by systems and institutions, dismantling racism means—above all—confronting and transforming the systems and institutions of our society. The previous chapters identified how institutional and cultural racism exist and function at levels far deeper than where change has thus far taken place in our society. Therefore, dismantling racism means addressing and changing systems and institutions at levels that have not been reached before. The rest of this chapter is dedicated to exploring how antiracist communities of resistance can become organizers of institutional and community transformation in order to end racism's misuse of power.

The Goal: "Antiracist Institutional Identity"

Just as "nonracism" is impossible for individuals, so also there can be no such thing as a "nonracist institution." A racist institution cannot just simply decide not to be racist anymore. A declaration by an institution that it is not racist or will no longer be racist without a long-term plan of implementation will inevitably be crippling and paralyzing, making true change impossible. The inherited designs and structures of our institutions ensure the preservation of white power and privilege. So long as those designs and structures remain in place, a single decision or even repeated pledges to act otherwise will only provide new cover for the original disease.

The goal for a racist institution is not to become a nonracist institution, but an "antiracist institution." While it is futile for an institution to proclaim itself as nonracist, it is excitingly possible for it to become antiracist. An antiracist institution will be committed to the long-term task of transformation, not only of itself, but of the society in which it is a part.

Building antiracist institutions requires a careful and intentional step-by-step process of deconstruction and reconstruction. We have been informed by our analysis in preceding chapters that change is required at the heart of an institution, and not just in its superficial, visible components. This is a long-term process that includes dismantling institutionalized racism, followed by redesigning and rebuilding in ways that ensure transformation and redistribution of power at all levels of the institution.

Moreover, transformation of a single institution is only the first part of a progressive process of change. As I described earlier, each institution in our society is intertwined with other institutions and communities, which are also a part of larger systems that function in interdependent ways. It is impossible to change one institution without affecting the system of which it is a part. An antiracist institution will inevitably need to become part of a network of institutions and systems that are antiracist. A transformed institution needs to be part of a transformed society. Only when that has been accomplished can one begin to speak of eventually attaining a vision of a nonracist institution or a nonracist society.

A New Institutional Identity

Just as with individuals, so also with institutions: antiracism begins with a new identity. Before an institution can implement antiracist practices and programs, it must become antiracist in its stated intentions and conscious identity.

As the result of the organizing work that I will describe in the next pages, the leadership of an institution needs to come to a profound understanding of how their institution has been a prisoner of racism, how its structures and mission have been instruments of promoting and preserving white power and privilege. And they need to make a decision and a commitment to become an antiracist institution that is committed to antiracist transformation.

Antiracist institutional transformation is neither quick nor easy. It is a process that requires long and laborious self-examination and long-term planning and change. It requires a process that leads the CEO, the board of directors, and all others connected to the institution to understand the infectious disease of Power[3] that has been decimating this particular institution and all its predecessor institutions for centuries with a design and structure that guarantees power and privilege for white people and strips people of color of authentic participation in and benefits from the institution.

Antiracist institutional transformation can only take place when it becomes clear that a sickness has been eating away at the very depths and foundations of the institution—a sickness that is as injurious to white people as it is to people of color. This transformation will take place only when it becomes clear that it is not a "sacrifice" for the sake of others, but a necessary step that serves the self-interests of the institution itself. In fact, antiracist institutional transformation is the only way to avoid death and gain new life and wholeness and a new sense of inclusive power at the heart of the institution.

Change at the Heart of an Institution

Turn back for a moment to page 167 and review the structural chart of an institution. Do you recall that the three upper levels of the chart—*Personnel, Programs and Services,* and *Community and Constituency*—are the outwardly visible levels of an institution? It is on these levels where superficial change is often attempted in order to look more colorful, while seeking to avoid change on the levels where real power resides.

The change I will now be discussing in order to shape an antiracist institution focuses on the lower levels of the chart, at the heart of the institution in its *Organizational Structure* and in its *Mission, Purpose, and Identity.* The goal must be to make changes at these foundational levels of an institution. These changes will redefine the purpose of an institution, undo structures of white power and privilege, and build new structures of institutional power that are fully inclusive of and accountable to communities of color. When this kind of transformation takes place, then it will become possible to say that an institution is recovering from racism and is becoming an institution that is powerfully and excitingly new. At the very depth of its being it is becoming an antiracist institution.

Introducing a Tool
to Measure Institutional Change

The goal of the next pages is to describe a path that an institution can follow in order to make these changes. In order to do this, I want first to introduce a tool that will help visualize this path. The tool is a measuring instrument called a "continuum" that portrays the path to become an antiracist/multicultural institution. This chart (fig. 7.1) on pages 234–235 measures the gradual movement of an institution through a series of six stages as it progressively deals with its institutionalized racism.

Please take a few minutes from your reading to study the continuum, including the commentary in each of the six stages. As you study the continuum, the primary message of the left half (Stages 1–3) and the right half (Stages 4–6) will hopefully become clear:

WHERE INSTITUTIONS ARE NOW		
MONOCULTURAL → → → MULTICULTURAL → →		
1. A SEGREGATED INSTITUTION	**2. A "CLUB" INSTITUTION**	**3. A MULTICULTURAL INSTITUTION**
• Pre–1960s legalized structures of segregation • Intentional and public exclusion of African Americans, Native Americans, Latinos/ Hispanics, Asian Americans and Arab Americans • White power and privilege and dominance of people of color is inscribed throughout institution • Intentional and public enforcement of racist status quo throughout institution • Institutionalization of racism includes formal policies and practices, teachings, and decision making on all levels • Institution usually has similar intentional policies and practices toward other socially oppressed groups such as women, gays and lesbians, Third World citizens, etc.	• Publicly obeys the laws of desegregation; removes signs of intentional exclusion • Is tolerant of a limited number of people of color with "proper" perspective and credentials **But . . .** • White constituency is still exclusive and paternalistic in its attitudes and actions, and often declares, "We don't have a problem." • Continues self-understanding in organizational structure and mission as a white institution serving a predominantly white constituency • Continues to maintain White power and privilege through its de facto policies and practices, teachings, and decision making on all levels of institutional life • May still secretly limit or exclude people of color in contradiction to public policies	• Develops official policies and practices regarding multicultural diversity and inclusiveness • Sees itself as "nonracist" institution with open door: to people of color • Carries out intentional inclusiveness efforts, recruiting "someone of color" on committees or staff **But . . .** • "Not those who make waves" • Little or no contextual change in power structure culture, policies, and decision making • Is still relatively unaware of continuing patterns of white privilege, paternalism and control • Increasing discord about diversity, and signs of failure of programs of multicultural diversity • People of color increasingly express dissatisfaction or leave institution

Fig. 7.1. © Crossroads Ministry[3]

WHERE INSTITUTIONS NEED TO GO		
→ → ANTIRACIST → → → ANTIRACIST MULTICULTURAL		
4. IDENTITY CHANGE— AN ANTIRACIST INSTITUTION	**5. STRUCTURAL CHANGE— A TRANSFORMING INSTITUTION**	**6. A CHANGING INSTITUTION IN A CHANGING SOCIETY**
• Programs of antiracism training are instituted, resulting in a common analysis of systemic racism and a growing understanding of racism as barrier to effective diversity • A consciousness of white power and privilege emerges, and an increasing commitment to eliminate inherent white advantage • Cross-racial relationships are deepened and white people begin to develop accountability to communities of color • Through auditing and evaluation, the analysis is applied to all levels of the institution • A critical mass of leadership and constituency claims an antiracist identity and a vision of an antiracist institution • A transition to Stage 5 is initiated by a formal decision to institutionalize an antiracist identity within the institution's identity documents and throughout the structures and culture of the institution	• Institution commits to new stage of redesigning, restructuring, and institutionalizing antiracist identity • Restructuring ensures full participation of people of color in decision making and other forms of power sharing on all levels of the institution's life and work • Inclusion of worldviews, cultures and lifestyles of people of color is ensured in all aspects of institutional life • Authentic and mutually accountable antiracist relationships are structured between people of color and white people within the institution • There are similar institutional changes toward other socially oppressed groups, including women, gays and lesbians, Third World citizens, etc. • There is within the institution a sense of restored community and mutual caring	• Institution affirms the necessity of antiracist relationships with other institutions and in the larger society • Institution commits to participation in the struggle to dismantle racism in the wider community • All relationships and activities between institution and community are redefined and rebuilt based on antiracist commitments • Clear lines of mutual accountability are built between the institution and racially oppressed people in the larger society • Institutional alliances with others in society ensure links to all aspects of social justice, particularly to issues of global interdependence and international structures of justice and equality

- *Where Institutions Are Now*: The left half of the continuum represents the historical path that most institutions have been following since the beginning of our country until the present time. It is possible for nearly every institution in this country to locate itself somewhere along the path of these first three stages.
- *Where Institutions Need to Go*: The right half of the continuum represents the future path toward change, as a result of organizing to design and shape anti-racist multicultural institutions. The text outlines a step-by-step organizing process of an institution moving through these last three stages.

An Outline of the Rest of This Chapter

In the three remaining subsections of this chapter, this continuum will be the focal point of our discussion of institutional transformation:

A. *The First Half of the Continuum: Where Are We Now?* Institutions are never static and changeless, but are always changing. In this section, we will see that nearly every institution can locate itself somewhere on the first three stages of this continuum, and see that where it is now is different from where it was thirty or fifty years ago.

B. *Principles of Organizing to Move Forward.* Institutional change can be guided, managed, and controlled. In this section we will look at some of the basic organizing skills needed to help an institution move forward across the rest of the continuum.

C. *The Second Half of the Continuum: The Three Stages of Institutional Transformation.* In this section, we will look at the organizing steps outlined in the last three stages of the continuum: "Identity Change," "Structural Change," and "A Changing Institution in a Changing Society."

The First Half of the Continuum:
Where Are We Now?

Institutions are never static and changeless, but are always changing. Where any particular institution is now on the continuum is different from where it was thirty or fifty years ago. If we are going to plan to move forward, the first thing we need to know is where the starting place is.

Where have we come from and where are we now on the continuum? As a way of looking at the continuum and answering this question, think of an institution that you know very well and with which you are closely involved: a local school or school system, a corporate office, a public agency, a congregation, a district or diocese of a church, and the like. Try to image where you think this institution is presently located on the first three stages of the continuum. As you do this, be aware that as institutions move through these stages of development, various pieces of the institution can be in two or more stages at the same time. In fact, the larger the institution, the more spread-out over the continuum it might be. It is possible to identify the principal place where an institution is located on the continuum, however, especially with regard to its publicly declared posture or position.

Movement through the First Three Stages

Now, let us begin our in-depth work with this continuum by looking at the first three stages, the places where most of our institutions have been since their beginning. The reader should be able to recognize that this review of the first three stages of the continuum is a reprise, or a summary of the history and analysis of racism that has been presented in the first six chapters of this book.

Stage 1: "A Segregated Institution." Please reread the description of Stage 1 of the continuum. Nearly every institution and community in the United States was in Stage 1 of the continuum for hundreds of years until legal changes took place in the 1960s. As we have documented in previous chapters, for 90 percent of our national history most of our institutions practiced overt and legal exclusion of African Americans, Native Americans, Latinos/Hispanics, Asian Americans, and Arab Americans. There was no apology for the blatant reality that all our institutions consciously and intentionally served the white society exclusively.

It should therefore not only be obvious that all of our institutions were once in this Stage 1, but also that most of our institutions are no longer there. Our nation came to the point of crisis where legalized segregation was no longer economically, politically, or socially feasible, and during the past fifty years most institutions have moved out of Stage 1. A tumultuous process of institutional change and resistance to change was initiated in the 1960s and still continues through today, a process that has moved most institutions out of Stage 1 and into Stage 2 and beyond. It is technically illegal for any institution that serves the public to still be in Stage 1. With the exception of private organizations like the Ku Klux Klan and the exclusive clubs of our millionaires and billionaires, very few institutions are still in this first stage.

At the same time, it is crucial to recognize the detrimental effects of this stage that continue long after an institution moves to the next stages. The tragic reality is that having once been in Stage 1 leaves a profound and permanent scar on an institution. When any given institution was in this first stage, a racist identity based on the ideology of white supremacy was inscribed in the institution's DNA by Power[3]. Although the outward practices of an institution may have since been altered, this subterranean identity still remains like a hidden virus and a hindering handicap as it moves through the next stages of the continuum. It is not possible for any institution to become truly antiracist/multicultural until this hidden identity has been transformed.

Stage 2: "A Club Institution." Please reread the description of Stage 2 of the continuum. The move from Stage 1 to Stage 2 is a step forward—but not very far. It is important to note that for most of our nation's institutions, this move from Stage 1 to Stage 2 was not voluntary. They were required by law to move there. Moreover, at least in the early part of Stage 2, most institutions were desperately searching for ways to resist change and to maintain white supremacy and control of people of color. Haunting images remain of Ruby Bridges being escorted by the National Guard to attend elementary school in New Orleans, as well as many other traumatic historical confrontations in places like Little Rock, Selma, Chicago, Wounded Knee, and so forth.

With great reluctance, but yet with some progress, by the mid-1970s most public signs of intentional exclusion were torn down, and "tolerance" became the watchword of the day. Slowly, gradually, white institutions—public schools, public utilities, banks, stores, commercial services, churches, and so forth—crossed over the color line and opened their doors to provide services for communities of color.

Tragically, the service they provided was with second-hand equipment and third-class style, while still reserving the best for the white community as before. Moreover, although formal lines of segregation were removed, below the surface powerful and less visible barriers of segregation remained in place, and the lives of people on either side of the barriers were for the most part still kept distant and far apart. *De facto* segregation, still separate and still unequal, is a predominant identifying characteristic of Stage 2.

Most importantly, despite some visible positive changes, institutions in Stage 2 of the continuum faced few requirements to make deeper changes in their internal organizational design and structure or in their underlying mission and identity. Even though there was increasing presence of people of color within institutions, there was almost no shifting of power. We need to be absolutely clear that in this second stage, whatever changes were made to relate differently to people of color, the power to make those changes remained almost fully in the hands of white people, and the priority mission and purpose of institutions to serve the white society was not seriously challenged.

Then, as institutions moved across Stage 2, beneath the thin veneer of openness and integration, fissures and eruptions began to appear. As the numbers and expectations of people of color in the workforce grew, the atmosphere of paternalism and uncomfortable "tolerance" on the part of institutional leaders caused increasingly strained relationships, and the white club style of institutional life became increasingly dysfunctional. Serious crises began to emerge that increasingly affected the internal life of institutions. Not many years after desegregation, Stage 2 on the continuum could already be seen as an abysmal failure. The pressure was on many institutional leaders to "do something."

As will become clearer in the following paragraphs, this pressure to "do something" signaled the beginning of movement toward Stage 3, while at the same time it caused deeper division inside most of our nation's institutions. It can best be described in terms of schizophrenia. As a result of that division, some parts of most institutions have moved forward toward Stage 3, while major parts of those very same institutions became stuck—and are still stuck today—in Stage 2.

In the daily news, it is still possible to see unmistakable signs that significant portions of every institution are stuck in Stage 2. These signs come to light whenever we read or hear about persistent court battles over school boundaries or affirmative action, legal battles over political and residential borders, resurgent police violence, and hundreds of other issues that appear regularly on the front pages of our newspapers.

The schizophrenia can best be imaged by overlaying the chart that portrays the five levels of an institution on top of the continuum, as is portrayed in the sketch below. The parts of the institution that are stuck in Stage 2 are the levels of *Organizational Structure* and *Mission, Purpose, and Identity*. Readers will recognize these parts as the institutional levels that are most hidden and that have been affected least by change in society during the past fifty years. While these levels are stuck in Stage 2 of the continuum, the top three levels become separated and are able to move forward. During the past fifty years, these top three levels in most institutions—*Personnel, Programs and Services*, and *Community and Constituency*—have been able to move with varying degrees of speed toward the next stage of the continuum.

Disastrously, the pressure has been pushing in opposite directions: one force demanding to stay and maintain the club more effectively, and the other force insisting on moving toward the next stage of the continuum. The tug-of-war served to deepen institutional schizophrenia. Even while the foundations of the club were being shored up in the early 1980s, the other levels of institutions began moving into Stage 3. If readers have been thinking of a particular institution during the last couple of pages, it should be possible to identify how these two forces have affected that institution, and to trace how each of these forces is still present today.

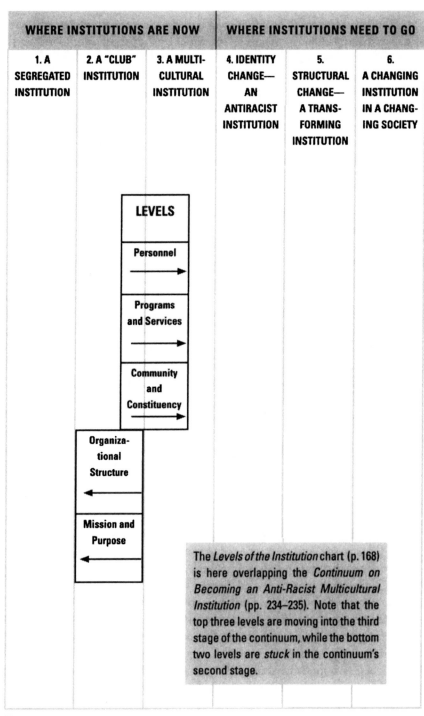

The *Levels of the Institution* chart (p. 168) is here overlapping the *Continuum on Becoming an Anti-Racist Multicultural Institution* (pp. 234–235). Note that the top three levels are moving into the third stage of the continuum, while the bottom two levels are *stuck* in the continuum's second stage.

Fig. 7.2.

Stage 3: "A Multicultural Institution." Please reread the description of Stage 3 of the continuum. As I described in greater detail in the previous two chapters, many of our nation's businesses and corporations began in the 1980s to develop the ideology and methodology of "multicultural diversity." As this new phenomenon became the rage, the vast majority of institutions and communities in our society followed the leadership of the corporate world, and began to place multicultural diversity somewhere in their top ten priorities.

To their credit, in this stage of the continuum many institutional leaders did—and are still doing—their best to open welcoming doors to everyone. There are many good things to say about the fact that our nation's institutions have been trying—at least in their public posture and their carefully crafted self-images—to become effectively multicultural.

Inevitable, however, because of the schizophrenia in the movement from stage 2 to stage 3, this third stage of the continuum is filled with even greater contradictions and volatility than the previous stages. Despite the good intentions and the efforts of many white people and many people of color working together to build new relationships within these institutions, the fatal flaw of inflexible and unyielding power that is built into white institutional structures causes the inevitable failure of multicultural diversity.

Thus in Stage 3 we see creative attempts made by *multicultural personnel* to create *multicultural programs* to serve *multicultural constituencies*, while they are still contained inside organizational structures and identities designed exclusively for and controlled almost exclusively by the white society. No matter how much progress an institution makes into Stage 3, the fundamental power structures still remain unchanged.

Since an institution's organizational structure and identity are still defined and controlled by the historic assumptions contained in the first and second stages, being in Stage 3 inevitably causes an internal contradiction between racism and multicultural diversity, and creates the impossible and monstrous reality that I named in chapter 5 as "racist multicultural diversity." It is a form of diversity that is racist and ultimately does not work. As a result of racist multicultural diversity, being in Stage 3 of the continuum inevitably leads an institution into the deepest crisis it has yet experienced, a crisis that produces severe internal disunity and fragmentation.

It is ultimately impossible for racism and multicultural diversity to coexist, and it is therefore also impossible for an institution to be in this third stage for very long before renewed crisis begins to emerge. The crisis then multiplies when it is discovered that there are yet more stages to go through and the institution must move on into Stage 4. This discovery of more stages beyond Stage 3 can be traumatizing. Most institutional leaders who promote multicultural diversity believe that the continuum only has three stages, with the stage of multicultural diversity as the last and final stage of successful change. But, no matter how hard an institution tries, racist multicultural diversity as it is formulated and implemented in most of our institutions is destined to fail.

At this point, it could be helpful if the reader recalls, or perhaps rereads, the section in the previous chapter on cultural racism entitled, "Why Multicultural Diversity Fails." It is crucial to comprehend the depth of schizophrenia being experienced by an institution caught in this conflict. Although entering Stage 3 may have taken place with the best of intentions, after having been there for some time, there is intense pressure from both directions: to move backward to Stage 2 or forward to Stage 4.

What are some of the signs of this crisis of the failure of racist multicultural diversity? The following are a few signs that readers may recognize in their own institutions:

- There is increasing discord about diversity in your institution, including growing conflict between white personnel and personnel of color. The conflict simmers most deeply between higher-ranking institutional white leaders and personnel of color who are usually in lower-ranking levels. If the discord is not permitted free expression, but is repressed by institutional authority, it may find alternate expression through passive resistance and even through expressions of institutional humor. Those few personnel of color who hold upper-level institutional positions are often caught in the middle and may feel forced to side with white institutional leaders.

- Training programs on multicultural diversity, aimed toward improving interracial relationships among personnel, have far less effect than they originally had and are either being scheduled less often or have been disbanded altogether.

- People of color increasingly express dissatisfaction more openly, or leave the institution in frustration. If the institution does exit interviews, these negative assessments are usually (and fruitlessly) expressed. Human resource personnel have to work overtime to find their replacements.

- In response to the growing crisis, institutional leaders are likely to be found attempting all kinds of maneuvers to remain in this stage in order to avoid moving backward *or* moving forward. They attempt to do the impossible—institutionalize racist multicultural diversity.

- Quietly and privately, small groups of personnel, including both white persons and persons of color, are having conversations trying to figure out what is going on and what can be done. Among these small groups there is increasing awareness of the crisis, and of the need for new understandings of racism and new directions for institutional transformation—the need to cross over into Stage 4. Often, there emerges from these groups an antiracist community of resistance that I described earlier in the chapter.

Thus, a picture emerges of an institution being pulled backward toward former patterns of resegregation, pushed forward toward new territory, and at the same time digging its anchor deeper, trying to stand fast and maintain the *status quo*. But the anchor can find no firm hold; it is dragged in both directions through the sand. The ensuing crisis more and more insistently demands that a decision must be made to move backward or to move forward.

In the next two sections I will explore the path of an institution that makes a decision to move forward to make the deeper changes that are required if dismantling racism is going to take place seriously.

Principles of Organizing to Move Forward

Crossing the Line into Stage 4
We have now arrived at the place where this entire book has pointed. There are three more stages on the continuum. These next three stages are filled with new hope and possibility. We need to enter them not only knowing that deeper change is needed, but even more importantly, that deeper change is truly possible. The subject now before us is organizing to dismantle racism at a much deeper institutional level than ever before.

Our goal now is to reach to the very center of an institution, to the level of its mission, purpose, and identity. Organizing must take place to change the very heart of an institution that was originally designed and structured to serve white power and privilege.

- Crossing the line from Stage 3, the new starting point is Stage 4, where the goal is to shape a new antiracist identity and mission.
- After completing Stage 4, Stage 5 will lead to the task of structural transformation and institutionalizing changes so they will become permanent.
- And the last stage, Stage 6, will make direct connections between a transforming institution and the movements in other institutions and communities to build an antiracist society.

We've Never Been Here Before
This is new and unknown territory. Our institutions have never before been antiracist, and we have never before been an antiracist society. This is new ground for all of us. Any institution that reaches this stage on the continuum is

joining with others who are shaping new antiracist paths. There are no guide-books, no historical reports on "how to institutionalize antiracism." The rest of this book, as it leads to these new stages of organizing, is relying on skills and experience that are still under development and are still being tested.

We are exploring new terrain that has no preexisting roads or paths. There are no travel agencies to make reservations in advance; there are no roadside tourist information booths to advise us on the best routes. We are making a path by walking on it, learning by doing, learning together, and sharing our learnings.

The second half of the continuum seeks to chart a path through this new and unknown territory. It is a description of three stages of institutional move-ment and the organizing process of moving through each stage. It is not a finished map, but rather a guide that is constantly evolving and changing. Through the work of Crossroads Ministry, People's Institute for Survival and Beyond, and other antiracism training organizations, hundreds of institutions and communities have crossed into the second half of the continuum and are carving new paths of antiracism. Each step that is described in these three stages is partly theory, partly knowledge, evolving and changing as experience teaches new and better ways of moving through this new territory.

Moving from racist institutions to antiracist institutions is a difficult and complex task. It is also exciting and rewarding. As we explore the final three stages of the continuum, let us do so with a sense of anticipation that it may yet be possible to redefine and restructure institutional power in ways that openness and trust can take the place of fear and hostility, that systems and institutions can be rebuilt that are just and egalitarian, and that the world's resources can be equally shared and received.

We Are Not Alone

Although we are in new and strange territory, we are not alone on this path of change; nor are we the first ones to walk along it. We have been brought this far by many people who have been on this path before us; and there are many joining with us now and many who will come after us. As I have already observed, the struggle against racism has been taking place for centuries from the moment European colonists invaded the Americas. The struggle has been led by people of color, but many courageous white people have also joined this struggle, following the path of resistance carved out by people of color.

White people must constantly be reminded that people of color are the best authorities on racism and antiracism. The analysis of racism in this book is based on teaching by people of color, and the experience and authority of people of color can provide guidance for predominantly white institutions seeking transformation. Moreover, since the major mark of a transforming antiracist institution is shared power with people of color, this is a critical moment for white people and people of color to be working together in a way that accentuates new ways that white communities can learn from and follow the leadership of communities of color.

"Don't Mourn, Organize"

The last words spoken by Joe Hill, famous union organizer just before he died, were "Don't mourn, organize!"[4] These words are a call to all who see a broken and unjust world and are longing for change. Yearning and praying, studying and talking about issues of injustice are all important, but unless these things are done in the context of intentional collective organizing for action that will actually make change happen, they can be a waste of time.

Change does not happen by accident. As we think together about the task of institutional transformation and the next three stages in the continuum, it is important to understand that institutional change can be guided, managed, and controlled. When institutions are left to evolve and change without careful guidance, they will change chaotically and eventually break down or wear out like a car without maintenance.

There is no magic formula for reaching the goal of an antiracist multicultural institution, but skillful organizing will help us get there. The task of dismantling racism and building antiracist multicultural systems and institutions requires the particular skills of intentionally organizing a path of change that is carefully planned one step at a time. Before examining more closely the path though the last three stages of the continuum, we need to have an important discussion about what it takes to prepare for this journey. It is a discussion about the art and skill of organizing for change. It is not enough to know what kind of change is needed. An equally important question is how we go about making change happen. We need to know how institutions and communities change, and we need to how to get the organizing skills and methods required to change them.

Learning to Organize

We need to learn to organize to dismantle racism. The more than five-hundred-year history of struggle against the forces of racism that we traced in chapter 1 would have never happened without persistent, courageous, and skillful organizing. Without this history, we would not be where we are today, at the gateway to another major step of change. We are part of this next step as we walk the path of the continuum of institutional change, and we need to learn the persistence, courage, and skills of those who came before us.

In recent years many people have been involved in the work of organizing to create antiracist institutions and communities. A rapidly increasing supply of experience, information, and resources is available to assist in this task. As has been referred to throughout this book, the information presented here tries to represent the experience of an antiracism training and organizing group in Chicago named Crossroads Ministry and other antiracism training and organizing groups such as People's Institute for Survival and Beyond in New Orleans. During the past twenty-five years, these and other organizations have led antiracism workshops and taught organizing skills to tens of thousand of people from hundreds of organizations, institutions, and communities throughout the United States.

The people who attend these workshops and participate in training programs are equipped and skilled in the task of institutional and community change. With a wonderful multiplying effect, these organizations, institutions, and communities have themselves become partners in the antiracism training and organizing work. Many schools, universities, churches, community-based organizations, and governmental institutions are on this new frontier, discovering and defining more accurately the nature of antiracist institutions and an antiracist society. A great deal has been learned that provides new directions for our path together.

Principles of Organizing for Change

In the next pages is a description of five primary antiracism organizing principles that can help to guide the work of organizing to dismantle racism. Then, in the final section of this chapter, I will indicate how these principles can be applied by moving through the last three stages of the continuum by building antiracist institutions and communities.

These five organizing principles are the product of the shared experience of a large number of people, and although the body of knowledge is growing with new learnings every day, these principles continue to provide a foundation for moving forward. Of course, these brief pages can only provide an introductory taste of the organizing principles and skills that we need to have to do this work. The resource section in the back of this book points to other books and organizing resources on organizing, and there are also other resources being written at this moment that will become available in the future. Most important, as the fourth organizing principle emphasizes, hands-on training is available for people who wish to implement these principles within their own institution.

The First Antiracism Organizing Principle:

There Must Be a Crisis

Human communities and organizations usually continue to function in normal patterns of organized behavior until a crisis occurs that interrupts the normal patterns, making it difficult or impossible to continue forward without making changes. It is especially the nature of institutions not to make major transformative changes except by necessity.

I have already noted that a major part of the motivation to move forward on each stage of the continuum is a serious institutional crisis. The step forward that is taken in each stage is also incomplete, however, and eventually results in another crisis. Thus, the response to one crisis is the inevitable cause for the next crisis, and so forth until the continuum is completed.

The biggest and most important crisis that institutions are currently facing is the failure of racist multicultural diversity. It is this crisis that propels an institution from Stage 3 toward Stage 4 on the continuum. This moment of transformation is dramatic and traumatic. All the changes thus far on the continuum have been leading toward this moment, and yet there has been little awareness that this moment is coming. This new crisis does not have the loud and confrontational expression of the civil rights movement, which was the crisis that moved institutions from Stage 1 to Stage 2, or the colorfully attractive and enticing appearance of the diversity movement, which was the crisis that moved institutions from Stage 2 to Stage 3. This new crisis has thus far been quieter, more hidden, and surrounded by denial that a crisis even exists. But it is a bomb waiting to explode.

I have also already noted that many institutional leaders entered into Stage 3 with the conviction that this would be the last stage on the continuum. It is a great surprise to many of them that it is only the halfway mark. It is a surprise that takes place only when the leading edge of the institution has passed entirely through Stage 3 and is approaching the farther edge. By this time, the institution is usually stretched over a long distance, covering the greater part of Stages 2 and 3. The institution's *Organizational Structure* and *Mission and Purpose* are still for the most part stuck in Stage 2. Its *Personnel, Programs,* and *Constituency* have moved at least partially into Stage 3. Eventually, a small contingent/expedition of institutional personnel reaches the end of Stage 3, discovers that it is not the end of the process, and detects the edge of another giant step that needs yet to be taken. This discovery inevitably leads to the new sense of crisis.

The new crisis is the inescapable product of racist multicultural diversity. It is a crisis that is inevitable, predictable, and inescapable. And it is a crisis that is an absolutely necessary step toward true antiracist multicultural diversity. How soon it arrives in a particular institution or community, how soon it is discovered, and how soon it is admitted are not quite so predictable. But its arrival and its unavoidability are certain. Like seriously ill persons who stay in denial and refuse to go to a doctor, the question is not whether the sickness will get worse, but when and whether the hurting will be severe enough to come out of denial and ask for help.

Nearly every institution in our society is currently in the midst of, or is being drawn inexorably toward, this crisis of the failure of racist multicultural diversity. In writing this book, one of my primary assumptions is that most readers of this book are searching for ways to understand this crisis and to help others to recognize and face this crisis.

Perhaps an appropriate question for the reader at this moment is, What is the particular crisis in the failure of racist multicultural diversity—either in your institution or in your community—that brought you to this book? I hope by now this question is clearer to you than when you began reading. I hope by this point in your reading you are better prepared to define the crisis within your institution or your community, and are prepared to proceed to the question of how this crisis can be addressed and who needs to be in your company as you develop the collective process of understanding and dismantling racism, and of building an antiracist multicultural institution and community.

Beyond the Crisis: Discovering the Opportunity

Bad news sometimes turns out to be a doorway to good news. A moment of crisis is also a moment of opportunity to organize. Look again at the solid line between Stage 3 and Stage 4 on the continuum. Try to picture this line becoming changed to a gateway to the rest of the continuum. Not only is crisis an unavoidable result of racist multicultural diversity; it is also a necessary step toward new opportunity to create antiracist institutions and antiracist multicultural diversity. As long as racist multicultural diversity seems to be working, an institution will not have to face its impossible contradictions. Once this reality begins to be clear, however, institutional leadership is given an opportunity to make a decision whether or not to move forward past the midpoint in the continuum to the next step in dismantling institutional racism.

In making this decision, there needs to be a healthy balance between awareness of how far an institution has come and how far it still needs to go. Because our society has moved so far since the days of apartheid, it is possible to have hope. And because we have come to this point of crisis it is possible to see the critical need and the opportunity to move farther. If no progress had been made at all during the past fifty or more years, there could be no constructive sense of crisis, but only a debilitating sense of despair and helplessness.

A prisoner who lies completely bound in chains has little or no hope. When a prisoner has gotten up on one knee and can look around and see the possibility of freedom, however, hope can be restored, and the remaining barriers to freedom can be addressed.

At the same time, the remaining barriers to freedom are formidable and extremely intimidating. An institution may have come a long way, but progress has slowed and come nearly to a standstill. Something has gotten in the way of forward movement. The crisis arises because the heart of the problem has not yet been reached, and everything that has thus far been gained is now being threatened. Acknowledging the crisis means becoming more aware than ever how serious is the disease of racism and how deep the surgeon must yet cut before the cancer is fully removed. The sense of crisis will help institutional leaders to become aware of how superficial the changes have thus far been, and how limiting racist multicultural diversity is.

When the crisis is perceived and the opportunity is acknowledged, the first antiracist decision by institutional leadership must be a commitment to take another step forward. As difficult as this decision can be, it will ultimately be a positive and energizing step. For it will provide new realization that the institution has not hit a dead end, but has found a gateway to move forward in the struggle for racial justice.

The Second Antiracism Organizing Principle:
There Must Be a Common Analysis

An institution needs to develop a clear understanding of its own systemic racism and the results it has produced. The cause of the crisis must be concretely addressed and understood. In order to move forward, institutional leadership needs to develop an analysis of racism such as that which is presented in this book. The analysis must be held in common by institutional leadership.

A common and collective analysis of racism does not come easily. As I have already emphasized earlier in this chapter, while describing the process of building antiracist communities of resistance, it requires a carefully constructed process in which participants are guided through an analysis and led to struggle together with it until there is growing agreement. Such an analysis does not get created by committee and cannot be based on the perceptions that are the result of past socialization. I do not know of any way for such an analysis to be developed other than through participation in antiracism training workshops. The purpose and function of antiracism training workshops are to help a group of people "deprogram" distorted experiences and misunderstandings and then to shape new understandings of systemic racism.

The analysis that is developed must not just be individual and personal, but must also contain a clear understanding of an institution's systemic racism and the results it has produced. It must deal concretely and accurately with the cause of institutional crisis. Moreover, it must not be general or theoretical, but a practical analysis that can be applied to the task of deepening institutional change. It must produce a clear understanding of what needs to be changed within the institution, along with why and how the changes can take place.

The Third Antiracism Organizing Principle:
Institutional Transformation Is an "Inside Job"

We are preparing to do heart surgery, to transform the heart of an institution. Such in-depth institutional transformation can be neither legislated nor implemented from the outside. The primary motivating force and transforming power for the last three stages of the continuum must come from within the institution. It must be an "inside job."

The transformative forces that moved our society's institutions through Stages 1 through 3 of the continuum came mostly from the outside. The civil rights movement and other movements of the 1960s, national and local legislation and civil rights laws, economic pressure, community pressure—all these forces had important and powerful effects on our institutions. These outside forces were necessary to move our institutions across the first three stages of the continuum.

But as a result, change was mostly motivated from the outside; it did not come voluntarily from within. As our nation's systems and institutions moved from legal segregation to "white clubs," and then from white clubs to superficial multicultural diversity, they were moved by outside forces that pushed them and shoved them to places they did not at first choose to go. Of course, there were persons within these institutions who welcomed these outside forces and rejoiced in the changes. But the initiation of these changes did not come from within.

Transformational Change from Within

Now, as the next steps of institutional transformation reach to the heart of an institution, the organizing must take place from within the institution, an inside job. It is not the detached work of outsiders, but the loving work of insiders. The primary motivating forces will not come from external sources, but must be internally generated. The energy to move forward on these next steps of our journey must come from people who are not only motivated by love for their institution, but also by the knowledge that their institution cannot survive without transformation at its very heart. If there is to be an effective response to the crisis, it will need to be generated by those who feel an ownership for the institution, who have a deep knowledge of the institution, and by those who have the power to endorse, mandate, and bring the changes to fruition.

In chapter 5, I introduced the distinction between "transactional change" and "transformational change." Transactional changes are more external, surface changes in which an institution's underlying design and structure remain untouched. Transformational change, on the other hand, reaches deep within an institution in order to fundamentally alter the underlying design and structure.

The changes that resulted from movement across the first three stages of the continuum were important, but they were transactional changes that had little effect on the heart of an institution. Although these transactional changes were, and continue to be, absolutely necessary, the results of these first steps were relatively superficial. They changed an institution's outward policies and programs, as well as many of the ways an institution related to the community it served, but they did not change an institution's internal mission and purpose, design and structure. As we have also seen, the result of transactional change was the bringing about of a crisis that cannot be resolved without deeper transformational change by those who are most deeply involved on the inside of the institution.

Of course, this "inside job" will still need a whole lot of outside help. There will still need to be outside forces from the rest of the society, applying continued pressure to help those within the institution remain aware of the need for change, and helping the change take place. These outside forces must be considered friendly allies by those who are working for change from within. Representatives of the community that is served by the institution need to be profoundly engaged in the transformative process.

Who are the "insiders" who can make this change happen? There are two answers to this question:

- The first answer has to do with who will initiate change. Who are the insiders who will get the antiracism work started in an institution? It is here that the "antiracist communities of resistance" that I discussed in the earlier part of the chapter need to be brought once again before the reader's consciousness. More often than not, such an *ad hoc* group will come into being when institutional crisis is first being perceived. This is the institution's "early warning system." These are the people who are first aware that the multicultural diversity efforts are superficial and dangerously support the continuation of racism. These are the people—people of color and white people—who come together, usually without institutional authorization, to reflect on the approaching crisis. They will begin, as I described earlier, by developing their own analysis and building their own community. But their eventual task will be to initiate an organizing process that brings the entire institution to an awareness of the crisis.

- The second answer to the question is that ultimately the persons who participate must be all the institution's "stakeholders" from the full range of the institution—from the top to the bottom of the organizational structure, from the CEO to the receptionist, from the consumer to the program leader, from every level of personnel, and especially from people of color whose power and participation in the institution will undergo significant change as a product of this transformation. The coming together of this wide range of people cannot be accidental or serendipitous. Rather, it must follow a careful and intentional organizing and skill-building process. Most important, as I will state even more explicitly below, the institution's highest leadership need to mandate and endorse internal change, and the entire constituency will ultimately need to accept and embrace it.

> ## The Fourth Antiracism Organizing Principle:
> ### Trained Organizing Teams Are Needed to Guide the Way

Implementing a transformational process such as suggested here requires organizing skills that do not ordinarily come naturally to the personnel and constituency of an institution. The pathway through these steps of institutional transformation is difficult and complex, and there are many barriers along the way. As awareness of the crisis and the need for transformation become clear within the institution, so also will there be a growing realization of the need for new abilities and capacities to lead through the process of change.

One of the best approaches to filling this need is the creation and training of organizing teams to develop the long-term and short-term step-by-step processes and to provide guidance for their implementation throughout the institution. These "antiracism organizing teams" must, of course, be mandated, endorsed, and supported by the central institutional leadership.

At this point, in order for the institution to do this "inside job," it will need to call upon "outside help." The outside help is *not* to do the transformative work *for* the institution, but to equip institutional personnel with the skills to do the transformative work themselves. Leadership for change at the heart of an institution must come from the inside, not from the outside; but help is needed from the outside to create and train organizing teams and provide them with the skills and capacities to do the transformative work. The objective is a well-equipped, in-house antiracism organizing team that will plan, design, and guide the institution through long-term transformation.

The Crossroads Antiracism Team-Training Program
Although there is not sufficient space in this chapter or in this book to present a complete description of the antiracism team-formation process of Crossroads Ministry, what follows is a brief summary description of their training program.[5] The work of Crossroads is to train teams within institutions, helping them to analyze racism and to develop and implement strategies to dismantle racism within their structures. Crossroads training begins with the ability to analyze systemic racism. Then, provided with a comprehensive understanding of racism, an intensive training process equips teams with organizing skills to lead their institutions toward long-term and permanent transformation.

The specific skills that teams develop are:

- *Analyzing systemic racism*: building and sharing a common understanding of racism;
- *Researching and evaluating*: the ability to identify and analyze racism in a specific context, as well as to evaluate and assess change;
- *Teaching*: the ability to educate about racism and provide local leaders with strategies and tools for its elimination;
- *Organizing*: the ability to develop and implement strategies for change.

During the past two decades, Crossroads has provided consultation and training services for many institutions and organizations, facilitating the development of more than two hundred internal transformation teams. Crossroads also designs programs, resources, and networks that provide teams with the necessary skills and tools that are needed to bring about systemic change, and lead toward the elimination of systemic racism within their institutions and organizations.

Crossroads provides a process to assist antiracism organizing teams in the development of specific action plans that help dismantle personal, cultural, and institutional racism, aimed toward institutional transformation. The Crossroads training model was developed through an action and reflection process that included development of experimental projects in various settings and throughout the United States.

The Forming and Equipping of Antiracism Teams
Crossroads has developed an intensive process to develop and train antiracism organizing teams. The entire training process normally lasts from twelve to

eighteen months. When the final phase is completed, the team members have developed a twenty- to thirty-year plan. After institutional leadership approves the plan, the team is prepared to lead their institution toward the long-term structural and programmatic transformation that is outlined in Stages 4, 5, and 6 in the continuum.

> ## The Fifth Antiracism Organizing Principle:
> ### Institutional Transformation Is a Step-by-Step and Long-Term Process

How long does it take to transform an institution? How many years of organizing are required to produce an institution that is antiracist from its internal heart to all of its external functions?

Institutional transformation is a long-term process that does not happen overnight. However, a step-by-step process can be developed that is aimed toward completing a long-term plan and design for transformation. Learning from historical experience, it is important to remember that it has taken institutions more than fifty years to move from Stage 1 to Stage 3 on the continuum. Using this experience as a guide, the path across the second half of the continuum must also be measured in numbers of decades. Antiracism training teams that are trained by Crossroads usually develop an initial twenty- to thirty- year timeline in their strategic plan. This does not assume the job will be finished in a predictable period of time, but it does provide for the teams a measuring tool to determine and evaluate progress in moving across the last three stages of the continuum. The teams make an assumption that by the completion of their twenty- to thirty-year plan, an institution can be well engaged in Stage 4 and Stage 5 of the continuum.

Why is it so difficult, and why does it take so long? It is extremely important to recognize that the very nature of an institution determines and controls the answer to this question. Institutional change is *supposed* to be long-term and difficult. The purpose of an institution is to be an instrument of preservation, perpetuation, and protection. By their very nature, institutions seek a stable existence and resist instability and change. At every level of institutional life, as I already described in the chapter on institutional racism, policies, procedures, and practices are "institutionalized" over a long period of time, and are measured by ongoing standards and criteria to ensure that their mission is being fulfilled and maintained.

When these institutionalized structures have been in place long enough, carrying out their functions becomes natural to all its participants. "The way things are done" becomes the institution's normal and accepted way of life. The policies and practices of the everyday life of an institution are embedded and rooted in long-standing purposes, traditions, and structures.

By definition, therefore, institutional transformation is intended to be a long and difficult task. It requires first the "deinstitutionalization" of that which we no longer want and then the "reinstitutionalization" of that which we do want. Ending institutionalized racism must not leave a vacuum, but be replaced with institutionalized antiracism. Whenever significant institutional transformation takes place, all of the intricate parts and subparts of an institution require reexamination and transformation.

Our goal is to "institutionalize" antiracism by redesigning and restructuring the institution at its deepest levels. The institutionalized racism that we are seeking to change was created over a period of five hundred years, and it will not be changed overnight. Think of all the carefully defined organizational structures, the process of making and implementing decisions, the training of personnel, the creation of programs and educational materials, the policies and practices that have evolved within an institution, all of which were shaped intentionally in the context of a mission and purpose to serve white power and privilege. Not only does all of this need to be undone and redone, but the personnel and constituency of the institution needs to learn about and accept these changes and then live with these changes long enough until they are as natural as was the previous institutional way of life. And when we have completed the creation of an antiracist institution, we want it also to be as difficult to change as was the previous racist institution.

The Second Half of the Continuum:
The Three Stages of Institutional Transformation

In this final section, we will look at the organizing steps outlined in the last three stages of the continuum. As we move through Stages 4, 5, and 6, it is important to keep in mind the organizing principles that were just reviewed. We need also to keep in mind that no one has yet completed this path and that we are all making a path by walking on it. Each step in the three stages on the second half of the continuum is part theory, part experiential knowledge; moreover, each step is evolving and changing as experience teaches new and better ways.

Stage 4: Identity Change—From Racist Institution to Antiracist Institution
As has already been stated, the most important principle in dealing with institutional racism is identity change. *Who we are* will determine *what we will do*. It is on this deepest level of institutional identity that racism's Power[3] infused its poison and accomplished its greatest destruction. And it is on this level that we must first focus our transformative efforts.

Before new structural changes can be institutionalized in Stage 5, new institutional identity must come into being in Stage 4. It is just as true with institutions as it is with individual persons: while still languishing within racism's prison, before concrete plans of escape can be implemented, a new identity must begin to be formed. The new identity being formed is an "antiracist institutional identity."

The continuum suggests a step-by-step process in Stage 4 to give birth to this identity. As we proceed to reflect on each of these steps, each item should be considered as part of a carefully organized and implemented process of transformation. And also keep in mind that at the completion of this stage the plan is to move to the next stage—Stage 5—in order to formally change the design and structure of the institution from the perspective of this new antiracist identity.

Step One: *Programs of antiracism training are instituted, resulting in a common analysis of systemic racism and a growing understanding of racism as barrier to effective diversity.* Through antiracism training and workshops, the predominantly white institutional leadership, working closely with communities of color within the institution and in the geographical area served by the institution, explore together and eventually agree upon, claim, and proclaim a common analysis of systemic racism. With this analysis, institutional leaders can begin to diagnose their institution's racism. Moreover, developing a common analysis of racism also results in building new relationships among and between white people and communities of color. As I stated earlier, this common analysis cannot come about simply by reading a book, or though some other form of individual personal change. Rather, it requires all institutional leaders to share the experience of together acquiring this analysis of racism, and being enabled to speak collectively with one voice about their common understanding.

Step Two: *A consciousness of white power and privilege emerges, and an increasing commitment to eliminate inherent white advantage.* As this new analysis of racism is shared more broadly, there develops among the institutional leadership and among the institutional constituency a new and deepening awareness of historically institutionalized white power and privilege, and of the resultant disempowerment of people of color. Along with this new consciousness, it will begin to be clear that one of the first priorities in Stage 5 will be the elimination of structures that foster white advantage.

Step Three: *Cross-racial relationships are deepened and white people begin to develop accountability to communities of color.* As white leadership works side by side with communities of color to develop a common analysis of racism, cross-racial relationships will begin to deepen in ways that have almost never before been present between these two groups. First, since white people will be learning an analysis of racism that originates from communities of color, they will develop a new ability to listen to, learn from, trust, and follow the leadership of communities of color. Second, white people will learn to be accountable to communities of color in ways that counteract the one-sided accountability that has defined cross-racial relationships throughout the centuries. At the same time, people of color will be learning to overcome the effects of their own socialization and experience of being dominated and of being divided from each other. Learning these new skills of accountability is a first step toward building mutually accountable relationships between white communities and communities of color, and structuring mutual accountability at the deepest levels of our institutions.

Step Four: *Through auditing and evaluation, the analysis is applied to all levels of the institution.* Within institutions, a process of auditing and other forms of assessment on every institutional level is initiated, resulting in a thorough awareness of white power and privilege and dominance over people of color, as well as an understanding of how they are institutionalized within the institutionalized design and structure. Applying the analysis throughout the institution is the means of identifying where change is needed. Only when there is a comprehensive picture of what needs to be changed is it possible to develop a strategy for changing it.

Step Five: *A critical mass of leadership and constituency claims an antiracist identity and a vision of an antiracist institution.* Although antiracism training and developing an analysis of racism is initiated within a relatively small group in the institution, that is only the beginning. Understanding and acceptance of the analysis must eventually expand to and be shared by all the personnel, the constituency, and other stakeholders in the institution. Only when there is a critical mass of people within the institution who share in this common analysis will it be possible to move to the next stage in the continuum and begin to make concrete and specific changes.

Step Six: *A transition to Stage 5 is initiated by a formal decision to institutionalize an antiracist identity within the institution's identity documents and throughout the structures and culture of the institution.* When a critical mass of institutional leadership and constituency have reached a consensus and broad acceptance of the shared analysis of racism, it is possible to declare a new antiracist institutional identity, and to inscribe it in the institution's formal identity documents: its constitution, by-laws, vision and mission statement. The institution will also now be ready for the long-term task of transforming its design and structure at every level. This is the decision that will complete Stage 4 of the continuum and prepare the institution to move to the next stage. It is now possible to redefine institutional power structures in such a way that they are fully shared with and accountable to communities of color.

Stage 5: Structural Change — A Transforming Institution

Now it is time to institutionalize antiracism. It is time to transform the *Mission and Purpose* and the *Organizational Structure* of the institution, along with its culture, programs, and everyday life. This is the payoff for an institution's antiracism organizing. This is the moment when power is redefined and the distribution of power is restructured. The official proclamation that an institution's life will now be based upon an antiracist identity is a signal to all people that everyday life will be different. Having worked through the crisis at the end of Stage 3 struggled with an analysis of racism and adopted a new antiracist identity in Stage 4, the institution is now ready to make and institutionalize the long-term changes that will enable it to become antiracist in all its organizational aspects and life.

Ever since the institution's power structures got stuck in Stage 2, the organizers for change have been working toward this moment. The institution entered into Stage 5 with the same organizational structure that existed in Stage 2, when the institution was still a "white club." But now the time has come for redefinition and restructuring of power and accountability. The official changes made in the institution's identifying documents at the conclusion of Stage 4 constitute a mandate that institutionalized changes can and must be made throughout the rest of the institution. Sustained and strengthened by the new identity of antiracism, the institution's leadership, constituency, and personnel—all of its stakeholders—now face the exciting task of step-by-step transformation of antiracist structures.

The central feature of an antiracist institution is the redefinition and restructuring of power. It must be institutionalized within the organizational structure, demonstrated in new leadership and new relationships, expressed in programs and services, and implemented by personnel. It will not all come to fruition at once. It will be a step-by-step creation, with a great deal of trial and error and practice before it becomes natural and fully accepted. It will be years before the transformation nears completion, when every program, every curriculum resource, every policy, protocol, and practice, every cultural occasion and special event have been addressed and subjected to rigorous examination, redesign, and evaluation. But those who have adopted a new antiracist identity will gladly participate in making and following a long-term plan, committed to its implementation.

As is indicated in Stage 5 of the continuum, an institution will go through the following steps:

Step One: *Institution commits to new stage of redesigning, restructuring, and institutionalizing antiracist identity.* Based upon the antiracist analysis and identity achieved in Stage 4 of the continuum, a formal commitment is made to enter into a process of intentional institutional restructuring. Although there are many prior experiences of organizational structuring and restructuring that will offer insight into this experience, it will nevertheless require a great deal of inventiveness. There are no generic models for an antiracist institution. And each institution's antiracist structures must reflect the specific purpose, language, and values of that particular institution. Leaders of the restructuring process will need to develop a planning, implementation, and evaluative process, with a clear timeline. All levels of the institution must be included in the commitment to change and in the process of bringing it about.

Step Two: *Restructuring ensures full participation of communities of color in decision making and other forms of power sharing on all levels of the institution's life and work.* As stated above, the primary mark of antiracist institutional restructuring will be change in the use of power. The goal is the right use of shared power by everyone. This means that for the first time there will be *full* participation of communities of color in decision making and other forms of power sharing on all levels of the institution's life and work. Restructuring and institutionalizing the right use of power means far more than pledges and personal commitments to do things differently. While goodwill and good intentions are necessary ingredients for reaching this stage of the continuum, they are not the primary marks of institutional change. Here we are talking about people of color and white people with goodwill and good intentions working together to create structures and defining clearly the standards and criteria by which the institution will function differently and in measurable ways at all levels of organizational life.

Step Three: *Inclusion of worldviews, cultures, and lifestyles of communities of color is ensured in all aspects of institutional life.* It is now possible to achieve a truly antiracist multicultural diversity. We have described "racist multicultural diversity" as a way of making a white controlled institution only look more colorful, a process of achieving the appearance of cross-cultural inclusiveness in a way that is still controlled by white people. By contrast, "antiracist multicultural diversity" means that the *power* to ensure the inclusion of worldviews, cultures, and lifestyles of communities of color in all aspects of institutional life will also be fully shared by people of color.

Step Four: *Authentic and mutually accountable antiracist relationships are structured between people of color and white people within the institution.* We have thoroughly discussed at various places in this book the necessity of white people learning to be authentically accountable to communities of color. In Stage 4 of the continuum, that achievement is presented as one of the major criteria of white antiracist identity. Without white people being accountable to communities of color, accountability continues to be completely one-sided, and therefore mutual accountability has been impossible. Now, however, the discussion must go beyond white accountability to communities of color, to a discussion of authentic and mutually accountable antiracist relationships that must be structured between people of color and white people within the institution. True accountability can never be one-sided. All of us must learn to be accountable to each other in an antiracist way and in a way that is based upon a shared analysis of racism.

Step Five: *There are similar institutional changes toward other socially oppressed groups, including women, gays and lesbians, Third-World citizens, and so forth.* In the introduction to this book, the interrelationship of all forms of oppression was affirmed. There cannot be changes in one form of oppression without the willingness to bring about changes in all forms of oppression. Although this book has focused only on transformation of racist oppression, it is time once again to note and to insist on this interrelationship and on the interdependency of liberation from all forms of oppression. Authentic antiracism requires also authentic antisexism, antiheterosexism, anticlassism, antinationalism, and so forth. An institution that has reached this stage of the continuum must be also working on similar institutional changes toward other socially oppressed groups.

Step Six: *There is within the institution a sense of restored community and mutual caring.* The conclusion of Stage 4 of the continuum will not be signaled by the end of struggle and the completion of change, but by the presence of a sense of well-being while continuing to implement change. There is in fact no timetable for concluding this stage. It is rather an ongoing, living, transformative process that should never end. There are no institutions that have completed all the steps in this stage of the continuum. There are not even many institutions that have entered into this stage. But it is the direction in which we all need to be headed. If our society, in its communities and in its systems and institutions, is to find authentically new and safe paths in which to continue our struggle for racial justice and reconciliation, then all of our institutions must eventually go through this stage of transformation.

Stage 6: A Changing Institution in a Changing Society

Racism is rooted in every aspect of our societal life. Therefore, working for change in a single institution is just one piece of the larger task of community and societal change. There must be a conscious and intentional linking of the transformation process within a single institution to the larger process of societal change.

Stage 6 of the continuum is not simply a sequential stage that follows the completion of Stage 5. Its intention must be clearly present throughout the second half of the continuum, and its implementation must at least have its beginning in a way that is parallel to Stage 5. Nevertheless, it is important to describe this stage in terms of a separate organizing process, with a distinct strategy of planning and implementation. As is indicated in the column describing Stage 6, an institution will go through the following steps:

Step One: *Institutions affirm the necessity of antiracist relationships between the institution and the larger society.* The ultimate vision that drives the process of institutional change is a future vision of an institution and wider community that has overcome systemic racism. Thus, to work toward shaping an antiracist multicultural institution must include an intentional process by which an institution shapes and reshapes its participation in changing the larger society.

Step Two: *Institutions commit to participation in the struggle to dismantle racism in the wider community.* Those working to shape and structure antiracism in a particular institution need friends and allies outside the institution. There are other individuals and organizations in the larger community with a commitment to dismantle racism. It is important for those working for change in an institution to be in contact with and to build relationships between the institution and these other groups. Moreover, it is by working with these other groups that the institution can begin to participate in the struggle to dismantle racism in the wider community.

Step Three: *All relationships and activities between institutions and communities are redefined and rebuilt based on antiracist commitments.* There are deep historic formal and informal relationships that already exist between any given institution and the larger society of which it is a part. Given the nature of racism, however, these relationships have been historically and are still currently defined in terms of the perpetuation of white power and privilege. Therefore, each of these relationships must now be redefined and rebuilt from an antiracist perspective. Of course, this will often entail extremely difficult work, since it cannot be assumed that the larger society shares the antiracist commitments of the institution. Thus, in these and other ways the task is not simply redefining and rebuilding relationships, but must also include the work of challenging and transforming the larger society.

Step Four: *Clear lines of mutual accountability are built between the institution and racially oppressed people in the larger society.* Just as we stressed in Stage 5 the importance of building mutually accountable relationships inside the institution between white people and people of color, so also clear lines of mutual accountability need to be built between the institution and racially oppressed people in the larger society. Once again, mutual accountability begins with predominantly white institutions learning for the first time to be accountable to racially oppressed communities of color. This accountability relationship must be defined and structured in measurable ways and not simply stated with good intentions.

Step Five: *Institutional alliances with others in society ensure links to all aspects of social justice, particularly to issues of global interdependence and international structures of justice and equality.* The ever-expanding concentric circles of change must lead us ultimately to global issues of poverty racism and related forms of injustice. As indicated throughout this book, the continued presence of white power and privilege within our society is a product of global colonialism that has left similar expressions of oppression throughout the world. Each of us, as well as each of our institutions and communities in the United States must ultimately be part of a global movement for change.

Conclusion:
Toward a Racism-Free Twenty-First Century

Although we have traveled all the way to the end of the continuum, that is not the place where this book ends. Rather, we need to return to the line between the first half and the second half of the continuum. That is where our organizing efforts must begin.

The leading edge of U.S. society stands at the threshold that leads from Stage 3 to Stage 4. We have come a long way, and we still have a long way to go. Our systems and institutions and our vast variety of residential communities are on the edge of discovery of a new path forward. Our nation must not go backward, nor can we stay where we are. Dismantling racism means moving forward to a new world of antiracism.

Already a growing number of our communities and institutions have begun to move across the line into the second half of the continuum. They are looking forward toward the struggle that lies ahead, and they are also looking back to call others who have not yet crossed the line to join them. Antiracist transformation is a long-term process that cannot be completed until all our institutions join the path toward antiracist change. The transformation of any single institution or community is a small piece of the larger effort and even longer-term process of shaping an antiracist society. The goal is not only transformation of an institution, but also for the institution to participate in transforming the community in which it exists.

As we were once reminded by Martin Luther King Jr., no person is free until all people are free; so also must we constantly remind ourselves of the connectedness between institutional transformation and the transformation of the society around us. No institution can be isolated or insulated from its community, and no community can be separated from the larger society. We cannot create islands of change floating in a sea of no change.

Even though the movements of the 1960s were cut short before they could complete their work, they are an important reminder to us that societal change is possible. We must see our task as continuing those movements. The eventual and ultimate goal of organizing for change within individual institutions and communities is the reigniting of a movement for racial justice in our nation, a movement that will not stop and is unstoppable until we have become an antiracist people.

Moreover, it is impossible to separate the movement for racial justice from the rest of the movements to end other forms of injustice in our society. They all form one single movement. And the movements for justice within our own society are even less separable from movements for global justice that are aimed toward ending poverty, racism, and other forms of national and international injustice globally.

How do we measure success in antiracism organizing? In one sense we can measure success by our step-by-step progress through the continuum. In another sense, we can measure our success by being an effective spark in the long-term process of building the movement for community, national, and global justice and peace.

News Stories of a Growing Movement

I began this book with three news stories that have been predominant in the media and in our minds during recent years. Now, as I write the conclusion and the final part to this book, these same stories still represent the storms of racism that are raging as strongly as ever in our country and throughout the world.

Each of these news stories represents both tragedy and hope: the tragedy of racism and the hope of struggle to dismantle racism:

- *New Orleans*: As the struggle to rebuild New Orleans continues, it has become increasingly clear to many people that it was not only a hurricane named Katrina that destroyed the city of New Orleans, but racism directed predominately toward African American people and toward the preservation of white power and privilege: racism in the inadequate response to people of color in a life-threatening and life-destroying emergency; racism in the inadequate construction of the levees in the first place and in the unwillingness to strengthen the levees over the course of decades when it was known that they would not withstand a hurricane such as Katrina; racism in the process of planning and implementing the restoration of New Orleans; and racism in the very denial that racism is involved. Racism has destroyed a city, and racism is hell-bent on preventing its rebuilding.

  And yet, new life, new struggles, and new organizing strategies are also emerging throughout New Orleans: on almost every block and street corner; in old community organizations reassembled and in newly organized community groups; inside old agencies being restabilized and in new agencies with new designs; among evacuees and their supporting allies in far-flung cities in temporary or in new permanent homes. Facing the inevitable evil of resurgent racism, thousands of people are organizing with a determination to rise again, insisting that racism will not win.

- *"Illegal Aliens"*: That which is euphemistically referred to as an "immigration crisis" concerning undocumented workers is targeting Latino/Hispanic peoples in the United States—particularly Mexican people. The need for low-cost labor in our society has always created a vacuum that sucks immigrants from other countries into our factories and fields. According to the definitions imposed by racism, Latinos/Hispanics are not white. They are people of color in a nation that is still living with the deep-seated belief that first-class citizenship in the United States of America is a status reserved for white people. Once again, in this latest oppression against people of color—not unlike the genocide of Native Americans and the enslavement of Africans—Latinos/Hispanics and other undocumented people are being made into the racial scapegoats for an economic system that cannot give up its addiction to white power and privilege

  And yet, it is impossible to see the millions of Latinos/Hispanics and their allies marching and demonstrating in every city and town in this country without marveling at the incredible and wonderful potential of the "Latino Power" that has been unleashed. Whether or not, by the time these words are being read, a temporary or permanent solution has been found to the immediate crisis of undocumented workers in our country, the important issue is that another significant mark is being made in the contribution of Latinos/Hispanics to the long-term task of resisting racism's systemic misuse of power. Every time the monstrous power of racism reasserts itself against people of color and antiracist white people in our society, we are given another opportunity to organize for racism's ultimate demise and for the institutionalization of antiracist/multicultural power.

• *9/11*: The destruction of the World Trade Center, successive terrifying Western military incursions into the Middle East, and continuing terrorist attacks throughout the world have once again demonstrated that the seeds of global colonialism and racism are still producing the deadly fruits of fanaticism and hatred—not just on one side, but on all sides. It will not end or even be diminished until we hear the message that the world is not only imprisoned by the failed forces of democracy, but even more so by the evil forces of racism, poverty, and the ungodly imbalance of wealth and power. And it will not end without all of the world's religions demanding that their teachings no longer be used for cruel and violent purposes.

9/11 has also added another layer of terror to domestic racism within our country against Arab Americans and Middle Eastern people. The attack on the World Trade Center and succeeding counterterrorism programs dramatically changed the racial and social status of Arab Americans and Middle Eastern peoples. They have become scapegoats, and have been made into the least trusted and most rejected people of color in the United States.

And yet, throughout our nation and the world, the horrifying insanity of war and its atrocities is once again awakening and strengthening among us greater forces for sanity and peace. In the brief moments following 9/11, in the name of counterterrorism, the large majority of U.S. citizens favored retaliation, supported the violence of vengeful war, and gave tacit permission to oppress Arab Americans as a necessary act of self-protection. As months and years passed and the toll of the dead and the cost of war increased without reducing the threat or producing solutions, the polls began to tell a different story: a dramatic reduction of support for politics and policies of the "war against terror" and an equally dramatic reenergizing of efforts to create alternate approaches to dealing with the escalating terror.

Perhaps by now the terror has become yet worse; or perhaps at least a temporary peace has been found. I hope a way is being found to counter the race-based attacks on Arab Americans. One thing is certain: a permanent solution will not be found without a commitment to dismantle the long-established systems of colonialism and racism. And one more thing is even yet more certain: wherever oppression continues, resistance to oppression will grow and flourish.

Inspiration and Hope for a New Beginning

I want to reemphasize that the perspective of this book is not despair, but hope. The basis for this hope is not a naïve belief in the potential of white people to change ourselves or to change our society, but rather a firm belief in the potential strength of reigniting a united movement for justice, particularly in the context of leadership of the oppressed. Even though our society has given up on the poor and especially poor people of color, we can be sure of two things: first, that God has not given up on the poor; and second, that the poor have not given up on themselves. Someone may have called them the "permanent underclass," but that is a name chosen neither by God nor the poor themselves. History shows that when people are pushed to the bottom, they refuse to stay there. Again and again, those who are stripped of dignity and basic human rights rise in strength, demanding justice for all people.

The Happiness Machine Revisited

. . . Then a new and even greater danger arose. The Happiness Machine became so large and productive that there was no place on earth left to put the dross. The piles of dross crept closer and closer to the homes of the happy people and to the place where the Happiness Machine was operating. The ominous threat was that the dross would back up into its own machine, and the machine would self-destruct. Now the happy people were threatened not only by the rebellion of the unhappy people, but also by their own Happiness Machine.

The new danger caused even greater internal conflict and tension among the happy people. Some people began to predict sorrowfully that the Happiness Machine would soon self-destruct. Others suggested that the only alternative was to build an even bigger Happiness Machine in order to deal with the crisis they were facing. Others began to see that the Happiness Machine was not the solution to their problems, but the cause. They wanted to reduce the size of the Happiness Machine, or even dismantle it altogether. Some even began to wish that they could join together with the unhappy people to find solutions to the problem and build a new society together without the help of Happiness Machines.

The end of this story has not yet been written. This book is an invitation to readers to see themselves as part of the story and to help write its ending.

The Happiness Machines are still working overtime to preserve white power and privilege, with the threat of their explosion or implosion as great as ever. The struggle between racism and antiracism continues unabated. The end of the story of the Happiness Machine is still being written. Chapter after chapter describe the ongoing conflict. In one chapter the forces of racism that protect the Happiness Machine seem to be winning. Then another chapter is written that signifies in undeniable terms that the forces of resistance are alive and well. There are numerous signs of hope and signs of promise that counteract and challenge the threat of new forms of racism. All over our society, in nearly every community and institution, people are joining together to write a new ending to the story of the Happiness Machine.

The ultimate hope for the United States and the rest of the world is that the poor and oppressed will develop the strength and leadership that will lead to a better world, and that we will follow them to that better world. More specifically, the hope for white America is that we will be able to relinquish unjust power and control, and join in writing a positive ending for our fable before it is too late. Not only because we're running out of time, and not only because we're afraid of what will happen if we don't change, but also because it is right and because it is just.

We Are Signs of Hope and Promise

From the beginning to the end of this book, an invitation and a challenge has been made to white people in our society to join the struggle to end racism. Resistance to racism cannot be left only to people of color. For their sake, for our sake, for the sake of all humanity, for God's sake, we are called to reject the prison of racism that has incarcerated us for centuries, and to join African Americans, Native Americans, Latinos/Hispanics, Asian Americans, and Arab Americans in creating an antiracist society.

Finally, as we commit ourselves to begin again, we affirm that we are neither the first, nor are we alone. Many have been here before us. Those of us now gathered to help write an ending to the story of the Happiness Machines should be aware of those before us as well as those gathering with us today in various parts of the world. Each of us has been carried into the struggle against racism on the shoulders of those who have struggled before us.

You and I are signs of hope and promise—in the antiracism work of Crossroads Ministry, of People's Institute for Survival and Beyond, and hundreds of other antiracism communities of resistance; in city halls and churches, in schools and universities, in factories and fields; wherever people are responding to their sense of crisis by analyzing and organizing in creative new ways.

New forms of racism call for new forms of resistance. Thousands upon thousands of people are responding to that call to action: million-man

marches, immigrant demonstrations, grassroots organizing, antiracism training, institutional transformation—the list goes on and on. This book and the
experiences that brought it into being are just one small part of the escalating
resistance that is matching, blow by blow, the rise of new forms of racism. As
it has been from the beginning, resistance to racism is a phoenix that always
emerges from the ashes of oppression.

A Tribute to Heroes and Heroines Who Resisted Racism, and Who Carried Us on Their Shoulders to the Place Where We Now Stand

Frederick Douglass, Sojourner Truth, Chief Seattle, J. Phillip Randolph,
Dolores Huerta, Gordon Hirabyashi, Clarence Jordan, Benito Juarez,
John Brown, Chief Powhattan, George Washington Carver, Chief
Cochise, Jackie Robinson, Cesar Chavez, Fred Hampton, Vincent Cin,
Bert Corona, Abbey Kelly, Denmark Vesey, Marcus Garvey, Jim Thorpe,
Thurgood Marshall, Rosa Parks, Denise McNair, Addie Mae Collins,
Carole Robertson, Michael Schwerner, James Earl Chaney, Andrew
Goodman, Eugene Crawford, Harriet Tubman, Angelina and Sarah
Grimke, Minoru Yasui, George Lee, Jesus Colon, Dr. Martin Luther
King Jr., Imani/Nadine Addington, Kenneth Jones, Pedro Albizu Cam-
pos, Brad Chambers, Chief Little Turtle, Crispus Attucks, Chief Crazy
Horse, Carlos Bulosan, Antonio Rodriguez, Abraham Heschel, Barbara
Jordan, Benjamin Franklin, Chief Tecumseh, Zora Neal Hurston, Chief
Joseph, Fannie Lou Hamer, Leonard Peltier, James Reeb, Mark Clark,
Robert Terry, Septima Clark, Gerry Conway, John Newton, Yick Wo,
Nat Turner, Mubarak Ale Khan, Carter G. Woodson, C. T. Vivan, Angela
Davis, Bob Moses, Viola Liuzzo, Malcolm X, Jim Dunn, Lillian Seng,
Chief Black Hawk, Benjamin Banneker, Chief Sitting Bull, Fred Kore-
matsu, Langston Hughes, Angel Luis Gutiérrez, James Baldwin, Cecilia
Alvarado, Robert Matsui, Anne Braden, Ida B. Wells, Chief Geronimo,
Pat Simpson-Turner, Mary Church Terrell, W. E. B. Du Bois, Dallip
Singh Saund, Emmett Till, Rudy Acuña, Medgar Evers, Jim Hayes, and
many thousands more.

**We Who Are Alive Commit Ourselves to the Sacred Task
of Remembering with Thanksgiving
as We Walk New Paths toward Justice**

NOTES

Introduction

1. W. E. B. Dubois, Preface, in *The Souls of Black Folk* (Chicago: A. C. McClurg, 1903), 1.

1. The Continuing Evil of Racism

1. Rev. Johnny Ray Youngblood is pastor of St. Paul Community Baptist Church in Brooklyn, N.Y., a church that has developed the "Maafa Suite," an annual commemoration of the catastrophe of African slavery, often thought of as the African holocaust. *Maafa*, a Kiswahili word for catastrophe, tragedy, or disaster, was introduced into contemporary African American scholarship by Dr. Marimba Ani to refer to the period in world history otherwise known as the "middle passage," or transatlantic slave trade. For Web site information, see resources section starting on page 277.

2. In most of this book, I have refrained from using the term *America* to refer to the United States, since America extends throughout North America and South America. In the minds of many people, equating America and the United States of America reflects a kind of nationalistic arrogance that is resented by people in the other Americas. Occasionally, however, in order to communicate in terms of popular language it becomes necessary to use such terms as "African American."

3. Several books can be recommended for further exploration of this interrelationship between colonialism and racism. See Mahmood Mamdani,

Citizen and Subject: Contemporary Africa and the Legacy of Late Colonialism (Princeton: Princeton University Press, 1996); Michael Omi and Howard Winant, *Racial Formation in the United States: From the 1960s to the 1990s* (New York: Routledge, 1994); and Howard Winant, *The World Is a Ghetto* (New York: Basic Books, 2001). I am also very grateful to Dr. Victor Rodriguez, California State University at Long Beach, and Robette Diaz, from the Crossroads Ministry organization, for their contributions emphasizing the importance of colonialism in order to understand racism in the United States.

4. Howard Zinn, *A People's History of the United States: 1492 to Present* (New York: HarperCollins, 2003), 16.

5. Bartolomé de Las Casas, *Tears of the Indians*, J. Phillips trans. *Brevísima relación de la destrucción de las Indias* (1552). To view the full text of this document, go to http://www.ciudadseva.com/textos/otros/brevisi.htm (accessed 5/1/07).

6. Zinn, *A People's History of the United States*, 29. For more statistical data, see also Brent Staples, *African Holocaust: The Lessons of a Graveyard*; for Web site information, see resources section below. See also Ira Berlin, *Many Thousands Gone: The First Two Centuries of Slavery in North America* (Boston: Harvard University Press, 2000); and Eugene D. Genovese, *Roll Jordan Roll: The World the Slaves Made* (New York: Random House, 1976).

7. Ian Haney-López, *White by Law: The Legal Construction of Race* (New York: New York University Press, 1996), 1.

8. Salah D. Hassan, "Enemy Arabs," *Socialism and Democracy* 33 (vol. 17, no. 1). See http://www.sdonline.org/33/salah_d_hassan.htm (accessed 5/1/07). Hassan is chair of the department of history of art and professor of African and African Diaspora art history and visual culture and director of the Africana Studies and Research Center at Cornell University.

9. Victor M. Rodriguez, *Latino Politics in the United States: Race, Class, and Gender in the Mexican American and Puerto Rican Experience* (Dubuque: Kendall-Hunt, 2005), 17.

10. Martin Luther King Jr., "Facing the Challenge of a New Age," Montgomery, Ala., December 1956, in *A Testament of Hope: The Essential Writings of Martin Luther King, Jr.*, ed. James M. Washington (San Francisco: HarperCollins, 1986), 141.

11. Zinn, *A People's History of the United States*, 539.

12. Martin Luther King Jr., "A Time to Break Silence," *A Testament of Hope*, 231.

13. See en.wikipedia.org/wiki/Students_for_a_Democratic_Society and en.wikipedia.org/wiki/Student_Nonviolent_Coordinating_Committee.

14. For further information on the FBI Counterintelligence Program, see "COINTELPRO: Supplementary detailed staff reports on intelligence

activities and the rights of Americans; book III; Final Report of The Select Committee To Study Governmental Operations With Respect To Intelligence Activities; United States Senate; April 23 (under authority of the order of April 14), 1976." Available online at http://www.icdc.com/~paulwolf/cointel-pro/churchfinalreportIIIc.htm (accessed 5/1/07).

15. Benjamin Hooks, quoted from a news conference report in the *New York Times,* July 10, 1989.

16. For further information about the Southern Poverty Law Center, see resources section below.

17. See http://thomas.loc.gov for information there on the Hate Crime Statistics Act of 1990.

18. For further information about Prison and Jail Project in Americus, Georgia, see "Additional Resources," below.

19. Remark by commentator Julianne Malvaux on ABC's *Prime Time: True Colors* (aired November 26, 1992). For further information on this video, see resources section below.

20. The "Foot Identification/Power Analysis" exercise was created by Dr. Jim Dunne and Ron Chisom, cofounders of the People's Institute for Survival and Beyond. The exercise has been used to help tens of thousands of people analyze racism in "Undoing Racism" workshops led by People's Institute. It is also used by Crossroads Ministry (with permission from People's Institute) in all their antiracism training. For further information about these organizations, see resources section below.

21. C. Eric Lincoln, *Race, Religion, and the Continuing American Dilemma* (New York: Hill and Wang, 1984), 10–11.

22. There are innumerable separate sources for all of the statistics cited in these pages. A reliable summary of these statistics and their sources can be found in an excellent article entitled "Wide Economic, Racial Gaps Exposed by Katrina," by the Friends Committee on National Legislation (FCNL10/14/2005 ©1998–2006 FCNL, 245 Second Street NE, Washington, D.C., 20002). For further information about this organization, see resources section below.

23. Cornel West, *Democracy Matters: Winning the Fight Against Imperialism* (New York: Penguin, 2004), 22–23.

2. Defining Racism

1. While Crossroads Ministry and People's Institute use similar workshop processes to explore this definition and analyze systemic racism, the step-by-step outline followed in this chapter and in succeeding chapters of this book is patterned after the specific process developed and used by Crossroads Ministry.

2. "Prejudice," in *Webster's New Twentieth Century Dictionary, Unabridged*, 2nd ed. (New York: World Pub. Co., 1964).

3. Ian Haney-López, *White by Law: The Legal Construction of Race* (New York: New York University Press, 1996), 90. It may seem at first to be a mark of progress when the Supreme Court in their ruling in *United States v. Thind* no longer recognized a scientific basis for the concept of race. However, the highest judges of the land were a long way from recognizing the absurdity of the construct of race itself. In place of a scientific basis for determining racial identity, the court substituted what can now be seen as an even more ludicrous basis for racial determination; namely, "the understanding of the common man." Thus, common knowledge and popular beliefs replaced science as the first line of legal defense of white supremacy.

4. "Race," in *Webster's New Twentieth Century Dictionary Unabridged*, 2nd ed.

5. Audrey Smedley, "Race," in *Encyclopedia Britannica*, 2005 ed. (Chicago: Encyclopedia Britannica, 2005).

6. Audrey Smedley, *Race in North America: Origin and Evolution of a Worldview* (Boulder, Colo.: Westview, 1999), 16–17.

7. Ibid., 150–68; Smedley here provides further information on the early racial classification of humanity by anthropologists.

8. Michael Omi and Howard Winant, *Racial Formation in the United States: From the 1960s to the 1990s* (New York: Routledge, 1994), 62.

9. The United States Congressional Naturalization Act of 1790 (1 Stat. 103) limited the right to become a naturalized citizen to "free white persons," thereby excluding indentured servants, African slaves, free African Americans, and later Asian Americans. The law, although modified somewhat over the years, remained in effect for 162 years, until 1952.

10. See Ronald Takaki, *From Different Shores: Perspectives on Race and Ethnicity in America*, (New York: Oxford University Press, 1994). Also see Haney-López, *White By Law*, and Smedley, *Race in North America*, for further study of the history of race.

11. Definition of race by People's Institute for Survival and Beyond and Crossroads Ministry. While this definition of race here presented is in no way substantially changed from Dr. Karenga's original conceptualization, its particular wording has evolved for teaching and training purposes through the work of People's Institute for Survival and Beyond and of Crossroads Ministry, and particularly through collaboration between Dr. Karenga and Dr. Michael Washington from People's Institute.

12. The specific wording of this definition is mine, but it is derived from the teaching and training methodologies of People's Institute for Survival and Beyond and of Crossroads Ministry.

13. The teaching device of describing the exponential increase of racism's misuse of power with the symbols "Power^1," "Power^2," and "Power^3" was developed while I was director of Crossroads Ministry, and is still used in their training programs.

3. White Power and Privilege

1. John Howard Griffin, *Black Like Me* (New York: Signet, 1960).

2. Tim Wise, *White Like Me: Reflections on Race from a Privileged Son* (New York: Soft Skull, 2005).

3. Many universities have developed programs of whiteness studies in recent years. For further information, see books on whiteness in resources section below.

4. Robert Terry, *For Whites Only* (Grand Rapids: Eerdmans, 1988), 17.

5. For further information on the concept of color blindness, see Eduardo Bonilla-Silva, *Racism without Racists: Color-Blind Racism and the Persistence of Racial Inequality in the United States* (Lanham, Md.: Rowman & Littlefield, 2006).

6. Peggy McIntosh, *White Privilege and Male Privilege: A Personal Account of Coming to See Correspondences through Work in Women's Studies* (Wellesley, Mass.: Wellesley College, 1988). For information about purchasing this document, see resources section below.

7. Kendall Clark, "Defining White Privilege"; http://whiteprivilege.com/definition/ (accessed 5/1/07).

8. Robert Jensen, "White Privilege Shapes the U.S."; http://uts.cc.utexas.edu/~rjensen/freelance/whiteprivilege.htm (accessed 5/1/07).

9. McIntosh, *White Privilege and Male Privilege.*

4. Individual Racism: The Making of a Racist

1. For further information and discussion on identity formation in general, see James E. Côté and Charles G. Levine, *Identity, Formation, Agency, and Culture: A Social Psychological Synthesis* (New Jersey: Erlbaum Associates, 2002). For further reading on the subject of racial identity formation in particular, see Michael Omi and Howard Winant, *Racial Formation in the United States: From the 1960s to the 1990s,* Critical Social Thought (New York: Routledge, 1994); and Beverly Daniel Tatum, *Why Are All the Black Kids Sitting Together in the Cafeteria?* (New York: Basic Books, 1997).

2. PBS-TV's *Frontline,* "A Class Divided." See the "Films and Video" section of the resources section below for further information on this video.

3. Although the concepts of "internalization of racist oppression" and "internalization of racist superiority" are broadly used in antiracism work,

these particular definitions were developed through the collaborative work of the Crossroads Ministry staff/board collective with input from partners in the Unitarian Universalist Association, Christian Church (Disciples of Christ), and the Tri-Council Coordinating Commission.

4. For further information on the internalization of racist oppression of people of color, see resources section below. I strongly encourage readers of this book to study and seek to understand the ways in which racism perpetuates itself through the socialization of people of color to cooperate and comply with racism's demands. It is important to listen to and learn from people of color, however, and not from white people, in order to understand the internalization of racist oppression.

5. Conclusion to Crossroads definition of internalization of racist oppression and internalization of racist superiority.

6. Tatum, *Why Are All the Black Kids Sitting Together in the Cafeteria?*

7. C. S. Lewis, *The Great Divorce* (New York: HarperCollins, 1973).

8. Omi and Winant, *Racial Formation in the United States*, 63.

5. Institutionalized Racism

1. Definition by Crossroads Ministry, which I have somewhat abbreviated and edited with permission from Crossroads Ministry.

2. Institutional Levels chart by Crossroads Ministry, which I have somewhat modified with permission from Crossroads Ministry.

3. William B. Johnston and Arnold E. Packer, *Workforce 2000: Work and Workers for the Twenty-First Century* (Indianapolis: U.S. Dept. of Labor, 1987).

4. Beverly Daniel Tatum, *Why Are All the Black Kids Sitting Together in the Cafeteria?* (New York: Basic Books, 1997).

5. From the Web site of Bachmann Global Associates, an organizational development consulting firm located in Atlanta that specializes in change management. See http://www.bachmannglobal.com/transformational_leadership.htm (accessed 5/1/07).

6. Cultural Racism

1. Mapping chart developed by Dr. Victor M. Rodriguez, Professor in the Department of Chicano and Latino Studies, California State University at Long Beach. Used by Permission.

2. Definition of cultural racism by Crossroads Ministry, which I have somewhat modified with permission from Crossroads Ministry.

3. See Kenji Yoshino, "The Pressure to Cover," *The New York Times*, January 15, 2006. Adapted from Yoshino's book, *Covering: The Hidden Assault on Our Civil Rights* (New York: Random House, 2006).

4. William B. Johnston & Arnold E. Packer, *Workforce 2000: Work and Workers for the Twenty-First Century* (Indianapolis: U.S. Dept. of Labor, 1987).

5. Israel Zangwill, *The Melting Pot: Drama in Four Acts* (New York: Macmillan, 1921), 35.

6. Noel Ignatiev, *How the Irish Became White* (New York: Routledge, 1995).

7. Karen Brodkin, *How Jews Became White Folks and What That Says about Race in America* (Rutgers: Rutgers University Press, 1998).

8. Quoted by permission from personal correspondence with Dr. Rachel Luft, who teaches sociology at the University of New Orleans and is a consultant and resource trainer with Crossroads and with People's Institute for Survival and Beyond. In addition to Dr. Luft, I have also been taught much about the relationship between anti-Semitism and racism by Louise Derman-Sparks, a nationally recognized expert in antibias curriculum for children, who also is a consultant and resource trainer for Crossroads Ministry.

9. See Alex Haley, *Roots: The Saga of an American Family* (New York: Doubleday, 1976).

7. Dismantling Racism

1. Robert Terry, "The Negative Impact on White Values," in *Impacts of Racism on White Americans*, ed. Benjamin P. Bowser and Raymond Hunt (Newbury Park, Calif.: Sage, 1981), 120.

2. Crossroads Ministry has published several documents on the principles of caucusing. Also, from within the People's Institute, there has emerged an organizing effort among white people entitled "European Dissent." For addresses to request information, see resources section below.

3. Continuum on Becoming an Antiracist Multicultural Institution by Crossroads Ministry, which I have somewhat modified with permission from Crossroads Ministry.

4. Joe Hill (born in 1879, died in 1915) was a radical organizer, labor activist, and songwriter. He was a member of the Industrial Workers of the World (IWW), also known as the Wobblies. He was executed for murder after a controversial trial. After his death, he became a hero and model of organizing for justice.

5. For more details on Crossroads team training program, please see additional resources below.

ADDITIONAL RESOURCES

The following select list of books, films, videos, and organizing tools may be helpful to readers who wish to continue pursuing the work of dismantling racism.

Books

Acuña, Rodolfo. *Occupied America: A History of Chicanos.* New York: Harper-Collins, 1988.

Allen, Theodore. *Invention of the White Race: The Origin of Racial Oppression in Anglo-America.* New York: Verso, 1997.

Bennett, LeRone, Jr. *Before the Mayflower: A History of Black America.* Chicago: Johnson, 2003.

Bonilla-Silva, Eduardo. *Racism without Racists: Color-Blind Racism and the Persistence of Racial Inequality in the United States.* Lanham, Md.: Rowman & Littlefield, 2006.

———. *White Supremacy and Racism in the Post-Civil Rights Era.* London: Lynne Rienner, 2001.

Bowser, Benjamin P., and Raymond G. Hunt, eds. *Impacts of Racism on White Americans.* 2nd ed. Newbury Park, Calif.: Sage, 1996.

Branch, Taylor. *Parting the Waters: America in the King Years 1954–63.* New York: Simon & Schuster, 1988.

Brodkin, Karen. *How Jews Became White Folks and What That Says about Race in America.* Rutgers: Rutgers University Press, 2000.

Brown, Dee. *Bury My Heart at Wounded Knee: An Indian History of the American West*. New York: Holt, Rinehart and Winston, 1971.

Bullard, Robert, ed. *Unequal Protection: Environmental Justice and Communities of Color*. New York: Random House, 1996.

Carr, Leslie G. *"Color-blind" Racism*. Thousand Oaks, Calif.: Sage, 1997.

Chisom, Ronald, and Michael Washington. *Undoing Racism: A Philosophy of International Social Change*. Chicago: People's Institute Press, 1997.

Davila, Arlene. *Latinos, Inc.: The Marketing and Making of a People*. Berkeley: University of California Press, 2001.

Deloria, Vine. *Custer Died for Your Sins: An Indian Manifesto*. Norman: University of Oklahoma Press, 1988.

Du Bois, W. E. B. *The Souls of Black Folk*. New York: Penguin, 1989 (reprint).

Feagin, Joe. *Systemic Racism*. New York: Routledge, 2006.

Frankenberg, Ruth. *White Women, Race Matters: The Social Construction of Whiteness*. Minneapolis: University of Minnesota Press, 1993.

Franklin, John Hope. *From Slavery to Freedom: A History of African Americans*. New York: Knopf, 1994.

Friere, Paulo. *Pedagogy of the Oppressed*. Chicago: Herder & Herder, 1970.

Gonzalez, Gilbert G., and Raul Fernandez. *A Century of Chicano History: Empire, Nations, and Migration*. New York: Routledge, 2003.

Hacker, Andrew. *Two Nations: Black and White, Separate, Hostile, Unequal*. New York: Scribner, 2003.

Haney-López, Ian F. *White by Law: The Legal Construction of Race*. New York: New York University Press, 1996.

Harding, Vincent. *There Is a River: The Black Struggle for Freedom in America*. New York: Vintage, 1983.

Hate Groups in America: A Record of Bigotry and Violence. New York: Anti-Defamation League of B'nai B'rith, 1982.

Higgenbotham, A. Leon, Jr. *In the Matter of Color: Race and the American Legal Process: The Colonial Period*. New York: Oxford University Press, 1978.

hooks, bell. *Ain't I a Woman: Black Women and Feminism*. Cambridge, Mass.: South End Press, 1981.

Hughes, Langston. *The Ways of White Folks*. New York: Vintage, 1990.

Ignatiev, Noel. *How the Irish Became White*. New York: Routledge, 1995.

Jaimes, M. Annette, ed. *The State of Native America: Genocide, Colonization, and Resistance*. Boston: South End Press, 1992.

Kozol, Jonathan. *Savage Inequalities: Children in American Schools*. New York: Harper Collins, 1991.

Lincoln, C. Eric. *Race, Religion, and the Continuing American Dilemma*. New York: Hill and Wang, 1984.

Loewen, James. *Lies My Teacher Told Me: Everything Your American History Textbook Got Wrong.* New York: Touchstone, 1996.

Malcolm X. *The Autobiography of Malcolm X.* New York: Grove Press, 1965.

Mamdani, Mahmood. *Citizen and Subject: Contemporary Africa and the Legacy of Late Colonialism.* Princeton: Princeton University Press, 1996.

Marable, Manning. *The Crisis of Color and Democracy: Essays on Race, Class and Power.* Monroe, Me.: Common Courage Press, 1991.

Myrdal, Gunnar. *An American Dilemma.* New York: Harper & Row, 1944.

Omi, Michael, and Howard Winant. *Racial Formation in the United States: From the 1960s to the 1990s.* New York: Routledge, 1994.

Rodriguez, Victor M. *Latino Politics in the United States: Race, Ethnicity, Class and Gender in the Mexican American and Puerto Rican Experience.* Dubuque: Kendall-Hunt, 2005.

Roediger, David. *Toward the Abolition of Whiteness: Essays on Race, Politics, and Working Class History.* New York: Verso, 1994.

———. *The Wages of Whiteness: Race and the Making of the American Working Class.* London: Verso, 1991.

———. *Working Toward Whiteness: How America's Immigrants Became White.* New York: Verso, 2005.

Smedley, Audrey. *Race in North America: Origin and Evolution of a Worldview.* Boulder: Westview, 1999.

Smith, Lillian. *Killers of the Dream.* New York: Norton, 1994.

Smith, Paul Chaat, and Robert Allen Warrior. *Like a Hurricane: The Indian Movement from Alcatraz to Wounded Knee.* New York: New Press, 1996.

Takaki, Ronald. *A Different Mirror: A History of Multicultural America.* Boston: Little, Brown, 1993.

———. *Strangers from a Different Shore: A History of Asian Americans.* Boston: Little, Brown, 1998.

Tatum, Beverly Daniel. *Why Are All the Black Kids Sitting Together in the Cafeteria? And Other Conversations about Race.* New York: Basic Books, 1997.

Terry, Robert. *For Whites Only.* Grand Rapids: Eerdmans, 1988.

U.S. Riot Commission Report. *Report of the National Advisory Commission on Civil Disorders.* New York: Bantam, 1968.

Washington, James M., ed. *A Testament of Hope: The Essential Writings and Speeches of Martin Luther King, Jr.* San Francisco: HarperCollins, 1986.

Winant, Howard. *The World Is a Ghetto.* New York: Basic Books, 2001.

Wise, Tim. *White Like Me: Reflections on Race from a Privileged Son.* New York: Soft Skull, 2005.

Wright, W. D. *Racism Matters.* Westport, Ct.: Praeger, 1998.

Wu, Frank. *Yellow: Race in America Beyond Black and White.* New York: Basic Books, 2002.

Zinn, Howard. *A People's History of the United States: 1492 to Present*. New York: HarperCollins, 2003.

Films and Videos

A Class Divided. Produced by Yale University Films. 60 min. 1985. A PBS *Frontline* video program that demonstrates the effects of racial conditioning to internalize racial superiority or inferiority. Watch the program at: http://www.pbs.org/wgbh/pages/frontline/shows/divided/etc/view.html (accessed July 6, 2007).

Ending Racism—Toward a Racism-Free Twenty-First Century. Produced by Crossroads Ministry. 35 min. 1996. VHS. This introductory-level video for adults helps viewers see the need for a comprehensive analysis of racism. Order by phone at (262) 637-2644 or e-mail ellen@crossroadsministry.org.

Eyes on the Prize: America's Civil Rights Years 1954–1965. Directed by Henry Hampton. PBS Home Video. 6 hrs. 1986. An excellent video series, using news and other film resources, portrays the history of the civil rights movement.

The Family of God: Helping Pre-Adolescents Respond to Racial Stereotypes. Produced by Crossroads Ministry with the Evangelical Lutheran Church in America. 1995. VHS. This faith-based video helps young people ages 8–12 deal with racial stereotyping. Order by phone at (262) 637-2644 or e-mail ellen@crossroadsministry.org.

True Colors. Produced by ABC News. 19 min. 1991. VHS. Northbrook, Ill.: MTI Film & Video. In this *PrimeTime* episode, Diane Sawyer and a video documentary team follow two men (one white and one black) through the course of a day in St. Louis.

Organizing Tools

Education and Organizing Manuals

Alinsky, Saul. *Reveille for Radicals*. New York: Vintage, 1989.

Bobo, Kim. *Organizing For Social Change: A Manual for Activists*. Washington, D.C.: Seven Locks Press, 1991.

Chisom, Ronald. Principles of Anti-Racist Organizing, a transcript of a presentation given in September 2005, available from the Peoles Institute for Survival and Beyond, 601 N Carrollton, New Orleans, LA 70119.

Derman-Sparks, Louise, and Carol Brunson Phillips. *Teaching/Learning Anti-Racism: A Developmental Approach*. New York: Teachers College Press, 1997.

Derman-Sparks, Louise, and Patricia G. Ramsey. *What If All the Kids Are White? Anti-bias Multicultural Education with Young Children and Families.* New York: Teachers College Press, 2006.

McIntosh, Peggy. *White Privilege and Male Privilege: A Personal Account of Coming to See Correspondences through Work in Women's Studies.* Wellesley, Mass.: Wellesley College, 1988.

McKnight, John, and Jody Kretzmann. *Building Communities from the Inside Out.* Chicago: ACTA Publications, 1993.

Menkart, Deborah, Alana Murray, and Janice View. *Putting the Movement Back into Civil Rights Teaching: A Resource Guide for K–12 Classrooms.* Oakland: Teaching for Change, 2004.

Shapiro, Ilana. *Training for Racial Equality and Inclusion.* Washington, D.C.: The Aspen Institute, 2002. This manual analyzes ten programs to eradicate racism and build antiracist multicultural diversity (including Crossroads Ministry and People's Institute for Survival and Beyond). Copies of Dr. Shapiro's manual can be acquired from the Aspen Institute, One Dupont Circle NW, Washington, D.C. 20036.

Antiracism Training Organizations

Throughout this book, it has been emphasized that the material for the book is derived from the author's experience with two organizations: Crossroads Ministry and Peoples Institute for Survival and Beyond. Following is material to further describe these two organizations.

Crossroads Ministry
Education, Training, and Organizing to Dismantle Racism and Build Anti-Racist Multicultural Diversity

Crossroads Ministry is an antiracist training and organizing collective, established in 1986, that provides education and training to dismantle racism and build antiracist multicultural diversity. Crossroads was directed for sixteen years by Joseph Barndt, the author of this book, from its founding in 1986 until 2002. The present coexecutive directors of Crossroads are Robette Dias and Chuck Ruehle. With an administrative and training staff of approximately fifteen people, Crossroads programs focus on systemic racism, seeking to address the root causes of racism through long-term institutional transformation.

The primary work of Crossroads is to train teams within community-based, governmental, and human-service organizations, as well as educational and religious institutions, helping them to analyze racism and to develop and implement strategies to dismantle racism within their structures. Crossroads training begins with the ability to analyze systemic racism. Then, provided with a comprehensive understanding of racism, an intensive training process equips teams with strategic skills to lead their institutions toward long-term and permanent transformation. For more than twenty years, Crossroads has facilitated the development of hundreds of internal transformation teams.

Crossroads also designs programs, resources, and networks that provide teams with the necessary skills and tools that are needed to bring about systemic change and lead toward the elimination of systemic racism within their institutions and organizations.

Crossroads' Mission Statement and Principles

The mission of Crossroads Ministry is to dismantle systemic racism and build antiracist multicultural diversity within institutions and communities. This mission is implemented primarily by training institutional transformation teams, and is guided by the following principles:

- The work of Crossroads is based upon a systemic analysis of racism and its individual, institutional, and cultural manifestations;
- The work of Crossroads is faith-based while at the same time nonsectarian, seeking to honor all expressions of spirituality that support and empower antiracism;
- Crossroads seeks to be accountable in its work to those who share a common analysis of racism, and especially to communities of color;
- Crossroads understands its antiracism work to be part of a national and global movement for racial justice and social equality;
- Crossroads recognizes that resistance to racism also requires resistance to all other forms of social inequality and oppression.

Crossroads Ministry Contact Information
Crossroads Ministry
Debra Russell, Administrative Director
P.O. Box 309
Matteson, IL 60443
Tel: (773) 638-0166
Email: xrdsinfo@crossroadsministry.org
Web site: http://www.crossroadsministry.org

The People's Institute for Survival and Beyond

The People's Institute for Survival and Beyond (PISAB) is a national and international collective of antiracist, multicultural community organizers and educators dedicated to building an effective movement for social transformation. Through Undoing Racism™ Community Organizing Workshops, technical assistance, and consultations, PISAB helps individuals, communities, organizations, and institutions move beyond addressing the symptoms of racism to undoing the causes of racism so as to create a more just and equitable society.

Founded in 1980 by long-time community organizers Ron Chisom of New Orleans and Dr. Jim Dunn of Yellow Springs, Ohio, The People's Institute understands that the fabric of racism is inextricably woven and constructed into the founding principles of the United States. Yet, since racism exists, it can also be undone through effective antiracist organizing with, and in accountability to, the communities most impacted by racism. The People's Institute believes that effective community and institutional change happens when those who are agents of transformation understand the foundations of race and racism and how they continually function as a barrier to community self-determination and self-sufficiency.

Antiracist Principles for Effective Organizing and Social Transformation
The People's Institute for Survival and Beyond believes that an effective, broad-based movement for social transformation must be rooted in the following antiracist principles:

- **Undoing Racism™.** Racism has been consciously and systematically erected, and it can be undone only if people understand what it is, where it comes from, how it functions, and why it is perpetuated.
- **Learning from History.** History is a tool for effective organizing. Understanding the lessons of history frees us to create a more humane future.
- **Sharing Culture.** Culture is the life support system of a community. If a community's culture is respected and nurtured, the community's power will grow.
- **Developing Leadership.** Antiracist leadership needs to be developed intentionally and systematically within local communities and organizations.
- **Maintaining Accountability.** To organize with integrity requires that we be accountable to the communities struggling with racist oppression.
- **Networking.** The growth of an effective broad-based movement for social transformation requires networking or "building a net that works."
- **Analyzing Power.** Through the analysis of institutional power, we identify and unpack the systems external to the community that create the internal realities that many people experience daily.
- **Gatekeeping.** Persons who work in institutions often function as gatekeepers to ensure that the institution perpetuates itself. By operating with antiracist values and networking with those who share those values, and maintaining an accountable relationship with the community, the gatekeeper becomes an agent of institutional transformation.
- **Identifying and Analyzing the Manifestations of Racism.** Individual acts of racism are supported by institutions and are nurtured by societal practices such as militarism and cultural racism, which enforce and perpetuate racism.

People's Institute Contact Information
The People's Institute for Survival and Beyond
Ron Chisom, Executive Director
Tiphanie Eugene, Administrative Director
601 N. Carrollton
New Orleans, LA 70119
Tel: (504) 301-9292
Email: tiphanie@pisab.org
Web site: http://www.pisab.org

For Additional Information

The Friends Committee on National Legislation. A nonpartisan Quaker lobby in the public interest, seeks to follow the leadings of the spirit as it speaks for itself and for like-minded Friends. For more information, contact the committee: by mail at, 245 Second St. N.E., Washington, DC 20002-5795; by phone at, 1-202-547-6000 or 1-800-630-1330; by e-mail at, fcnl@fcnl.org; or visit http://www.fcnl.org.

The MAAFA Suite—A Healing Journey. A dramatic and moving event performed every year by St. Paul Community Baptist Church in Brooklyn, New York, memorializing "The Maafa" (a Kiswahili word meaning "disaster" or "holocaust," the catastrophe of enslavement of Africans). For information and brochure, write MAAFA Commemoration Resource Center, 859 Hendrix St., Brooklyn, NY, 11207; Tel: (718) 257-1300.

Prison and Jail Project. A courageous and effective confrontation of continuing racist institutional practices by law-enforcement agencies, courts, and prisons in Georgia. The newsletter *Freedomways* is available by writing Prison and Jail Project, P.O. Box 6749, Americus, GA, 31709; Tel: (229) 924-7080.

Southern Poverty Law Center. A nonprofit organization that combats hate, intolerance and discrimination through education and litigation. For more information, write Southern Poverty Law Center, 400 Washington Ave., Montgomery, AL 36104, or visit http://www.splcenter.org.

accountability
  absence of, 150, 180, 196, 198–
    199
  definition of, 152, 178
  institutional, 148–149, 152–153,
    168, 174–177
  mutual, 153, 203, 228, 228–229,
    235, 257, 260, 262
  and power, 179, 228, 258
  to communities of color, 180,
    199, 229, 235, 256, 257
abolition of slavery, 26, 27–28,
  92–93, 197
affirmative action, 33, 35–36, 45,
  159, 173, 239
African American/black
  black history month, 133, 202–
    203
  culture and identity, 4, 7–8, 87,
    176, 185, 193–194, 199, 206,
    213, 269,
  oppression and resistance, 8, 20,

    27, 23–24, 30, 36, 41,
    47–48, 92, 180, 264
  and other people of color
    See people of color
American Revolution, 17, 155
anti-racist/anti-racism
  communities of resistance, 221–
    223, 226–231
  definition of, 223–225
  identity formation 223–232,
    255–257
  institutional identity formation,
    231–233
  organizing
    See organizing for change
anti-Semitism, 11, 140, 211
  and racism, 11, 64, 69, 210–212,
    275, 277
apartheid
  economic, 37
  global, 52
  South African, 29, 52, 158

U.S. style, 20, 27–28, 30, 35, 93,
  155, 248
Arab American/Middle Eastern
  culture and identity, 7, 21, 22,
    65, 185
  oppression and resistance, 28, 37,
    41, 64, 156, 265–266
  and other people of color
    See people of color
Aryan Nation, 38, 138
Asian American
  culture and identity, 7, 21–22,
    65, 185, 191, 193–194
  oppression and resistance, 28, 30,
    41, 47, 92, 156, 272
  and other people of color
    See people of color
assimilation, 171, 200, 205–206,
  211–212

Bell, Sean, 39, 135
Bernier, Francois, 66
bigfoot, 40–41
Black Panthers, 32
black history
  See African American
black people
  See African Americans
black power
  See power
Blumenbach, Johann, 66
Bridges, Ruby, 111, 238
Brodkin, Karen, 211, 275
Brown Berets, 30
Brown power
  See power
Byrd, James, 38, 135

Carmichael, Stokely
  See Kwame Ture
Chin, Vincent, 38
Chinese exclusion act, 24

Chisom, Ronald, xiii, 8, 271
Church
  and racial identity formation,
    120, 123, 140, 147, 188–189
  supporting racism, 6, 38, 40, 56,
    60, 68, 74, 138, 146, 148,
    157, 179, 197
  resisting racism, 31, 35, 38, 50,
    226, 236, 246
Cisneros, Henry, 180
civil rights movement
  accomplishments and limitations,
    3, 14, 24, 28, 29–35, 43,
    50–51, 93–94, 112–113,
    158, 206, 247
  heroes and heroines of,
    31
Clark, Kendall, 96, 273
COINTELPRO, 31–32, 270–271
Cole-Vodicka, John, 39
colonialism
  See racism and colonialism
colorblind ideology, 37, 51, 88–89,
  128, 132, 134, 140, 273
Columbus, Christopher, 15
Crossroads Ministry, 8, 59, 106,
  125, 187, 221, 226, 228, 244,
  267, 271–272
culture
  cultural appropriation, 195, 198–
    199
  cultural curtain, 193–200, 203–
    207, 215–219
    definition of, 195–197
  cultural oppression, 37, 137, 174
    definition of, 186–189
  cultural racism, 185–217
  and individualism, 187–188,
    197–198
  race-based culture, 166, 185–186,
    190–194
  white culture, 195–201, 207–215

Diallo, Amadou, 38, 135
diversity
    See multicultural diversity
Douglass, Frederick, 7
Du Bois, W. E. B., 8, 269

Elliot, Jane, 123–124
emancipation
    See abolition of slavery
ethnicity
    See racism and ethnicity
European American
    See white racial identity
Executive Order 9066, 21

Gandhi, Mahatma, 7, 222
gentrification/regentrification, 131, 176
Griffin, John Howard, 87

Haley, Alex, 213
Haney Lopez, Ian F., 18
Harlem Renaissance, 28
Hassan, Salah D., 22, 270
Hill, Joe, 245, 275
Hispanic American
    See Latino/Hispanic
Hooks, Benjamin, 33, 271
Hoover, J. Edgar, 31
Hudson Institute, 170, 202

identity formation
    anti-racist identity formation
        See Anti-racist/Anti-racism
    racial identity formation, 82, 120–124, 137–139, 273
    institutional identity formation 154–157, 169, 182
        See also Power³
Ignatiev, Noel, 210, 275
individual racism, 111, 115–118, 127, 141,169–170, 190
    See also Power³
institutions
    and accountability
        See accountability
    function and purpose of, 3, 75, 145–149
    and identity formation
        See identity formation
    levels and structure of, 165–169
    and systems, 146
institutional change
    transformational and transactional, 95, 182–183
    continuum of, 233–243, 255, 262
institutional organizing
    See organizing for change
institutional racism
    and accountability
        See accountability
    definition of, 56–57, 76, 81, 84, 90, 153–154
    history of, 18, 19, 35, 44, 92–94, 100, 154–158
    institutionalized, legalized, and self-perpetuating, 92–94, 143, 151–152, 156
    levels of, within institutional structures, 166–182
    new forms of, 159–165
integration
    See race and integration

Jackson-Chaves, Donovan, 38
Jensen, Robert, 99, 102, 273
Jones, Nathaniel "Skip", 39

Karenga, Maulana, 72
Keillor, Garrison, 211
Kennedy, John Fitzgerald, 210
King Jr., Martin Luther, 7, 29, 31,

123, 133, 134, 198, 222, 263, 270

King, Rodney, 38, 164, 203

Ku Klux Klan (KKK), 20, 28, 31, 38, 138, 237

La Raza, 30, 32

Las Casas, Bartolomé de, 17, 270

Latino/Hispanic

culture and identity, 9, 21, 65, 72, 185, 191, 193, 205

oppression and resistance, 5, 16, 23, 28, 30, 36, 41, 37, 47, 92, 156, 264–265

and other people of color

See people of color

Lewis, C. S., 131, 274

Lincoln, C. Eric, 41, 111, 271

Linnaeus, Carolus, 66

Luft, Rachel, 211, 275

Major, Barbara, xiii

Malcolm X, 31, 82

Mandela, Nelson, 7, 29, 222

Manifest Destiny, 23

McIntosh, Peggy, 89, 106, 110, 273

melting pot, 192, 209–215, 275

minutemen, 238, 138

multicultural diversity, xii, 35–37, 52, 174, 185–186, 202–203

racist and anti-racist, 234–235, 247–251, 259

Nation of Islam, 32

Native American

boarding schools, 20, 197

culture and identity, 19, 62, 65, 92, 185, 192–194

oppression and resistance, 7, 11, 16–17, 20, 23, 26–27, 30, 36, 41, 47, 64, 92, 132, 155– 156, 188, 199, 201, 230

and other people of color

See people of color

Naturalization act of 1790, 18–19, 155, 272

Omi, Michael, 68, 133, 270, 272, 273

Organizing for change, xii, 8, 12, 15, 28, 33, 220–221, 223, 226– 227, 230–233, 236, 358, 261– 264, 267–268, 275

principles of organizing, 243–255

people of color

explanation of term and use, 8–10

See also African American, Asian American, Native American, Arab American, Latino/ Hispanic, People's Institute for survival and beyond, xii, 8, 40, 59, 86, 221, 226, 246, 267, 271–272

power

analysis, 40, 175, 271

black power, xi, 113

brown power, xi, 75, 117

definition of, 74–75

misuse of, 59, 73, 76–77

systemic power, 56–57, 59–60, 117, 128, 196

yellow power, xi, 30, 75, 117

and accountability

See accountability

See also Power[1], Power[2] and Power[3]

Power[1]

meaning of concept, 76–78, 84, 105

racism's power over people of color, 15–25, 31–34, 38–41, 46–48

Power²
  meaning of concept, 76–77,
    79–81, 84, 85–86
  See also white power and privilege
Power³
  meaning of concept, 76–77,
    81–82, 84
  See also racialization,
    internalization,
    institutionalization
prejudice
  See race prejudice
Puerto Rico, 15, 21, 23–24, 191,
  193

race
  classification by, 19–24, 66–72
  definition of, 64, 72–73
  and ethnicity, 63–64, 191, 272
  and integration, 33, 36, 52, 130,
    176, 199–205
  origins and history of , 64–72
  and science, 63–64, 66, 73, 272
  segregation by, 20, 28, 30, 50–51,
    76, 130, 158–159, 176, 191,
    204–207, 237–239
race prejudice, 56–61, 74, 83, 115–
  117, 153, 272
racialization, 62, 120–123, 190–
  193, 207–215
racial identity formation,
  See identity formation
  See also Power³
racism
  and colonialism, 15–16, 22, 52,
    68, 91, 265–266, 269–270
  correlate racism, 164–165, 172
  definition of racism, 58–60
  definition of racist, 115–118, 128
  detecting and measuring, 42–46,
    84, 94, 159, 166–169, 233,
    237

linguistic racism, 198
and other "isms", 10, 117, 260
resistance to
  cultural white racism, xi, 6,
    81, 115–117, 127, 141
  See resistance to racism
  See also individual racism,
    institutional racism,

Reconstruction, 20, 28, 232
red power, xi, 75, 117
redlining, 163
resistance to racism
  history of, 15–16, 25–32, 49, 53,
    102, 126, 157–158
  building communities of, 221–
    231, 243–244, 249, 251,
    267–268
  tribute to heroes and heroines in,
    268
Rodríguez, Victor M., 24, 189, 270,
  274

segregation
  See race and segregation
slavery, 7, 16, 17–18, 20, 24, 29–30,
  44, 70, 156, 192, 269–270
  See also Abolition of slavery
Smedley, Audrey, 64, 272
South Africa, 29, 52, 155, 158
Southern Christian Leadership
  Conference (SCLC), 32
St. Paul, 222
Stewart, Anne, 187, 204–206
Students for a Democratic Society
  (SDS), 32, 270
Student Nonviolent Coordinating
  Committee (SNCC), 112
Superiority
  See race and superiority
Supreme Court decisions
  Brown v. Board of Education of

Topeka, Kansas, 94
defining whiteness, 18, 22, 63, 71, 192, 208, 272
Plessey v. Ferguson, 20, 28
regarding civil rights laws and affirmative action, 33, 44
systems
See institutions and systems
systemic power
See power

Tatum, Beverly Daniel, 130, 176, 273, 274
Terry, Robert, 85, 88, 224, 273, 275
Thomas, Timothy, 39
Treaty of Guadalupe Hidalgo, 23
Ture, Kwame, 12

United Farm Workers, 30

Villaraigosa, Antonio, 180

Washington, Harold, 180
West, Cornel, 52, 271
white citizens' councils, 20, 28, 31, 113
white power and privilege
concept of, 85–90, 115–120
defining *white power,* 91–95
defining *white privilege,* 95–98

exploring, 81, 100, 102–110, 136–137, 147, 162, 182, 212–213, 224, 233, 256–257, 267
See also Power²
white race
culture and identity, 207–218
history and origin of, 18, 65
use of term, 9
See also Identity formation, racialization, Power³
white racism
See racism
white prison, 82, 112, 114, 116, 118–119, 141, 216
freedom from, 112–114, 119, 141, 212–216, 221, 224
Winant, Howard, 68, 133, 270, 272, 273
Wise, Tim, 87, 273
Workforce 2000, 170, 202, 272
World Church of the Creator, 38

yellow power
See power
Yoshino, Kenji, 200, 274
Young, Coleman, 180
Youngblood, Johnny Ray, 14, 269

Zangwill, Israel, 209, 275
Zinn, Howard, 16, 31, 270